Know it All,
Find it Fast
for Academic
Libraries

Know it All, Find it Fast for Academic Libraries

Heather Dawson

facet publishing

© Heather Dawson 2012

Published by Facet Publishing
7 Ridgmount Street, London WC1E 7AE
www.facetpublishing.co.uk

Facet Publishing is wholly owned by CILIP: the Chartered Institute of
Library and Information Professionals.

Heather Dawson has asserted her right under the Copyright, Designs and
Patents Act 1988 to be identified as author of this work.

British Library Cataloguing in Publication Data
A catalogue record for this book is available from the British Library.

ISBN 978-1-85604-759-3

First published 2012
Reprinted digitally thereafter

Text printed on FSC accredited material.

Mixed Sources
Product group from well-managed
forests and other controlled sources
www.fsc.org Cert no. SA-COC-1565
© 1996 Forest Stewardship Council

Typeset from author's files in 10/13 pt Aldine 721 and Nimbus Sans by
Flagholme Publishing Services.
Printed and made in Great Britain by MPG Books Group, UK.

Contents

CONTENTS

Introduction

What this book covers

The title of this book makes a very big claim. No one can possibly know the answers to all the questions that a student, researcher or academic might ask, nor should they claim to do so. Information resources are constantly evolving and one of the key tasks of the librarian is to make sure that he or she keeps up to date.

What this book does offer is a survival guide for front-line staff to help them find appropriate information quickly, whether they are answering questions at a physical help desk or remotely by telephone, e-mail or instant messaging service.

The entries cover a range of queries commonly encountered in the academic library. They are also of relevance to public library staff assisting visiting students. The key categories covered are:

- *Study skills*. Citing and referencing; literature-searching techniques; social research methods and avoiding plagiarism.
- *Locating different types of resources*. Starting-points for finding commonly requested types of material, including: archives; dictionaries; book reviews; biographical information; conference papers; encyclopedias; images; films; statistical data; maps; market research reports; opinion polls; newspapers; government publications; quotations and speeches.
- *PhD and researcher questions*. Basic guidance to common queries such as how to trace theses and dissertations; locating sources of funding; and searching for books and journals in other libraries.
- *Academic staff questions*. Starting-points for tackling questions relating to open access publishing; copyright licences; finding bibliometric data; and tracing online teaching and learning resources.
- *Subject literature searching*. Some basic starting-points for beginning research in a number of commonly encountered academic subject areas. The full list of these is: Accountancy; Art; Business Studies; Computer Science; Criminology; Development Studies; Economics; Economic History; Education; Engineering; Environment; European Union; Geography; History; Human Rights; International Relations; Languages; Law; Literature; Management; Marketing; Mathematics; Media Studies;

Medicine and Nursing; Music; Philosophy; Religious Studies; Science; Social Welfare and Social Work; Sociology; Sports Studies; Tourism; Women's Studies.

- *Area studies resources*. In addition, key resources for those studying a number of specific regions: African Studies, Asian Studies, Latin American Studies, Slavonic and East European Studies are also provided.

How to use this book

Each of the chapters highlights key places to look for information. These are intended to offer starting-points for research. Read the **Points to Consider** section first in order to identify common questions and links to related sections (these are indicated in **bold type** in the text).

The subject categories generally contain the following sub-sections:

- *Key organizations*. Trade, industry and/or scholarly bodies whose websites can be used to locate news and details about recent projects.
- *Libraries and archives*. Useful for searching library catalogues to locate key books and journals. However, do remember to check access agreements before urging students to visit!
- *Dictionaries and encyclopedias*. Useful for checking terminology and providing basic overviews of topics.
- *News services*. Specialist resources which are intended to supplement the national daily newspapers.
- *Journal article indexing services*. There is a general chapter on journal article indexes, which focuses on resources that cover a wide range of subject areas. The sections on journal article indexes in the individual subject chapters have a narrower focus and are designed to be used in addition to it. They include both subscription and free services. Remember that libraries can purchase e-resources via different packages, so local holdings need to be checked.
- *Internet gateways and portals*. In this category are websites which contain directories of links to academic-quality websites. Limitations of space mean that this book cannot list all the resources that students may need. It is therefore recommended to explore these resources in order to retrieve more detailed references to subject sub-fields.

Finally, remember that in order to use this book successfully library staff must combine its content with basic knowledge of their own local services.

A basic checklist of extra information should include knowledge of:

IT questions

- How to access computer networks on and off campus
- How to obtain and reset passwords
- How and where to report IT problems
- How to print/photocopy
- If and how visitors can use library computers/e-resources
- Availability and booking of IT courses

Building/campus questions

- Library opening hours
- Admissions policies – including ID required for entry
- Library/campus room numbers and locations
- Availability and booking facilities of study rooms, lockers
- Facilities for students with special needs
- How to report building maintenance problems

Questions relating to library printed collections

- How to borrow, return, reserve and renew books
- Fines and policies for overdue books
- Borrowing allowances for different categories of library user
- Library class mark locations
- How to report missing books
- How to request items for purchase
- How to request interlibrary loans
- How to contact subject librarians/specialists
- Access agreements with other libraries

Questions relating to library electronic resources

- How to obtain and reset passwords
- How to locate and log on to e-journals and other databases on and off campus
- Whom to report password and/or access problems to
- Availability and range of e-resources available to different categories of library users, including walk-in visitors

ACCOUNTANCY

Typical questions

- Where can I get access to the latest Accounting Standards?
- Are GAAP and Accounting Standards the same?
- Which chartered accountancy firms employ trainees?

Points to consider

- Accountancy courses often use specialist terminology which can be difficult to understand. Good starting-points are the websites of the main professional bodies, which have introductory guides. Particularly recommended is that of the Institute of Chartered Accountants in England and Wales (ICAEW).
- Another frequently requested resource is Accounting Standards. Again, guides can be found on the websites of the main professional bodies. Remember to check dates and jurisdiction.
- Students seeking journal articles may also find it useful to consult the resources listed in the **Economics** and **Business Studies** sections.

Where to look

Key organizations

Association of Certified & Corporate Accountants (ACCA)
   uk.accaglobal.com
   Leading organization which offers the Certified Accounting Technician qualification. Website has large selection of resources for students, including syllabuses, sample exam papers and study guides.

Institute of Chartered Accountants in England and Wales (ICAEW)
   www.icaew.com
   Website includes advice for students on careers and qualifications in accountancy. Also available are news stories, job listings and discussion forums. Free access to the **ICAEW Directory of Firms**, listing over 20,000 accountancy offices worldwide, **www.icaewfirms.co.uk**.

Institute of Chartered Accountants of Scotland
   www.icas.org.uk/icas

International Federation of Accountants
   www.ifac.org

1

Global organization for the accountancy profession. Membership list has links to websites of main national bodies.

Libraries

Institute of Chartered Accountants in England and Wales (ICAEW) Library

www.icaew.com/en/Library

Specialist library with the world's largest collection of historic accounting and finance books (covering 1494 to 1914), plus extensive holdings of current books and journals. Website offers free access to excellent guides on the structure of the accounting profession and how to find specific types of accounting information.

Accounting standards

Generally Accepted Accounting Principles (GAAP)

A term used to refer to the standard framework of guidelines for financial accounting used in any given jurisdiction. GAAP includes the standards, conventions and rules accountants follow in recording and summarizing transactions and in the preparation of financial statements.

International accounting standards

Accounting standards issued by the International Accounting Standards Board (IASB) and its predecessor, the International Accounting Standards Committee (IASC).

An excellent starting-point for understanding and comparing standards is the **ICAEW**, which lists and links to useful research resources,

www.icaew.com/en/Library/country-resources.

Accounting Standards Board (ASB)

www.frc.org.uk/asb

National standards setter. Website includes information on regulation, plus free access to many documents, including standards and discussion papers.

Financial Accounting Standards Board (FASB)

www.fasb.org

American national organization. Get news and information about standards.

Hussey, R. (2010) *Fundamentals of International Financial Reporting and Accounting,* World Scientific Press

Useful introduction to accounting and financial reporting, describes the development of international standards and the present structure, role and operations of the International Accounting Standards Board.

IAS Plus

www.iasplus.com/index.htm

Maintained by Deloitte. Free access to news about international financial reporting. Includes comparisons of International Financial Reporting Standards (IFRSs) and various local GAAPs, e-learning modules for students and many full-text Deloitte publications.

International Accounting Standards Board (IASB)

www.ifrs.org/IFRSs/IFRS.htm

Currently provides free access to the current year's consolidated unaccompanied IFRS (i.e. the core standards, without implementation guidance). Full access is via the **eIFRS** online subscription service, **eifrs.ifrs.org/eifrs**.

International GAAP (subscription required)

www.wiley.com/legacy/igaap09/index.html

Available in print or online. Compiled by Ernst & Young. Guide to interpreting and implementing International financial standards.

Dictionaries

Accounting Terminology Guide

www.nysscpa.org/glossary

Glossary produced by the New York State Society of Certified Public Accountants (NYSSCPA) for financial journalists, serves as a good introduction to American accounting terms.

Essential Accountancy Abbreviations

www.icaew.com/en/Library/subject-gateways/accounting/abbreviations

Directory developed by the ICAEW's Library and Information Service, includes the abbreviations of organizations, qualifications and other acronyms of accounting documents. The emphasis is on the UK, but the directory also includes the most important worldwide abbreviations. Includes some coverage of organizations which are now defunct.

News services

Accountancy Age

www.accountancyage.com

Free access to articles, news and job listings for UK accountancy and tax professionals.

ACCOUNTANCY

Accounting Web
www.accountingweb.co.uk
Online news and blogs for the accounting profession.

Internet gateways and portals
Use these to locate links to recommended online resources.

AccountancyStudents
www.accountancystudents.co.uk
Site founded by qualified accountant Mark Ellis to help students pass exams. Provides free access to useful online articles, discussion forums, plus links to key organizations and job websites.

AccountantsWorld
www.accountantsworld.com/default.aspx
Gateway to US accounting resources. Free access to news, research resources, sample letters and forms.

AccountingEducation.com
www.accountingeducation.com
A site aimed at accountancy teachers. It includes international news, an articles database, book reviews, job listings and links.

ACRONYMS AND ABBREVIATIONS

Typical questions

- I need to find an article published in WLR – where should I look?
- What does WIPO stand for?
- My reading list refers to mimeo.

Points to consider

- Many student reading lists use acronyms and abbreviations, and some of these may be non-standard! Always check the original source first, to see if it has a key to those used. If it doesn't, then try these general sources listed below. Other good starting-points (especially for specialist terminologies) are the subject-based sections of this book. Look in particular at **Law** and **International Organizations**.
- Remember that many library catalogues will not search properly for abbreviated journal titles or author/organization names. Students will usually need to find the full title first.
- Some problematic abbreviations that commonly appear on reading lists/book bibliographies are:
  - *Ibid:* an abbreviation of the Latin *ibidem*, meaning the same place. The citation refers to the same work as that cited in the preceding reference.
  - *Mimeo:* an unpublished academic paper.
  - *Op. cit.:* an abbreviation of the Latin *opere citato*, meaning in the work already cited. Look back to earlier in the list to find the full publication details, e.g., for Milan, *op. cit.*, p. 5, refer to the previous mention of Milan to get the full citation.
- Finally, check the date of publication. Many dictionaries of abbreviations are not updated frequently and so they may not include the latest journal titles.

Where to look

Acronym Finder

> www.acronymfinder.com
> Well regarded free website. Over 1 million acronyms and abbreviations covering all subject areas, many with encyclopedia-length explanations. Includes some journal abbreviations.

Acronyms, Initialisms and Abbreviations Dictionary (2011), 45th edn

> Up-to-date resource which covers all subject areas. Annually reproduced in a new edition by an editorial team.

Alkire, L. G., Westerman-Alkire, C. (2006) *Periodical Title Abbreviations,* **16th edn, Gale Research Inc**

Useful multi-volume set which covers journal title abbreviations, database abbreviations and selected monograph abbreviations in science, the social sciences, the humanities and law. Includes foreign language publications.

Bonk, M. R. (2001) *International Acronyms, Initialisms and Abbreviations Dictionary,* **5th edn, Gale Research**

Guide to over 210,000 international acronyms, abbreviations and alphabetic symbols used worldwide in all subject fields.

De Sola, R., Stahl, D. A. and Kerchelich, K. (2001) *Abbreviations Dictionary,* **10th edn, Taylor & Francis**

Classic work covering acronyms and abbreviations for all subject areas. Special sections include: international vehicle licence letters, government agencies, legal terms, American states and capitals.

Oxford Dictionary of Abbreviations **(1998), Oxford University Press**

Available in print or online via electronic reference packages from Oxford University Press. Covers over 20,000 everyday and specialist business, scientific and technical abbreviations and acronyms. Emphasis on those used in English-speaking nations.

AFRICAN STUDIES

Typical questions

- Can you recommend any free sites which cover African news?
- I need to do a literature search on ICT and development in Africa.
- Where can I find statistics on health in sub-Saharan Africa?

Points to consider

- This section focuses on resources for area studies of Africa. Many students will also need to supplement them with those recommended in the appropriate subject sections. Closely related topics include **Anthropology, Development Studies.**
- Also useful is the **Country Information** section. Remember that many nations in developing areas may not have the resources to update their national websites regularly. In these cases the international organizations resources recommended may be useful starting-points for research.

Where to look

Key organizations

Use these websites to find lists of events, conferences and recent research publications.

African Studies Association
  www.asauk.net
  UK subject-specialist organization founded in 1963. Website provides free access to a directory of Africanists, plus lists of theses accepted at UK universities since 2005.

African Studies Association of the USA (ASA)
  www.africanstudies.org
  Leading North American organization. Find information on events and specialist research.

Council for the Development of Social Science Research in Africa
  www.codesria.org
  Established in 1973 as an independent Pan-African research organization with a primary focus on the social sciences. Access useful information on research produced within Africa. This includes some full-text articles and conference papers.

Libraries and archives

Explore these resources to find references to key books and journals.

African Studies Centre, Leiden
www.ascleiden.nl/Library

Largest African studies collection in the Netherlands. Website provides free access to useful research guides, directories of African studies websites and *African Studies Abstracts*, which indexes recently published journal articles.

Bodleian Library of Commonwealth and African Studies at Rhodes House
www.bodleian.ox.ac.uk/rhodes

Part of the University of Oxford. Strong African archive collections, especially of the papers of British colonial officials.

Cambridge University Library
www.lib.cam.ac.uk/deptserv/rcs

Holds the collections of the library of the Royal Commonwealth Society. Search the catalogue and view online historical photographs of the British Commonwealth.

School of Oriental and African Studies (SOAS)
www.soas.ac.uk/library

Specialist library which is part of the University of London. Particularly strong missionary archives.

SCOLMA (Standing Conference on Library Materials on Africa)
www2.lse.ac.uk/library/scolma

UK libraries and archives group on Africa, runs a co-operative acquisitions scheme and publishes information on library holdings on Africa.

Encyclopedias

McIlwaine, J. (2007) *Africa: a guide to reference material*, 2nd edn, Hans Zell

Award-winning reference work which reviews over 3000 resources useful for researchers. Covers key journals, books, handbooks and other resources. Indexed by topic area and country.

Zell, H. (2007) *The African Studies Companion: a guide to information sources*, 4th edn, Hans Zell
www.africanstudiescompanion.com

Regularly updated guide, available in print or online. Evaluates useful resources for researchers. Includes lists of African studies organizations, libraries and reviews of e-resources.

E-journals and journal article indexing services

It is recommended that these be used in conjunction with the indexes listed in the appropriate subject section/general **Journal Article Indexes** section.

Africa.bib.org

www.africabib.org/databases.htm

Offers free access to several major databases:

- *Africana Bibliographic Literature.* Covers over 500 multilingual journals that specialize in African Studies. Dates from 1974 onwards. Indexed by country and topic.
- *African Women Bibliographic Database.* Contains over 35,000 citations from 1986 onwards, includes references to books and government documents; journal articles; Masters theses and PhD dissertations.

Africa Bibliography (subscription required)

africabibliography.cambridge.org

Published as an annual supplement to *Africa: the Journal of the International African Institute,* since 1984. It covers all subject areas and nations of Africa. Includes articles, book chapters and monographs.

Africa-Wide Information (subscription required)

www.ebscohost.com/public/africa-wide-information

Produced by NISC South Africa. A combination of many bibliographic databases including: *South African Studies, African Studies* and *African HealthLine.* They provide references to journal articles, research reports, conference books and dissertations.

African e-Journals Project

africa.isp.msu.edu/AEJP

Collaborative effort of Michigan State University with the Association of African Universities and the African Studies Association. Provides free access to a digital archive of a small number of historic humanities and social science titles published in Africa.

African Journals OnLine (AJOL)

www.ajol.info

Non-profit organization based in South Africa which seeks to increase the transparency of African-based research. Offers free tables of contents and abstracts from over 400 titles covering all subject areas. Access to the full text requires (in most cases) prepayment or a subscription.

African Studies Abstracts

www.ascleiden.nl/Library/Abstracts/ASA-Online/AllIssues.aspx

Compiled quarterly by the the African Studies Centre, Leiden. Indexes and abstracts articles from over 400 journal titles, plus selected book chapters from their collection. All subject areas of the humanities and social sciences are covered. Issues from 2003 onwards are free online.

Current Bibliography on African Affairs (subscription required)
www.baywood.com/journals/previewjournals.asp?id=0011-3255

Quarterly index to recent articles and publications covering all subject areas. Published since 1968.

Index to South African Periodicals
www.nlsa.ac.za/NLSA/databases/isap-online-public

Subject index of articles in periodicals published in South Africa. Entries date back to 1919. Some free online access. Older issues offered to subscribers only.

International African Bibliography (IAB) (subscription required)
www.degruyter.de/journals/iab

Well established source compiled and edited by David Hall in association with the Centre of African Studies, University of London. It lists details of more than 4000 publications each year. These include journal articles and book chapters covering all subject areas. Indexes by subject and country. Includes a section for the African diaspora.

Quarterly Index of African Periodical Literature
lcweb2.loc.gov:8081/misc/qsihtml

Compiled by the Library of Congress Office, Nairobi, Kenya. An index of over 300 selected periodicals (mostly scholarly) which are acquired regularly from 29 African countries.

Newspapers and news services

Africa Confidential (subscription required)
www.africa-confidential.com

Based in London, a well regarded leading fortnightly newsletter on politics in Africa.

African Newspapers Union List (AFRINUL)
www.crl.edu/grn/afrinul

Catalogue of holdings information for newspapers (all formats and all languages) published in sub-Saharan Africa that are held by member libraries of the Cooperative African Newspapers Project. Mainly American Libraries.

allafrica.com

allafrica.com

Largest electronic distributor of African news and information worldwide. It aggregates the reporting of more than 130 media organizations. Current news stories on the site (up to one year old) are free. A subscription is required to access the complete archive from 1996 onwards.

IRIN – Integrated Regional Information Network

www.irinnews.org

Produced by the UN Office for the Coordination of Humanitarian Affairs. While it covers the whole world, it often has excellent news on humanitarian issues affecting the African continent.

New Africa Analysis (subscription required)

newafricaanalysis.co.uk/index.php

Fortnightly analysis of political social and economic events from a progressive perspective. Includes coverage of the activities of aid agencies.

Statistical data

A number of international organizations regularly produce reports and data covering individual African nations. Key examples are listed below. You may also find it useful to consult the more general series listed in the **Development Studies** and **Statistical Data** sections.

African Development Bank

www.afdb.org

Supports economic and financial development. Key publications include *African Statistical Yearbook*, published annually by the African Development Bank in association with the African Union. It includes social, demographic, economic and financial data, also individual country reports. Reports from 1998 onwards are free online.

Afrobarometer

www.afrobarometer.org

African-led series of national public attitude surveys on democracy and governance in Africa. Partners include the Institute for Democracy in South Africa (IDASA). Use the website to get free access to polls and data from 1999 onwards covering 20 African nations.

Commonwealth Secretariat

publications.thecommonwealth.org

Regularly publishes papers on its activities in Commonwealth nations. Key topics include economic and social development, education, gender equality and election monitoring. Free access to some materials from its website.

Economic Commission for Africa (ECA)
www.uneca.org
Established in 1958 as a regional body of the United Nations. Wide-ranging remit. Its website provides free access to reports and statistics. Key publications include the annual *Economic Report on Africa*, regular reports on women, regional integration and progress towards the Millennium Development Goals.

IMF
www.imf.org/external/pubs/ft/reo/reorepts.aspx
Produces a number of regular reports discussing economic policy and prospects in a specific region. Free access to reports covering sub-Saharan Africa from 2002 onwards via its website.

OECD
www.oecd.org, www.africaneconomicoutlook.org
Produces the Annual *African Economic Outlook* in association with the African Development Bank, the OECD Development Centre and the United Nations Economic Commission for Africa. This covers over 50 nations and includes profiles and cross-country and cross-time analysis. Some materials online. Also available via the OECD iLibrary service (subscription required), where it can be cross-searched with other full-text reports.

UNDP
hdr.undp.org
United Nations Development Programme (UNDP) commissions the *Human Development Report* series, which aims to assess the political, economic and social well-being of populations. Its website provides free access to hundreds of national and international reports, many of which cover individual African nations. Materials from 1990 onwards.

World Bank
web.worldbank.org
Publishes *African Development Indicators*. It contains more than 500 macroeconomic, sectoral and social indicators, covering over 50 African countries, with data from 1965 onwards. Free datasets online at **data.worldbank.org**.

Internet gateways and portals

Explore these to find links to well regarded academic resources.

Africa Portal

www.africaportal.org

Special project of the Centre for International Governance Innovation (CIGI), Makerere University (MAK), and the South African Institute of International Affairs (SAIIA). Includes a digital library of over 2500 books, journals and digital documents related to African policy. Some of these are published by African organizations. Also available is an online directory of experts, and an events calendar of forthcoming conferences.

African Studies Internet Resources

www.columbia.edu/cu/lweb/indiv/africa/cuvl

Excellent site maintained by Columbia University Library. Includes a link to the International Directory of African Studies Scholars.

ANTHROPOLOGY

Typical questions

- How can I find out if there are any ethnographic films about the Ashanti?
- Where can I find recent articles on kinship?
- Are there any examples of fieldwork photographs online?

Points to consider

- Anthropology is traditionally divided into a number of sub-fields: physical anthropology (which focuses on the study of human populations, often using biology or evolutionary theory) and social or cultural anthropology (which focuses on the study of culture). These are quite different fields of study. Therefore it is always wise to ask what aspect the student is interested in!
- Social Anthropology is often associated with ethnography. This is a method of research based upon participant-observation field studies. It is also a term commonly used to describe anthropological monographs and films. Therefore students may ask for lists of ethnographies. Be aware that a search of many library catalogues for the term ethnography will simply retrieve those items which mention the word in the title, tables of contents or abstract. This will not be exhaustive. More extensive reading and film lists can often be retrieved from the websites of the main professional organizations.
- Many social anthropologists focus upon particular regions of the world. Therefore they may also be interested in using the broader geographically based resources designed for area studies specialists. Further information on these can be found in the **African Studies, Asian Studies, Latin American** and **Slavonic and East European Studies** sections.

Where to look

Key organizations

American Anthropological Association (AAA)

> www.aaanet.org
>
> World's largest professional Anthropology body, supporting over 21 key journals and numerous special-interest groups. Its serials are available on subscription as an e-journal database called *Anthrosource*. Check its blog for the latest research and publication news.

Association of Social Anthropologists UK & Commonwealth (ASA)

> www.theasa.org
>
> Founded in 1946, a key body for the study of Social Anthropology. Its website also includes online articles and films from ASA members.

Royal Anthropological Institute of Great Britain and Ireland
www.therai.org.uk
World's longest established scholarly association, dedicated to all aspects of physical and social anthropology. Its website is a key starting-point for tracing new research and forthcoming events. It also has links to a detailed listing of ethnographic films, its library catalogue and the *Anthropological Index to Journal Articles*, which it produces.

World Council of Anthropological Associations (WCAA)
www.wcaanet.org
Network of national and international associations that aims to promote worldwide co-operation in Anthropology. Use its website to find links to important national associations worldwide.

Libraries and archives

British Museum Anthropology Library
www.britishmuseum.org/the_museum/departments/africa,_oceania,_ americas/facilities_and_services/anthropology_library.aspx
Contains the holdings of the Royal Anthropological Institute Library. It covers all aspects of Social and Physical Anthropology and all regions of the world, with particularly strong collections on the British Commonwealth, Eastern Europe and the Americas (notably Mesoamerica). Search the British Museum collections online database to view photographs and images of many of its rare treasures! The library is open to the public for reference access.

National Anthropological Archives and Human Studies Film Archives
www.nmnh.si.edu/naa
Based at the Smithsonian Institution. Extensive holdings include field notes, journals, manuscripts, correspondence, photographs, maps, sound recordings, film and video. In addition to online guides to its own collections, it also has a directory of Anthropology archives worldwide.

School of Oriental and African Studies (SOAS)
www.soas.ac.uk/library
One of the world's most important academic libraries for the study of Africa, Asia and the Middle East. Forms part of the University of London. Collections include extensive archives.

Dictionaries and encyclopedias

Barfield, T. (ed.) (1997) *The Dictionary of Anthropology*, Blackwell Press
Focuses primarily on topics, theories and persons in Cultural and Social Anthropology, offering long articles with extensive bibliographies to guide further reading.

Birx, J. (ed.) (2006) *Encyclopedia of Anthropology*, SAGE
Award-winning five-volume set. Over 1200 entries that focus on topics in Physical Anthropology, Cultural Anthropology, Linguistics and Applied Anthropology.

Jacoby, J. and Kibbee, J. Z. (2007) *Cultural Anthropology: a guide to reference and information sources*, 2nd edn, Libraries Unlimited
An annotated bibliography which directs users to key handbooks, bibliographies, indexes, databases, literature reviews and conference proceedings. Sections on specific anthropological specialisms, including Urban Anthropology and Visual Anthropology.

Ethnographic film resources

ARD – Anthropology Review Database
wings.buffalo.edu/ARD
Maintained by the staff at the University of Buffalo. It provides free access to book and film reviews covering all areas of Anthropology.

Ethnographic Video Online (subscription required)
anth.alexanderstreet.com
Provides access to hundreds of key 20th-century anthropological films. Also offers transcripts and study notes. Educators may embed clips in online learning environments.

Royal Anthropological Institute film library
www.therai.org.uk/film/film-library-a-archive
Provides free access to online versions of its film catalogue. This is a good starting-point for locating the existence of ethnographies covering specific regions of the world. It also offers a current DVD/video film sales and hire service.

Visual Anthropology.Net
www.visualanthropology.net
One-stop shop to a wealth of online resources relating to all aspects of Visual Anthropology which is maintained by Ethnodoc, a cultural

association based in Matera, Italy. Find lists of events and courses, reviews and links to some free clips of online documentaries and films.

Journal article indexes

Anthropological Index Online
aio.anthropology.org.uk

Published by the Royal Anthropological Institute in co-operation with the Centre for Anthropology, British Museum. It indexes over 780 journals published in more than 40 languages which are currently taken by the library. This version is accessible free of charge on the internet. A subscription-based service with enhanced functionality is offered as part of the *Anthropology Plus* subscription service.

Anthropology Plus (subscription required)
www.oclc.org/support/documentation/firstsearch/databases/dbdetails/details/AnthropologyPlus.htm

Combines the contents of *Anthropological Index Online* with the index *Anthropological Literature* compiled by Harvard University's Tozzer Library. Together they cover over 2500 Physical and Social Anthropology journals from the 19th century to the present day.

International Bibliography of the Social Sciences (IBSS) (subscription required)
www.proquest.co.uk/en-UK/catalogs/databases/detail/ibss-set-c.shtml

Interdisciplinary database, one of the main areas covered is Social Anthropology. Materials from 1952 onwards.

Online archives and field notes

These resources contain examples of field notes, photographs and artefacts. In addition, many museums now offer online collection pages on their websites where you can search for and locate photographs of holdings.

CSAC Ethnographics Gallery
lucy.ukc.ac.uk

Project of the Centre for Social Anthropology and Computing at the University of Kent. Site includes an online version of Paul Stirling's ethnographic data archive, *45 Years in the Turkish Village – 1949–1994*, as well as other examples of fieldwork projects.

Digital Archives of the School of Oriental and African Studies
digital.info.soas.ac.uk

Provides free access to the photographic archive of Christoph von Fürer-

Haimendorf (1909–95), which is recognized as the world's most comprehensive visual documentation of tribal cultures in South Asia and the Himalayas.

Yale Peabody Museum – Department of Anthropology
www.peabody.yale.edu/collections/ant
An example of the growing number of online databases of museum collections. Anthropologists can use it to locate images of material culture artefacts such as ritual objects.

Internet gateways and portals

Anthropology Resources on the Internet
www.anthropologie.net
Maintained since 1999 by Bernard-Olivier Clist. Forms part of the WWW Virtual Library. Offers a directory of links to different resource types, university departments, regions of the world and more.

ARCHIVES

Typical questions

- Where is the Labour Party archive located?
- How can I find out if any private papers from Neville Chamberlain are available?
- Where can I find primary source materials relating to the British in India?

Points to consider

- Many students need to use primary source materials (items such as diaries, letters and manuscripts which provide first-hand evidence) in their dissertations. Archives are excellent sources of these. Their holdings can include private papers of individuals (including diaries, notes, photographs), organizational archives (including minute books, documents and photographs), government archives (minutes of meetings, notes and declassified documents) and military records.
- Note that in some cases there may be restricted access to government documents (which may be classified as secret for a specific period of time) or to personal or medical records (due to issues of confidentiality). Local archivists should be able to advise on this. The **Freedom of Information** section also covers how to make requests for items to be 'declassified'.
- Archives can be held by national or local organizations, universities and/or charities. Most have their own online catalogues. Note that entries in these may not be indexed in the main university catalogue. Check the website for archive or special collections pages where information on this can usually be found.
- Archive catalogues may differ in their levels of detail. Some provide general, collection-level details, others in-depth descriptions of the contents of individual files. Check the website for information because sometimes more detailed handlists may be available in the archive or elsewhere on the website.
- A good starting-point for tracing relevant archives are national record offices. These usually hold major collections of government documents and their websites should have links to any national archive registers and recommended research guides.
- Increasingly examples of digitized materials are accessible via archive websites. In some cases charges are made for downloading individual records. However, it is worth checking whether local or national record offices offer free access on site.
- This section covers general catalogues of archives; references to subject-specific resources are listed in each of the main subject sections.

Where to look

Research guides and tutorials

These sites will help students get started in using archives for their dissertations.

Archival Research Techniques and Skills (ARTS)

www.arts-scheme.co.uk/index.htm

Intended for use by novices. Information for students on how to locate and use archives. Includes advice on handling archives and using both printed and digital archives in research.

The National Archives

www.nationalarchives.gov.uk

Official record office of the British government. Offers comprehensive advice for researchers. This includes specialist guides covering political, military and social history. These highlight key documents and series held within the archives. Other features of the website include online exhibitions and a section for teachers with online lessons using primary source documents.

US National Records and Archives Administration (NARA)

www.archives.gov

Website has a really useful education section which offers catalogues plus general advice on using and citing archives. It also includes collections of lesson plans for teachers which offer guidance on using archives in the classroom.

Directories and catalogues

UK

Archives Hub

archiveshub.ac.uk

Designed to help researchers locate relevant archives in UK colleges and universities. Excludes archives held in other record offices. Search by subject, individual and organizational name. General collection-level descriptions and contact details.

Archon directory

www.nationalarchives.gov.uk/archon

Comprehensive list of record offices and archives in the UK (including colleges, local record offices and private organizations). Also covers institutions overseas which have substantial collections of manuscripts relating to British economic, social or political history. Basic overviews of collections with links to websites and access details.

Foster, J. and Sheppard, J. (2000), *British Archives: a guide to archive resources in the United Kingdom*, **4th edn, Palgrave Macmillan**

Well regarded listing of major UK archive collections. Has name, subject and organizational indexes.

National Register of Archives

www.nationalarchives.gov.uk/nra/default.asp

Covers archives relating to British history. Search the catalogues by person, organization and place names. Subject indexes not currently provided. Entries give brief details of location and access conditions. Note that fuller descriptions can often be obtained by checking the websites of the organizations concerned.

Political Parties and Parliamentary Archives Group (PPPAG)

www.bodley.ox.ac.uk/pppag.htm

Specialist network of archivists and librarians in charge of political archives and the private papers of politicians. Website has a guide to political records and a directory of key record offices.

International

Archive Finder (subscription required)

archives.chadwyck.com/home.do

Directory which describes over 220,000 collections of primary source materials held in thousands of repositories across the USA, the UK and Ireland. Search by subject, name or location.

Archives Made Easy

www.archivesmadeeasy.org

Hosted by the International History Department at the London School of Economics and Political Science. A collection of links, tips and reviews on using archives worldwide which has been created for students by the research community.

MICHAEL: Multilingual Inventory of Cultural Heritage in Europe

www.michael-culture.org

Supported by the European Union. Aims to provide a searchable catalogue of museums, libraries and archives from European nations which have digital collections. It is possible to view the collections by subject area, time period and place. Links are provided to the websites. A good starting-point for tracing online primary source materials.

ARCHIVES

OCLC WorldCat (Manuscript materials)

www.loc.gov/coll/nucmc/index.html

The Library of Congress website provides free access to this service which enables WorldCat to be searched for records relating to archives and manuscripts. Website has advice on how to do this plus links to key North American organizations and archives.

UNESCO – Archives portal

www.unesco-ci.org/cgi-bin/portals/archives/page/cgi

International index. Locate links to the websites of archives and record offices worldwide. Includes specialist indexes for government and military archives, archives held by universities and online digital archives. Also available are lists of archives in specific countries and research finding aids.

ART

Typical questions
- Where can I find out about the Glasgow School?
- I want to access data on recent art auction prices.

Points to consider
- This section highlights resources for tracing articles, art prices and art works online. There is also a separate section on **Images and Photographs** which covers photographs and other visual resources.
- Copyright can be a difficult issue for images. Consult the **Copyright** section for guidance.

Where to look

Key organizations

Metropolitan Museum of Art

    www.metmuseum.org

    World-famous New York museum. Use the website to consult a timeline of art history and search a collections database of over 250,000 images of works of art held by the museum.

Royal Academy of Arts

    www.royalacademy.org.uk

    Leading UK body renowned for its summer exhibition. In addition to exhibition listings, the website offers information on its history and an online archive of podcasts of key events covering historical and contemporary arts (including architecture and sculpture).

Libraries and archives

Arlis.net

    www.arlis.net

    Maintained by the National Art Library at the Victoria and Albert Museum, for the Art Libraries Society (ARLIS/UK & Ireland). A quick finding aid for tracing art and design journals located in UK libraries.

artlibraries.net

    artlibraries.net/index_en.php

    Cross-search the catalogues of many major art libraries in Europe and North America to locate books and journals.

Getty Research Institute
www.getty.edu/research
Extensive research library focusing on the history of art and architecture. Its website offers a selection of really useful research guides as well as an Art and Architecture thesaurus.

National Art Library
www.vam.ac.uk/nal
National Art Library at the Victoria and Albert Museum is a major reference library which is open to the public. It covers fine and decorative arts from around the world. Its website provides free access to study guides on researching auction house catalogues, biographical information about artists and art prices.

Dictionaries and encyclopedias

Clarke, M. (2001) *The Concise Oxford Dictionary of Art Terms*, Oxford University Press
Definitions of over 1600 terms covering art techniques, styles, methodologies and theories.

Turner, J. (ed.) (1996) *Dictionary of Art*, Grove
Also known as the *Grove Dictionary of Art*, this major 34-volume work covers all time periods and art styles. There are biographies of leading artists with references to the standard works about them, including exhibition catalogues. The dictionary is also available as part of the **Oxford Art Online** database (subscription required), **www.oxfordartonline.com public**, which also includes the full text of a number of other key art reference encyclopedias published by Oxford University Press including the *Oxford Companion to Western Art* and *Concise Oxford Dictionary of Art Terms*.

Images and paintings online

Note that more detailed advice on searching the internet for images is given in the **Images and Photographs** section of this book. However, in general, good starting-points are the websites of major galleries and museums, many of which have collections databases. Users should, however, be advised to check copyright conditions carefully before use.

ARTstor (subscription required)
www.artstor.org
Digital library of over a million images taken from famous art collections

worldwide. They include the Museum of Modern Art (MoMA) Architecture and Design Collection, the Metropolitan Museum of Art and the Bodleian Library.

British Printed Images to 1700
www.britishprintedimagesto1700.org.uk

Provides free access to a searchable database of several thousand historic images, mainly taken from the holdings of the Department of Prints and Drawings at the British Museum and the National Art Library at the Victoria and Albert Museum. Search by keyword or browse by subject. Headings include: agriculture, industry and commerce; buildings; military and war; nature; politics; and the Bible. A resources section provides contextual detail on understanding images of this time period plus links to related websites.

Google Art Project
www.googleartproject.com

Amazing site launched in 2011. Current partners (with more planned) include major galleries such as the Van Gogh Museum, Amsterdam; Metropolitan Museum of Art; Tate Britain; National Gallery, London; and the Uffizi Gallery, Florence. Explore the galleries using street-view technology and zoom in on pictures for an in-depth view.

VADS
www.vads.ac.uk

Free access to over 12,000 images designed for use in teaching and learning. They include paintings, prints, propaganda posters and fashion designs taken from major UK collections.

Journal article indexes

ARTbibliographies Modern (subscription required)
www.csa.com/factsheets/artbm-set-c.php

Provides abstracts of journal articles, books, essays, exhibition catalogues and reviews of all forms of modern and contemporary art from the late 19th century onwards, with an emphasis on lesser known artists. Articles published from 1974 onwards.

Bibliography of the History of Art
www.getty.edu/research/tools/bha/index.html

Free access to *Bibliography of the History of Art* (BHA) and to the *Répertoire international de la littérature de l'art* (RILA) via the Getty website. This indexes over 1200 titles of importance to art historians. Note that coverage is from 1975 to 2007. After this date it is succeeded by the *International Bibliography of Art.*

International Bibliography of Art (subscription required)

www.proquest.com/en-US/catalogs/databases/detail/iba.shtml

Successor to the *Bibliography of the History of Art* (BHA). Covers European art from late antiquity to the present, American art from the colonial era to the present and global art since 1945, indexing articles, exhibition catalogues and papers published in more than 500 titles since 2007.

Art prices and sales

Art Sales Prices

www.artinfo.com/artsalesindex

Freely available basic information on recent art sales.

Artprice.com (subscription required)

www.artprice.com

Database of over 27 million auction prices and indices from over 500 international auction houses. Covers 1986 onwards. It is possible to use the database to track information about prices for individual artists or trends in the market.

SCIPIO

www.oclc.org/support/documentation/firstsearch/databases/dbdetails/details/SCIPIO.htm

Information on auction sales catalogues from all major North American and European auction houses as well as many private sales from the 16th century to forthcoming sales.

Internet gateways and portals

Artcyclopedia

www.artcyclopedia.com

Offers thousands of links to famous artists, museums and galleries online. These include individual images of famous paintings.

arthistoricum.net – Virtual Library for Art History

www.arthistoricum.net

Project of the Library of the Zentralinstitut für Kunstgeschichte in Munich, Heidelberg University Library and other partners. Marvellous resource for students of art history, offering an index to recent dissertations and theses, *ARTicles online* (an index of art history articles), plus links to library catalogues, online image collections and news sources.

ASIAN STUDIES

Typical questions

- I need to trace data on economic development in South-East Asia.
- I want to know which libraries have large collections of Chinese-language materials.
- Where can I find articles on Islam in Asia?

Points to consider

- This is an area studies section. It should be used in conjunction with the appropriate subject sections. Also useful is **Development Studies**, as some nations may not have the resources to regularly update their own websites.
- Definitions of what constitutes South Asia or South-East Asia may differ. Always check if the user is interested in a specific nation. They may instead require information about the Asian diaspora overseas! The large number of nations covered means that it is essential that these resources are used as starting-points that should be explored further.

Where to look

Scholarly societies

UK

Use these to find information on the latest conferences, publications and research projects.

Association of South-East Asian Studies in the United Kingdom (ASEASUK)
aseasuk.org.uk
Leading subject organization.

British Association for South Asian Studies
www.basas.org.uk
Largest UK academic association for the study of India, Pakistan, Bangladesh, Afghanistan, Sri Lanka, Nepal, Bhutan, Maldives and the South Asian diaspora.

Royal Asiatic Society of Great Britain and Ireland
www.royalasiaticsociety.org
Established 1824. Leading learned society. Promotes science and the arts. Use the website to consult its library catalogue and find out about its renowned lecture series and support for research.

Royal Society for Asian Affairs (RSAA)

www.rsaa.org.uk

Promotes greater knowledge and understanding of Central Asia and countries from the Middle East to Japan. Use the website to find out about its public lectures and search the library catalogue.

International

Association for Asian Studies

www.asian-studies.org

Largest worldwide organization. Its website has an extensive directory of useful links to Asian Studies programmes and organizations worldwide as well as details about its publications, including the *Journal of Asian Studies*.

European Alliance for Asian Studies

www.asia-alliance.org

Network of European-based Asian Studies research institutes.

International Convention of Asia Scholars (ICAS)

www.icassecretariat.org

Seeks to promote research in Asian Studies by academics and civil society organizations. Find out about its regular conferences and publications.

Libraries and archives

UK

British Library

www.bl.uk/reshelp/findhelpregion/asia/southasia/sereources.html

Contains a world-famous collection covering contemporary and historical Asian studies. Highlights include the India Office records, which contain the official archives of the East India Company (1600–1858), India Office (1858–1947) and other government agencies, as well as private papers from individuals and historic newspapers. It also maintains a special family history search service, **indiafamily.bl.uk/UI/Home.aspx**.

School of Oriental and African Studies (SOAS)

www.soas.ac.uk/library

Specialist library of the University of London which has extensive holdings of books and journals covering the social sciences and humanities. Website provides access to the catalogue and a subject guide.

To trace other useful collections try the following sites. They are particularly useful for locating Asian-language resources. The websites also have events listings, details of digitization projects and contacts for language specialists.

South Asia Archive and Library Group
www.bl.uk/reshelp/bldept/apac/saalg

Southeast Asia Library Group
www.sealg.org

UKIRA
www.asiamap.ac.uk/index.php
Provides information on resources relating to Asia, the Middle East and North Africa held in university, public and research libraries. General descriptions of collections plus a union list of newspaper collections.

International

Centre for Research Libraries Global Resources Network
www.crl.edu/collections/topics/south-asian-studies
An international consortium of university, college and independent research libraries which seeks to improve access to area studies resources. Use the website to find information about Asian projects.

European Association of Sinological Librarians (EASL)
www.easl.org
Get news and information on European libraries with significant Chinese Studies collections.

EVOCS: European Virtual OPAC for Chinese Studies
www.sino.uni-heidelberg.de/evocs
Cross-search catalogues of European academic libraries with major collections.

Libraries of Asia and the Pacific Directory
www.nla.gov.au/lap
Maintained by the Conference of Directors of National Libraries of Asia and Oceania. Trace information about college, university, research and national libraries in nations of the Asia-Pacific.

Current awareness
Use these in conjunction with the main **Current Awareness Tools** section.

H-Asia
www.h-net.org/~asia

Free mailing list which forms part of H-Net Humanities & Social Sciences Online. Access recent book reviews, conference listings and discussion covering Asian history and culture.

ResearchSEA

www.researchsea.com

Research news portal, offers latest press releases from universities and research bodies in South-East Asia. Coverage includes business, science, technology and culture.

Journal article indexes

Bibliography of Asian Studies (subscription required)

www.aasianst.org/aboutbas.htm

Premier service covering Western-language social sciences and humanities journal articles, book chapters and reports published since 1971.

Index Islamicus (subscription required)

www.brill.nl/indexislamicus

Leading bibliography on Islam and the Muslim world. Indexes over 3000 journal titles, plus monographs and book chapters. From 1906 onwards.

Southeast Asian Serials Index

anulib.anu.edu.au/sasi

Maintained by Australian National library. Indexes academic journals about South East Asia published in a range of countries including Indonesia, Malaysia, Japan, Australia and the Netherlands. Includes Indonesian-language titles. Coverage from 1990 onwards.

Electronic libraries and internet portals

Use these to supplement the journal article indexes. They often offer links to relevant working paper series plus high-quality websites.

AccessAsia

www.accessasia.org

Maintained by the National Bureau of Asian Research. A specialist search engine which locates and cross-searches the personal websites of Asian studies specialists worldwide.

AsiaPortal

www.asiaportal.info

Maintained by universities that are members of the Nordic NIAS Council. It provides free access to topical news, articles and research reports about

Asian nations from Nordic universities (based in Iceland, Denmark, Norway and Sweden).

CrossAsia: Virtual Library East and South-East Asia
crossasia.org
Developed by the East Asia Department of the Staatsbibliothek zu Berlin to provide a single point of access to academic resources relating to the region. Search journal articles, newspapers, catalogues and browse key internet sites. Note that some services require a subscription. Excellent for locating Asian-language materials from China, Korea, Taiwan and Japan.

Digital South Asia Library
dsal.uchicago.edu
A project of the Center for Research Libraries and the University of Chicago. Highlights include Asian-language digital dictionaries, online maps, historic statistical data (from the colonial period to the present), maps, e-books, e-journals, bibliographies and other finding aids.

Savifa: Virtual Library of South Asia
www.savifa.uni-hd.de
Created by the library of the South Asia Institute (SAI) in co-operation with Heidelberg University Library. Offers scholars access to a wealth of online resources relating to all aspects of the history, politics and culture of South Asian nations (India, Pakistan, Bangladesh, Sri Lanka, Nepal, Maldives, Tibet (before 1950) and Bhutan). It includes e-journals, library catalogues, selected internet sites and a directory of Asian Studies scholars. **SavifaDok, archiv.ub.uni-heidelberg.de/savifadok/index.php?la=en**, contains many open access scholarly articles and papers.

Sarai: South Asia Resource Access on the internet
www.columbia.edu/cu/lweb/indiv/southasia/cuvl
Maintained by Columbia University. Contains hundreds of links to high-quality internet sites covering Bangladesh, Bhutan, India, Nepal, Pakistan, Tibet and Sri Lanka. Includes a searchable *International Directory of South Asia Scholars*.

Statistical data

Note that these resources should be used in conjunction with those in the general **Statistical Data** and **Development Studies** sections.

APEC – Asia-Pacific Forum
www.apec.org

Economic forum for the region. In addition to a meetings and documents database, its website also offers free access to **StatsApec, statistics.apec. org**, which contains major economic, social and bilateral trade indicators.

APECLIT

www.apec.info/lib/apeclit.html

Bibliography of published materials about APEC compiled by the Australian APEC Study Centre, Monash University. Includes publications about and by APEC. Links are provided to full-text versions where available.

Asian Development Bank

www.adb.org

Multilateral development bank which works to reduce poverty. Website provides free access to *Asian Development Outlook (ADO)*, its annual survey of economic trends. It also offers access to online databases, including investment climate surveys.

Asian Productivity Organization (APO)

www.apo-tokyo.org

Website includes growth maps, plus news, reports and data on economic trends, industry and agriculture.

Association of Southeast Asian Nations (ASEAN)

www.aseansec.org

Intergovernmental economic and security organization. Website has some country profiles, trade, economic and macroeconomic indicators.

South Asian Association for Regional Co-operation (SAARC)

www.saarc-sec.org

Website includes summit declarations and publications covering regional socio-economic co-operation.

United Nations Economic and Social Commission for Asia and the Pacific (ESCAP)

www.unescap.org

Regional body. Access press releases, reports, documents and data. ESCAP online database includes country-level data related to demography, migration, education, health, poverty, gender, employment, economy and environment. It is also possible to consult the *Statistical Yearbook for Asia and the Pacific* and the *Asia and the Pacific Trade and Investment Report*.

ASSOCIATIONS

Typical questions
- Is there a professional association for travel agents?
- Can you give me a list of key bodies that represent British accountants?

Points to consider
- Associations can refer to voluntary organizations, trade/industry groups or professional bodies.
- Students often find association websites useful for tracing information about careers and qualifications. In addition, many also sponsor conferences, journals and projects, so they can be used to find out about the latest research.
- This section covers general resources. Refer to the subject sections for links to information on key organizations in specific subject fields.

Where to look

UK

Directory of British Associations: and associations in Ireland (2011) 20th edn, CBD Research Ltd

Published since 1965 and regularly updated. Covers trade, professional and learned associations. Each entry gives contact addresses and membership information and lists key publications. There is also an index to acronyms.

Trade Association Forum (TAF)
www.taforum.org

Maintains an authoritative directory of UK trade organizations. Includes non-TAF members. Entries give summaries of remit and contact details.

International

Encyclopedia of Associations: international organizations (2010) 50th edn, Gale

Extensive three-volume set which covers national, regional and international bodies worldwide. Entries include contact details, history, budgets and key publications. Associations can be traced by geographic region and subject area. Normally updated annually.

ASSOCIATIONS

Encyclopedia of Associations: national organizations of the U.S. (2010), 49th
  edn, Gale
Trace information on national membership organizations based in
America. Contains geographic and chief executive indexes. Annual
updates.

BANKING

Typical questions

- I need to read the latest Monetary Policy Committee minutes.
- Where can I access international banking statistics?

Points to consider

- This section should be used in conjunction with the **Business Studies** and **Economics** sections, which list relevant libraries, journal article databases and working paper series.

Where to look

Key organizations

Trade associations

These provide news on the profession, lists of members and basic statistical data. Most also contain materials on banking regulation.

British Bankers Association
> **www.bba.org.uk**
> Publishes the *Annual Abstract of Banking Statistics* covering the UK industry (subscribers only). Other less detailed statistics can be downloaded free of charge. These include high street banking, credit card and mortgage data.

Building Societies Association
> **www.bsa.org.uk**
> Includes statistics on building society assets.

International Banking Federation (IBFed)
> **www.ibfed.org**
> Represents national banking associations. Useful links to websites of members.

UK Payments
> **www.ukpayments.org.uk**
> Formerly the Association for Payment Clearing Services (APACS), trade association of organizations providing payment clearing services.

Central banks

These websites usually provide information on the state of the national economy, national reserves and assets as well as data on banking systems and policies.

Bank of England
www.bankofengland.co.uk

Free access to Monetary Policy Committee minutes, the *Inflation Report* and *Financial Stability* reports. The statistics section *BankStats* has time series of financial and monetary data. Issues covered include financial institutions' balance sheets, public sector borrowing, interest rates and exchange rates. Check data coverage of series on the website.

Bank for International Settlements
www.bis.org

International organization which promotes international monetary and financial co-operation between central banks. Its website has a central bank hub with free access to useful directories of national authorities, speeches from bank governors and research reports. The statistics section provides free access to some international and national banking statistics. These include cross-border lending and borrowing of internationally active banks, securities, derivatives, external debt and property prices.

Board of Governors of the Federal Reserve
www.federalreserve.gov

Central bank of United States. Website has explanations of the system as well as a large number of publications and statistical reports. Users with a specific interest in statistical data should also consult the **St Louis Federal Bank FRED** site, **research.stlouisfed.org/fred2,** a free database of over 27,000 economic time series.

European Central Bank (ECB)
www.ecb.int

Responsible for conducting monetary policy for the euro currency area. Website provides free access to detailed information on the policy and governance of banks in eurozone nations. It includes convergence reports, financial stability reports and an extensive statistical section with euro data.

To trace other national bank websites see the list maintained by the **Bank for International Settlements (BIS), www.bis.org/cbanks.htm.**

Multilateral development banks

Provide financial aid for economic and social development activities in developing countries. Key organizations are the World Bank Group and four regional development banks. All provide some data, project and policy reports on their websites. A list of other development banks can be located on the World Bank website. The **Development Studies** section has a statistics sub-section which may also be relevant.

African Development Bank
www.afdb.org

Asian Development Bank
www.adb.org

European Bank for Reconstruction and Development
www.ebrd.com/pages/homepage.shtml
Includes specialist information on transition economies of Eastern Europe
and the Balkans.

Inter-American Development Bank Group
www.iadb.org

World Bank
www.worldbank.org

Statistical data

In addition to the websites listed above, refer also to the statistical resources in
the **Business Studies** section. Other specialist sources of banking statistics series
are the following.

BankScope (subscription required)
www.bvdinfo.com/Products/Company-Information/International/
Bankscope.aspx
Contains detailed financial information on over 30,000 individual banks
worldwide. Includes credit ratings and analyst reports.

Joint External Debt Hub (JEDH)
www.jedh.org
Maintained by the Bank for International Settlements, the International
Monetary Fund, the Organization for Economic Co-operation and
Development (OECD) and the World Bank. Brings together in one place
data relating to external debt of developing countries.

OECD Banking Statistics (subscription required)
www.oecd.org
Annual data from OECD nations from 1979 onwards.

BIBLIOMETRICS

Typical questions

- Who are the most highly cited authors in Economics?
- How can I identify influential journals in my field?

Points to consider

- Bibliometric data is a quantitative method which is increasingly being used to track and assess the impact of research. Further information on this can be found on the UK Research Excellence Framework (REF) website, **www.hefce.ac.uk/research/ref**.
- Researchers may wish to measure the number of times their individual articles have been cited by others. They may also want information on the impact factor of particular journals where they intend to publish.
- Institutions often want to measure and compare the number of citations/impact of a department with competitors in other institutions.
- However, journal citation data are not without controversy. Critics often point to problems relating to differences in publications between disciplines. For further discussion see the e-mail forum **www.jiscmail.ac.uk/lists/LIS-BIBLIOMETRICS.html**.
- As a result, many commercial databases offer several measures. These can be complex and difficult to understand. Recommend that enquirers consult help screens for explanations of the definitions and methodology used.

Where to look

Tutorials

MyRI

> **www.ndlr.ie/myri/about.html**
> Excellent open access site created by four Irish university libraries which teaches librarians and researchers how to use bibliometrics. It covers the main commercial products, explaining the strengths and weaknesses of each and how to use them effectively. It includes online tutorials and classroom materials for teachers that can be tailored for local use.

Commercial databases

Many journal article indexes, such as **ISI Web of Knowledge, wok.mimas.ac.uk**, allow users to sort their search results by number of times cited and to follow cross-references to the citing articles. They also allow registered users to receive alerts when their article has been cited by others.

ISI Journal Citation Reports (subscription required)

thomsonreuters.com/products_services/science/science_products/
a-z/journal_citation_reports

Provides information on the most frequently cited journals in individual subject fields. Note that these rankings cover only those titles indexed in ISI (Institute for Scientific Information) databases. Free tutorials are available from the website. The publisher also maintains a free Citation Impact Center website, **science.thomsonreuters. com/citationimpactcenter** with news.

Scopus (subscription required)

www.scopus.com/scopus/home.url

Competitor to ISI. Results will differ because it indexes a different list of journals and uses other methods of calculation. Citation data is from 1996 onwards. This is a shorter time span than that covered by ISI. However, reviewers often feel that it indexes more non-English-language titles and medical/scientific titles. It is possible to conduct citation analyses on individual authors, journal titles or institutions.

Free websites

ISI Highly cited com

isihighlycited.com

Maintained by Thomson Scientific, publishers of ISI Web of Science. Provides information on 250 of the most important scientists worldwide. Individuals are selected using analysis of the most highly cited papers from over 20 years of data taken from the ISI Web of Science databases.

Publish or Perish

www.harzing.com/pop.htm

Software programme which uses Google Scholar to analyse citations. Note the caveat on the site relating to varying subject coverage of Google Scholar and the fact that it may retrieve items which may not have been peer reviewed.

SCImago

www.scimagojr.com

Developed by a research group from the University of Granada, Extremadura, Carlos III (Madrid). Uses Google page-ranking technology and journals taken from the Scopus database. Ranks the impact and number of citations for journal titles, subject areas and countries (where researchers are based). Coverage from 1996 onwards.

BIOGRAPHICAL INFORMATION

Typical questions

- What university did the prime minister attend?
- When was Nelson Mandela born?

Points to consider

- Find out as much as you can about the individual. What does the user already know? Do they know the nationality; occupation; approximate date of birth; subject area of work; university affiliation? All these may help in tracing further leads.
- Many nations publish dictionaries of national biography which contain summaries of the lives of some of their key men and women. These can often be traced via the national library website, which in some cases may even offer free versions. However, do remember to check the date range covered because they may not include people who are still alive.
- Some professions, such as the military and the clergy, also publish information about their leading members in annual directories. Try consulting the **Associations** section for further ideas.
- Increasingly, governments are placing CVs and other biographical information about prime ministers and presidents online. These can be more detailed than reference books, offering online speeches and articles not available elsewhere.
- Many university lecturers also have their own home pages, which can list and even provide free access to journal articles and working papers. Often these can be traced by searching for the name of the university or individual via Google. However, do remember that these may not always be kept up to date. Check for information about when the page was last updated.

Where to look

Oxford Dictionary of National Biography (DNB) (subscription required)
www.oxforddnb.com
National record of over 55,000 men and women who have shaped British history from earliest times to the current day. All subjects are deceased. Entries include bibliographies and links to related websites; many also have portraits or photos. Non-subscribers can sign up to receive via e-mail free biographies of the day.

American Dictionary of National Biography (subscription required)
www.anb.org
More than 18,000 entries for important historic Americans. Entries include portraits, lists of biographical sources for further reading. Free access to a biography of the day.

Australian Dictionary of Biography Online
adbonline.anu.edu.au/adbonline.htm
Free access to over 10,000 entries for famous Australians from all walks of life. The site is searchable by name and occupation. Currently no entries for individuals who died after 1980, although there is a programme to expand this.

Who's Who (UK) (subscription required)
www.acblack.com/whoswho
Offered in print or online, this annual volume is a major source for tracing information on famous living people. Online versions often also include a subscription to *Who Was Who* (covering earlier editions from 1897 onwards). Includes information on show business, media, political and sports persons worldwide. Non-subscribers can access a brief listing of persons born on the current day.

World Who's Who (subscription required)
www.worldwhoswho.com
Comprises more than 60,000 biographies. Strong coverage of world leaders, heads of state.

Occupational directories
A key example is

Crockford's Clerical Directory (subscription required)
www.crockford.org.uk
Available online or in print. Contains biographies of over 26,000 Anglican clergy in the UK. Online version covers from 1968 onwards.
Other key trade associations are listed in the **Associations** section.

BOOK REVIEWS

Typical questions

- Are there any reviews of Freeman's book on Margaret Mead?
- I want to find out who has reviewed my latest book.

Points to consider

- Many students are familiar with user-created comments or reviews on websites such as Amazon. This section will direct them to more 'academic' resources which they can use in their essays.
- Find out as much information about the book as you can because this will help in tracing reviews. When was it published? What was its subject area?
- Book reviews may take a long time to appear. Usually the best starting-points for reviews of recently published items are newspapers or specialist review publications.
- Many journal indexes also include book reviews. Often you can restrict your search by resource type in order to retrieve these. Recommended databases are in the **Journal Article Indexes** section.

Where to look

Current review publications

Choice: Current Reviews for Academic Libraries (subscription required)
www.ala.org/ala/mgrps/divs/acrl/publications/choice/index.cfm
In print or online. Associated with the American Library Association and often used by US library staff for collection development.

H-Net Reviews
www.h-net.org/reviews
Online scholarly book review service which forms part of the H-Net Humanities and Social Sciences website hosted by the University of Michigan. Offers free access to a searchable database of reviews of academic books in all fields of the social sciences. Users may sign up to receive e-mail updates.

London Review of Books (subscription required)
www.lrb.co.uk
Established in 1979. Has a reputation for publishing longer critical essays, some of which challenge 'received ideas'.

New York Review of Books (subscription required)
www.nybooks.com
> In print or online. Renowned fortnightly journal covers American literature and a range of philosophy, social, political and cultural titles. From 1963 onwards. Free access to the archive (prior to the current year).

Times Literary Supplement (subscription required)
www.the-tls.co.uk
> In print or online. Major British intellectual review journal. Published since the 1920s. Online archive currently from 1994 onwards.

Historic materials

These mainly cover English Literature. A good listing of volumes is available on the British Library website, **www.bl.uk/reshelp/findhelprestype/refworks/intenglit/intenglit.html**.

Key examples include:

Ward, W. S. (1972–79) *Literary Reviews in British Periodicals: a bibliography [1789–1826]*, **4 vols, Garland**

Wellesley Index to Victorian Periodicals (1824–1900) (subscription required for online version)
wellesley.chadwyck.com/home.do
Indexes 45 major 19th-century British titles.

BUSINESS STUDIES

Typical questions

- I want to find articles on entrepreneurship.
- How can I get information on turnover for the top 50 pharmaceutical companies?

Points to consider

- The needs of Business Studies students can range from advice on business planning to detailed company data. This section offers academic starting-points. Related topic areas are **Management, Banking, Economics, Marketing, Company and Stock Market Information**.

Where to look

Key organizations

Educational

Use these websites to trace news, conferences and links to key business schools.

UK

Association of Business Schools
 www.the-abs.org.uk
 Represents British business schools. Offers free access to annual reports and some statistics that give insight into recent trends.

Higher Education Academy
 www.heacademy.ac.uk
 Acts to support lecturers in UK higher education. Subject coverage includes business and management. Website highlights teaching and learning news and projects.

International

Academy of International Business (AIB)
 aib.msu.edu
 International association of scholars. Website has an excellent directory of links to academic websites worldwide.

African Association of Business Schools
 www.aabschools.com

Association to Advance Collegiate Schools of Business
www.aacsb.edu
Oldest accreditation board for business education in the USA.

Latin American Council of Management Schools (CLADEA)
www.cladea.org

Trade associations

Use these to trace news, views and comment on business policy from industry. All also have sections on career development.

British Chambers of Commerce
www.britishchambers.org.uk
National network of chambers of commerce.

Confederation of British Industry (CBI)
www.cbi.org.uk
UK's largest business lobbying group. Website is a useful starting-point for tracing business reaction to UK economic policy. Also includes regular surveys of business prospects.

Federation of Small Businesses
www.fsb.org.uk
Key starting-point for tracing information on small businesses in the UK. Useful directory of members.

Institute of Directors
www.iod.com
Membership organization of business leaders. Website has many factsheets on practical business skills.

US Chambers of Commerce
www.uschamber.com

International Chambers of Commerce
www.iccwbo.org

Libraries

Business Librarians' Association (BLA)
www.bbslg.org
Specialist membership organization for practitioners in UK and Ireland. Offers support, training and advice in business research techniques. Website often has materials from its events.

BUSINESS STUDIES

British Library Business and IP Centre
www.bl.uk/bipc

Supports business entrepreneurs and researchers by providing access to books, journals and databases. Search its online catalogues and consult the detailed industry research guides on its website.

City Business Library
www.cityoflondon.gov.uk/corporation/LGNL_Services/Leisure_and_culture/Libraries/City_of_London_libraries/cbl.htm

Leading UK public library for business information. Materials focus on current information.

European Business Schools Librarians' Group
www.ebslg.org

Has information and membership lists on a Europe-wide level.

Dictionaries

Law, J. (2009) *Dictionary of Business and Management*, 5th edn, Oxford University Press

Over 7000 definitions covering all areas of business and management, including US terms. Associated website has useful links, **www.oup.com/uk/booksites/content/9780199234899**

Journal article indexes

Use these in conjunction with the **Economics** section.

ABI/Inform (subscription required)
www.proquest.com/en-US/catalogs/databases/detail/abi_inform.shtml

Coverage from 1935 onwards. Includes journal articles, case studies, business news.

Business Source Complete (subscription required)
www.ebscohost.com/academic/business-source-complete

Indexes more than 1300 academic and trade journals, reports and case studies covering all aspects of business, management and marketing. Includes some titles from the19th century!

Emerald (subscription required)
www.emeraldinsight.com/products/first/index.htm

Produces a range of business and management e-journals and journal indexing services.

News services

Use these to supplement the national newspapers.

Business Week
www.businessweek.com

News and stock market prices from Bloomberg. Includes US business school news, advice and rankings.

Economist (subscription required to access some features)
www.economist.com

Provides up-to-date news and comment. Also has a business education section with news from business schools worldwide, regional rankings and MBA advice.

Financial Times (subscription required)
www.ft.com

Latest UK and international business news. Website includes continuously updated stock market prices plus news about business education, including regular global MBA rankings.

Wall Street Journal
europe.wsj.com (Europe Edition) (subscription required)
online.wsj.com

Get US and international business, finance and market news.

Internet gateways and portals

Biz/ed
www.bized.co.uk

Free teaching and learning resource for UK business students and lecturers. Access to online lesson plans, interactive tutorials, articles, podcasts and dictionaries covering all aspects of business and management education. Includes access to some company financial data.

British Library Business and Management Portal
www.mbsportal.bl.uk

Excellent starting-point. Register to use effectively. Cross-search the collection of the British Library for books, journal articles, reports series and case studies. Set up research alerts. Increasing numbers of full-text papers can be downloaded from the website (where copyright allows). Access to other items requires a subscription. Students are advised to check their own library/journal subscriptions as some of these may be offered locally.

BUSINESS STUDIES

globalEDGE

globaledge.msu.edu

Maintained by the International Business Center at Michigan State University. Provides an excellent directory of links to international business internet sites. Also includes lesson plans, online business statistics, country and industry profiles.

CAREERS GUIDANCE

Typical questions

- Can I become a solicitor if I have a degree in maths?
- Where can I find out the dates of forthcoming careers fairs?

Points to consider

- Most colleges will have specialist careers guidance services. These usually offer leaflets/advice on common queries relating to CV preparation, interview skills and preparing for psychometric tests. Many have websites which contain full-text guides and links to information on local events. Always check these first.
- The resources below are recommended services which can supplement these. Students should also be encouraged to contact subject-related professional associations because most maintain lists of courses, funding and employment opportunities. Subject sections in this book highlight key ones.

Where to look

Association of Graduate Careers Advisory Services (AGCAS)
www.agcas.org.uk
Professional association for UK higher education careers advisors. Website is designed to offer support to practitioners with online news and reports relating to the quality, content and service delivery of careers information. However, it does have a useful resource directory of links to key organizations and suppliers of careers advice.

Careers in Europe
www.careersineurope.hobsons.com
Site maintained by Hobsons for graduates. Includes country and employer profiles and a job-search facility. The same company also has sites covering opportunities in Australia, North America and Asia. Links to these are provided on the website.

High Fliers Research
www.highfliers.co.uk
Conducts a number of regular surveys, most recent examples of which can be downloaded from the website. The *Graduate Market* provides a snapshot of opportunities in the graduate jobs market in the UK. It includes data on starting salaries in specific sectors.

International Centre for Guidance Studies (iCEGS)
www.derby.ac.uk/icegs

Based at University of Derby, holds the UK's largest collection of guidance literature. Search its online catalogue to find references to books, articles and journals covering careers, employment and training. The website also highlights recent research and news about graduate careers opportunities.

Prospects
www.prospects.ac.uk

Graduate Prospects is the commercial arm of HECSU (Higher Education Careers Services Unit), a registered charity. Its website provides free access to a wealth of useful information. It includes general careers advice; sample CVs; a directory of all UK university careers services; plus graduate job-search databases and news about forthcoming careers events.

SKILL
www.skill.org.uk

National organization offering support and advice on careers, education and training for disabled students in the UK.

TargetJobs
targetjobs.co.uk

Another well regarded site designed specifically to offer graduates careers advice. It includes the **Careers Report, targetjobs.co.uk/careers-report**, which uses questionnaires and psychometric tests to guide students towards appropriate employment. Other features are course, jobs and career events listings for the UK.

Times Top 100 Graduate Employers
www.top100graduateemployers.com

Annual survey conducted by High Fliers Research. Website has basic rankings. The published book (which can be purchased and is often distributed by university careers services) has more detailed information, plus general careers advice on job applications.

Students may also be interested in viewing the regular listing of top UK gay-, lesbian- and bisexual-friendly employers on the **Stonewall** website at **www.stonewall.org.uk.**

CENSUS RESEARCH

Typical questions

- Can I get access to any sample data from UK censuses?
- When was the last Indian census held?
- I need to locate historic population distribution data for 19th-century London.

Points to consider

- Censuses are used by governments to collect statistical data on population size and distribution. They may also cover employment and living conditions. Frequency and range differs between nations. Students often find them useful in tracing historical demographic and social data at both local and national levels. They are also of value to family historians seeking information about their ancestors.
- Remember that data protection issues will restrict access to individual records from recent censuses, although statistical results and some anonymized samples are often available.
- Increasingly, commercial companies are making available on the web older census materials. Remember to check the authenticity of these and whether they contain images of the original transcriptions. The latter may be desirable to researchers checking for accuracy and seeking examples of their ancestors' handwriting! Note that public record offices may offer free access to selected online census services. Check before purchasing!
- Those interested in population issues may also find it helpful to consult the **Statistical Data** section.

Where to look

UK

Census records

The first modern census is generally regarded as having taken place in 1801. Individuals seeking earlier materials are advised to look at parish registers. Information is usually available in public record offices and The National Archives. A good website to use as a starting-point is **www.parishregister.co.uk**.

Note that records for Scotland and Northern Ireland are collected and stored separately.

These starting-points focus mainly upon individual household and personal records. Students wishing to engage in large-scale data queries are advised to use the resources listed in the census data sub-section.

Northern Ireland Statistics and Research Agency (NISRA)

www.nisra.gov.uk/Census/CensusHome.html

Covers census information in Northern Ireland. Website provides information on where and how to trace historical materials.

Office of National Statistics

www.ons.gov.uk/census

Provides basic information on the history, content and collection of the Census. It also links to recent population statistics.

ScotlandsPeople

www.scotlandspeople.gov.uk

Official website maintained in association between General Register Office for Scotland and the National Archives of Scotland. Contains a searchable catalogue of census materials from 1841 onwards. The site offers free access to a selection of records from famous Scottish people, plus detailed guides on finding and using archives.

Society of Genealogists

www.sog.org.uk

Membership organization offering a national library and education centre for family historians. Website provides free access to leaflets offering guidance on useful research resources. These include introductions to using the census for family history research.

The National Archives

www.nationalarchives.gov.uk/records/census-records.htm

Offers a searchable catalogue of census records from 1801 to 1911, plus guides to research using census records. Note that online access to most transcripts requires payment. Record offices which may offer free access are indicated on the website.

Census statistical data

Cathie Marsh Centre for Census and Survey Research (CCSR)

www.ccsr.ac.uk

Specialist research body based at the University of Manchester that plays a key role in developing and disseminating Samples of Anonymized Records (SARs) from the British Census. Website provides free access to news, events listing and the full text of recent working and conference papers. It is possible to register to get access to some anonymized data from 1991 onwards.

Census.ac.uk

www.census.ac.uk

Home of the ESRC Census Programme, managed by the Economic and Social Research Council. A key starting-point for academic researchers, offering guidance on how to find and access census-related datasets. This includes microdata, aggregate statistics and boundary data. The site links to handy online guides, training events, major census-related projects and research groups. Datasets from 1971 onwards can be downloaded (subject to registration requirements) by members of the UK educational community.

Census Teaching and Learning materials

cdu.mimas.ac.uk/materials

Developed for the UK higher education community as part of a publicly funded project. Access to tutorials and to case studies designed to support students and lecturers new to using census materials.

Online Historical Population Reports (OHPR) collection

www.histpop.org

Provides online access to the complete population reports for Britain and Ireland from 1801 to 1937. In addition to the Census, the site also contains enumerators' notebooks, essays from historians which set the materials in context and bibliographies to guide further reading.

International

IPUMS-International (Integrated Public Use Microdata Series, International)

international.ipums.org

World's largest international collection of micro-level (household/individual) census data. Currently housed at the Minnesota Population Center. Find information and access data variables from hundreds of censuses conducted worldwide since 1960. The site also has a good listing of when individual nations conducted censuses (post 1960).

United Nations Statistics Division

unstats.un.org/unsd/demographic/default.htm

Has a specialist demographic and social statistics section, which is an excellent starting-point for tracing news and information about population censuses being held worldwide. It includes links to the websites of national statistical offices plus a useful census knowledge base, **unstats.un.org/unsd/censuskb20/Knowledgebase.aspx**. The latter is a repository of information (guidelines, articles and documents) relating to the conduct, management and enumeration of censuses worldwide. It covers both theory and case studies relating to specific recent censuses.

US Census Bureau

www.census.gov

Responsible for conducting surveys of the American population. Website provides free access to a wealth of data. It is possible to download all censuses of population and housing from 1820 onwards: **www.census. gov/prod/www/abs/decennial/index.html**. The University of Virginia maintains a useful historical browser website based on this data which enables the user to generate online maps of selected state and county statistics: **mapserver.lib.virginia.edu**.

CHARITIES

Typical questions

- I need to find a list of UK charities involved in childcare.
- How can I get information on the financial regulation of charities?
- I need data on the income of a specific charity.

Points to consider

- Charities are increasingly involved in running community health, welfare and social development projects. Their websites often provide free access to blogs, videos and full-text reports. These can be a useful supplement to journal articles because they are often up to date and can offer an evidence-based perspective.
- However, students may need help in locating lists of charities for other reasons. These can include advice on grants/bursaries and volunteering opportunities. Separate sections on **Grants and Funding** and **Volunteering** cover these in more detail.
- This section provides advice on general resources. Browse the subject-specific sections to find other references. The **Non-governmental Organizations (NGOs)** section offers links to resources which include charities in their remit.
- Finally, remember that regulations are often country specific, so get as much information as you can on the exact nature of the enquiry.

Where to look

UK

Charities Aid Foundation
   www.cafonline.org
   Specializes in providing financial advice and training to charities. Website has guidance and events listings. It also offers free access to research reports containing data on levels of charitable giving in the UK and worldwide. Its Charity Trends website, **www.charitytrends.org**, enables users to locate, generate and download recent financial data about charities in England and Wales.

Charity Commission for England and Wales
   www.charity-commission.gov.uk
   Official regulator of charities in England and Wales. Get advice on charity legislation and consult the official register. Entries for individual charities include contact addresses and financial returns. For Scotland see **OSCR – Office of the Scottish Charity Regulator, www.oscr.org.uk.**

CHARITIES

***Charity Market Monitor*, Caritas Data. Annual**

Contains detailed analysis of the largest UK charities (with detailed breakdown of income, expenditure and assets). Plus information on the largest corporate donors to charities and trends in charitable giving.

Directory of Social Change

www.dsc.org.uk

Assists small and medium-sized voluntary organizations by providing training and information. Topics covered include management and fund-raising techniques. Some free access to news and events listings. Subscribers can view specialist databases on sources of grants and funding.

National Council for Voluntary Organizations (NCVO)

www.ncvo-vol.org.uk

Supports and acts on behalf of all community and voluntary organizations in the UK, including charities. Its website has a directory of organizations, plus news and events information.

New Philanthropy Capital

www.philanthropycapital.org

UK-based think-tank which specializes in research and consultancy destined to aid the financial effectiveness and impact of charities. Website includes headlines and the full text of many of its publications. These include evaluations of the charity sector.

Third Sector Research Centre

www.tsrc.ac.uk

Focal point for tracing recent research-based evidence about civil society (charities, pressure groups and NGOs) operating in the UK today. Read news, research reports and papers. These cover both theory and practice.

***Top 3000 Charities*, Caritas Data. Annual**

Offers key financial and contact information for the top 3000 UK charities. Each profile contains data for up to five years, including income, assets and expenditure.

***Who's Who in Charities*, Caritas Data. Annual**

Contains thousands of biographies of leading executives. Also lists and gives information on the largest charities.

United States

Charity Navigator

www.charitynavigator.org

Independent evaluator. Use the website to view its top-ranking charities by sector. You can also search for the income and expenditure of individual charities, plus assessments of their organization and financial efficiency. Methodology is explained on the website.

Internal Revenue Service (IRS)
www.irs.gov/charities/topic/index.html
Has responsibility for the regulation of American charitable organizations. Its website has detailed legal and financial information. This includes a searchable list of registered charities.

International

Catalog of Non-profit Literature
foundationcenter.org/gainknowledge/cnl/contents.html
Based on the library holdings of the Foundation Center. Provides thousands of references to materials covering philanthropy, charities and the non-profit sector. These cover books, articles and reports. Topics covered include charity management, grant proposals and research and statistics. Some emphasis on North America.

Europa International Foundation Directory, **Routledge. Annual**
Provides a guide to foundations and trusts worldwide. Indexed by region and subject area. Entries include contact addresses, aims, publications and some financial information.

CITING AND REFERENCING

Typical questions

- My tutor says I need to use APA style?
- How do I cite something I found on a website?

Points to consider

- Some universities and/or courses have recommended citation and referencing styles. Students should be advised to refer to their course handbooks or regulations to check this.
- Some journals also have a prescribed or house style; authors should check the specific journal's website.
- If a particular style is not prescribed, the best advice is to choose one style and use it consistently.
- Three of the most well known styles are: Chicago, APA and MLA
  — The *Chicago Manual of Style* is a style guide for American English published since 1906 by the University of Chicago Press. It covers American English style, grammar and punctuation and citations.
  — The *MLA Style Manual,* first published by the Modern Language Association of America in 1985, is an academic style guide widely used in North America which provides guidelines for writing and citing in the humanities.
  — American Psychological Association (APA) style is widely used as a standard for writing and citing in the sciences and social sciences.
- Always choose the most recent version of the guide. These are more likely to cover new forms of publication such as blogs, websites and online articles which students may need to cite.
- Students/researchers with large numbers of references may find it profitable to learn how to use referencing software such as EndNote or RefWorks because these can format bibliographies into the main styles automatically. See the **Reference Management Tools** section.

Where to look

General guides

Lipson, C. (2006) *Cite Right: a quick guide to citation styles – MLA, APA, Chicago, the sciences, professions, and more,* 2nd edn, University of Chicago Press
  Best-selling guide. Includes an introductory essay on why it is important to

cite correctly, plus simple-to-use explanations (with examples) of the main styles.

Pears, R. and Shields, G. (2010) *Cite Them Right: the essential referencing guide*, **8th edn, Palgrave Macmillan**
Covers when and why to cite, includes many practical examples. Main emphasis is on the Harvard system.

Purdue University Online Writing Lab
owl.english.purdue.edu
Excellent free collection of online tutorials maintained by Purdue University. The section on citing and referencing is particularly detailed and clear to understand, even for the novice student. Includes worked examples from APA and MLA.

APA style

APA website
www.apastyle.org
Offers free access to supplementary materials, a tutorial on the basics of the style and a blog where experts answer questions and discuss its usage.

Concise Rules of APA Style **(2009) 6th edn, American Psychological Association**
Pocket-sized version of the APA style guide (see next entry), focuses more narrowly on the APA style rules.

Publication Manual of the American Psychological Association **(2010) 6th edn, American Psychological Association**
Definitive guide covering the writing process and scholarly publication as well as the rules of the APA style.

Chicago style

Chicago Manual of Style: the essential guide for writers, editors and publishers **(2010) 16th edn, University of Chicago Press**
The official manual.

Chicago Manual website
www.chicagomanualofstyle.org
Online version of the guide. The full text and forum for users can be accessed by subscribers only. Non-subscribers can look at a useful questions and answers section.

MLA style

MLA Handbook for Writers of Research Papers (2009) 7th edn, **Modern Language Association of America**

Intended for undergraduates and college students. It covers each stage of the research process, from selecting the research question to writing up. Includes the authoritative guide to using MLA.

MLA Style Manual and Guide to Scholarly Publishing (2008) 3rd edn, **Modern Language Association of America**

Intended for graduates, researchers and academic staff. It covers scholarly publishing in more detail.

Further information about the handbooks and some web features can be viewed on the MLA website, **www.mla.org/resources**.

COMPANY AND STOCK MARKET INFORMATION

Typical questions

* Who is the chief executive of Tesco?
* How can I trace recent mergers in the airline industry?
* I need daily return data for the FTSE 100.

Points to consider

* Commonly requested items include: company accounts and annual reports, biographical information about directors, share prices, mergers and acquisitions information and analysts' forecasts. Queries can relate both to specific companies and to the top players in a sector.
* It can be difficult for students to obtain this type of high-quality data free on the internet. Always check for local subscriptions first. The mega databases listed below have the widest coverage. If they are not available, consult the libraries listed in the **Business Studies** section because all offer services to the public. For historical information refer to the **Economic History** section.

Where to look

Commercial mega databases

Note that these are large, powerful tools covering all aspects of company and stock market data. Navigation may require an understanding both of financial terminology and of using spreadsheets. If expertise is not available locally, most offer a staffed help desk. Alternatively, seek advice on the website of a major business school library. Manchester University maintains an excellent blog, **bizlib247.wordpress.com**.

Bloomberg (subscription required)
www.bloomberg.com/professional
Real-time analysis of international companies and markets. Company profiles include descriptions, company and industry news, five to ten years of financial statistics, interest rates, share prices and analysts' reports. It is possible to search and locate industry time series.

Datastream (subscription required)
thomsonreuters.com/products_services/financial/financial_products/a-z/datastream

Covers markets and international companies. Well regarded historical time series analysis. Company profiles include company accounts, share prices.

ISI Emerging Markets (subscription required)
www.securities.com
Focuses on emerging-market countries in Latin America, Central and Eastern Europe and Asia. Covers companies and industries. Coverage varies from country to country.

Company reports

UK

Bureau van Dijk databases (subscription required)
FAME (Financial Analysis Made Easy)
www.bvdinfo.com/Products/Company-Information/National/FAME.aspx
Useful tool for student use. Covers UK and Irish companies. Gives ten years of financial data, plus listings of board members and news. Covers companies registered at Companies House. The same company also markets a number of international company databases. These include *Amadeus* (Europe) and *Orbis* (international), **www.bvdinfo.com/ ProductsCompany-Information/International**.

Companies House
www.companieshouse.gov.uk
Official register of UK companies. Search for a company by name or registered number and request (for a fee) further information. Subscribers can obtain lists of disqualified directors.

SCoRe
www.score.ac.uk
National catalogue of printed company reports held in UK libraries. It does not provide links to online versions. Valuable for tracing older materials.

***Waterlow Stock Exchange Yearbook incorporating Crawford's Directory of City Connections*, Waterlow. Annual**
www.crawfordsonline.co.uk
Available in print or online. Financial information for approximately 2500 London Stock Exchange-quoted companies and 2000 of the largest unlisted companies. Includes board member details and cross-references to advisers, enabling connections to be quickly identified.

Other possible sources for company reports include:

• General internet searches for company home pages.

- **Annual Reports** website, **www.annualreports.co.uk**, which offers a free service to request printed reports.
- **RBA Information Service** (maintained by Karen Blakeman) also has an extensive collection of links to company information websites, **www.rba.co.uk.**

International

European Business Register
www.ebr.org/section/2/index.html
Information from 26 European nations.

Securities and Exchange Commission (USA)
www.sec.gov
Search for company filings online using the Edgar system. Website has tutorials on coverage and data.

World-wide Registries
www.companieshouse.gov.uk/links/introduction.shtml
Companies House maintains an excellent directory of links to the websites of national company registration authorities worldwide. Key examples include:

Mergers
In addition to the mega databases listed above, try:

Competition Commission (UK)
www.competition-commission.org.uk
Independent public body which conducts in-depth inquiries into mergers. Offers free access to all reports going back to the 1950s. Plus news about on-going inquiries.

Federal Trade Commission
www.ftc.gov
Information and cases from the USA.

Stock markets
In addition to the mega databases listed above, the news services in the **Business Studies** section have basic current prices and the websites of the exchanges themselves all offer news, glossaries, listings and some statistical data.

American Stock Exchange
www.amex.com

COMPANY & STOCK MARKET INFORMATION

NASDAQ
www.nasdaq.com
Includes, news, prices and companies listed on the stock exchange.

Federacion Iberoamericana de Bolsas de Valores
www.fiabnet.org

Federation of Euro-Asian Stock Exchanges
www.feas.org

Federation of European Securities Exchanges
www.fese.be
Website offers free access to statistics on trading from European stock exchanges.

London Stock Exchange
www.londonstockexchange.com
Website provides details of listings on the Main Market, Alternative Investment Market (AIM) and Professional Securities Market (PSM). It is also possible to consult some UK and international company statistics free of charge.

South Asian Federation of Exchanges
www.safe-asia.com

World Federation of Exchanges
www.world-exchanges.org
Useful starting-point for tracing information and links to stock exchanges worldwide. Offers news and statistics from 52 members worldwide. Some data from 1990 onwards.

COMPUTER SCIENCE

Typical questions

- Have any books been written about the history of Apple?
- Where can I get a definition of cloud computing?

Points to consider

- It is easy to find large amounts of information about computing on the internet. However many sites are of low quality and commercially orientated. This section will direct students to academic resources which they can use for literature searching.
- As information technology is a rapidly moving field, many research reports are published in journal or working paper series and can quickly become out-dated. Advise students to use these resources and check dates of publication.

Where to look

Key organizations

Use these to locate specialist research groups, forthcoming conferences and key journals for IT professionals.

Association for Computing Machinery (ACM)
www.acm.org
World's largest computer society.

BCS, the Chartered Institute for IT (formerly known as the British Computer Society)
www.bcs.org
Professional organization promoting the needs of the IT industry, academics, practitioners and government users.

IEEE
www.ieee.org
Renowned society, promoting research into all forms of technology, including electrical engineering, computer and IT specialisms. Website has free access to news and online videos.

Libraries

Radcliffe Science Library
www.bodleian.ox.ac.uk/rsl

The main science reference library of Oxford University, holds scientific material obtained on legal deposit.

UCL Library
www.ucl.ac.uk/library/guides/subjcs.shtml
University College London. Website includes a useful guide to databases and key websites.

Dictionaries

Daintith, J. and Wright, E. (eds) (2008) *A Dictionary of Computing*, **6th edn, Oxford University Press**
Covers over 6000 terms, including biographical entries. Useful companion website, **www.oup.com/uk/booksites/content/9780199234004**, contains recommended web links.

FOLDOC: Free Online Dictionary of Computing
foldoc.org
Supported by Department of Computing, Imperial College. Check over 14,000 definitions, terms, jargon and computing theories.

Journal article indexes

Use these to find references to journal articles. Remember to remind students that not all items found will be available in full text and advise them to use the working paper resources to pick up examples of the latest research.

ACM Digital Library (subscription required)
portal.acm.org
Access the full text of articles, transactions and conference proceedings from the Association for Computing Machinery, plus abstracts of key computing articles from other publishers.

Collection of Computer Science Bibliographies
liinwww.ira.uka.de/bibliography
Maintained by Alf-Christian Achilles. Free access to a searchable database which contains over 3 million references to articles, conference papers and reports in Computer Science. These are taken from open access repositories and open access indexes to journal articles compiled by leading universities and societies.

IEEE Computer Society Digital Library (subscription required)
www.computer.org/portal/web/csdl

Provides online access to IEEE magazines and transactions and more than 3300 conference publications.

Inspec (subscription required)

www.theiet.org/publishing/inspec

Contains over 11 million abstracts to journal articles, conference proceedings and technical reports covering science and technology. Extensive coverage of computer science and IT.

Working papers

Cogprints

cogprints.org

Provides free access to thousands of working papers covering Psychology, Linguistics and Computer Science. Key areas covered by the latter include artificial intelligence and human–computer interaction.

Computing Research Repository (CoRR)

arxiv.org/corr/home

Sponsored by a number of leading organizations, including ACM and Association for the Advancement of Artificial Intelligence (AAAI). It forms a specialist section of the *arXiv* e-print service based at Cornell University. Free access to thousands of abstracts (and many full text) papers covering all aspects of Computer Science.

News services

Computer Weekly

www.computerweekly.com

Keep up to date with the latest news, blogs and job listings for UK IT professionals. Many stories can be accessed free.

Computerworld

www.computerworld.com

Leading American fortnightly publication, includes job listings, headlines and stories. Free access to many.

Internet gateways and portals

Good starting-points for internet searching and tracing links to academic resources.

CiteSeerX

citeseer.ist.psu.edu

Originally developed by Princeton University, a specialist search engine and digital library which specializes in Computer Science literature.

DBLP Computer Science Bibliography
www.informatik.uni-trier.de/~ley/db/index.html
Maintained by the Computer Science Department of the University of Trier. Offers links to tables of contents of leading journals, major conference proceedings and the websites of computer science organizations.

TechXtra
www.techxtra.ac.uk
Specialist search engine for Engineering, Mathematics and Computing created by Heriot Watt University. Quickly find academic working papers, news, technical reports and announcements. Many have links to full text.

CONFERENCES

Typical questions

- How can I sign up to conference alerts?
- Can you recommend a website which lists forthcoming Philosophy conferences?

Points to consider

- Researchers often need dates of forthcoming conferences. They may also require access to the texts of papers given at conferences.
- Often the best sources of information on conferences are the websites of the main national and international professional organizations. These can be traced using the appropriate subject sections of this book. Most have events calendars. Some have archives of past papers.

Where to look

Conference alerts

AllConferences.com
> **www.allconferences.com**
> Free directory includes trade exhibitions, business conventions and meetings worldwide.

Conference Alerts
> **www.conferencealerts.com**
> Free worldwide listings and alerts covering a wide range of academic subject areas.

H-Net Academic Announcements
> **www.h-net.org/announce**
> Good example of a general academic mailing list which includes alerts to forthcoming conferences (often North America-based) as well as new publications.

ResearchResearch
> **www.researchresearch.com**
> Company specializing in information relating to research news and opportunities. Includes coverage of UK, Europe and Africa. Some services offered to subscribers only. Website has some free listings of forthcoming research events.

CONFERENCES

Conference papers

References to conference papers are often included in journal indexing services. Refer to the subject sections for details. Two general services which are particularly recommended are:

Conference Proceedings Index from ISI (subscription required)
thomsonreuters.com/products_services/science/science_products/
a-z/conf_proceedings_citation_index
Often integrated with other ISI databases such as the Web of Science. Coverage 1998 onwards. See website for selection criteria. Note that it does not contain full-text papers.

Zetoc (subscription required)
zetoc.mimas.ac.uk
Includes references to conference proceedings from a wide range of subject areas. Coverage from 1993 onwards.

Full-text conference papers themselves can be difficult to locate because many remain unpublished. Good starting-points are the conference website, the website of the organization which sponsored the conference and any home pages of speakers. Another possibility is **OpenDoar, www.opendoar.org,** a directory of open access repositories that often includes references to papers given by academic staff at universities worldwide.

COPYRIGHT

Typical questions

- How much of this book can I copy?
- Are there any limits to the numbers of articles I can put in a course pack?

Points to consider

- Students may need advice on copyright relating to photocopying and to the use of materials in their dissertations.
- Lecturers often enquire about copyright in relation to course packs and online learning materials.
- These questions frequently require specialist legal advice. The resources below offer general starting-points for help. However, do check whether the university has a local copyright specialist first!

Where to look

Note that it is important to check the jurisdiction and type of material (e.g. images, film, and printed text).

UK

CILIP: Chartered Institute of Library and Information Professionals
www.cilip.org.uk/get-involved/advocacy/copyright/pages/default.aspx
Professional body for UK librarians and information specialists. Provides basic copyright advice to members. The website includes links to recommended online resources.

Copyright Circle
www.copyrightcircle.co.uk
Long established commercial service which offers advice and training for library and museum staff.

Copyright Licensing Agency Limited (CLA)
www.cla.co.uk
Licenses organizations for copying extracts from print and digital publications on behalf of authors, publishers and visual creators. Its website provides access to the text of licensing agreements. These include those relating to further and higher education.

Cornish, G. P. (2009) *Copyright: interpreting the law for libraries, archives and information services*, 5th edn, Facet Publishing
Invaluable, easy-to-understand guide, covering all aspects of printed and

digital copyright. Includes lists of useful contact addresses for further help. Other similar publications covering different aspects of copyright can be located on the **Facet Publishing** website, **www.facetpublishing.co.uk**.

Educational Recording Agency (ERA)
www.era.org.uk

Issues licences relating to broadcast material (TV/radio recordings) for UK educational use. Website contains the text and advice about its licences.

Heron
heron.publishingtechnology.com/heron/home.htm

Offers a service to the UK academic community for copyright clearance, digitization and delivery of book extracts and journal articles for use in course packs and online learning environments.

Intellectual Property Office
www.ipo.gov.uk

Official government body responsible for granting intellectual property rights in the UK. Website contains a section on copyright, with advice on the law and an enquiry service.

JISC Digital Media
www.jiscdigitalmedia.ac.uk

Offers free help and advice to the UK higher and further education community on creating and managing digital media (including still and moving images). The website contains advice, factsheets and information on training.

JISC Legal
www.jisclegal.ac.uk

National organization which provides information on legal compliance and legal issues to UK higher and further education institutions. Its broad remit includes copyright. The website offers free factsheets and advice.

International

World Intellectual Property Organization (WIPO)
www.wipo.int

Specialized agency of the United Nations concerned with intellectual property (copyright and patents). Its website offers specialist legal news and texts relating to copyright. It includes a useful directory of links to the websites of national copyright agencies worldwide.

COUNTRY INFORMATION AND RANKINGS

Typical questions

- What is the population of Jordan?
- Which countries in Africa are considered to be the most democratic?
- I want to find political and economic risk assessments for Indonesia.

Points to consider

- The sources listed below are good starting-points for tracing recent facts and figures about nations worldwide. Other recommended sources are the websites of international and human rights organizations. These are explored in more detail in the appropriate sections of this book.
- Other rankings of nations regularly appear in the press. Always check who produced the index (are they politically motivated or neutral?), the methodology used and the currency of the index.

Where to look

Background information

CIA World Factbook

www.cia.gov/library/publications/the-world-factbook

Provides factual information about the history, population, government, economy, geography, communications and military of over 267 nations. Includes maps, images of flags and some comparative ranking tables.

Economist Intelligence Unit Country Reports (subscription required)

www.eiu.com

Well regarded series. Provides analysis and forecasts of economic and political trends in nations worldwide. Also includes regularly updated risk assessments. Website includes reports from 1996 onwards.

Library of Congress Country Studies

memory.loc.gov/frd/cs

Presents a description and analysis of the history and current social, economic, political and national security systems of countries.

Country rankings

Bertelsmann Transformation Index (BTI)

www.bertelsmann-transformation-index.de

73

International ranking of over 120 nations that measures development and transformation processes. It ranks how nations are countries progressing toward democracy and a market economy and analyses their political management. Produced since 2003.

Freedom House
www.freedomhouse.org
Independent watchdog which publishes a number of well regarded surveys:

- *Freedom in the World*. A comparative assessment of global political rights and civil liberties. Published annually since 1972. Available free online from 2002 onwards.
- *Freedom of the Press*. An annual survey of media independence in over 190 countries. Available free online from 2002 onwards.

Human Rights Index for the Arab Countries
www.arabhumanrights.org
Sponsored by the United Nations Development Programme on Governance in the Arab Region (UNDP-POGAR). Analyses and measures the extent of compliance with international human rights legislation of individual Arab nations.

COURSES

Typical questions

- How can I get a list of universities in London which run part-time courses in anthropology?
- Are there any distance learning courses in maths?

Points to consider

- Find out what type of information is needed e.g. full-time or part-time courses, level of study, location and subject area.
- Remember that universities have their own admissions departments. If information is required about entry to a specific course, students should be referred directly to the academic department concerned. Those requiring more general careers information about the suitability of certain courses for entry into a profession may find it useful to consult the local university careers advisory service and/or the professional association concerned. Listings of key organizations can be found in each of the subject sections of this book.
- It is very easy to find websites offering lists of courses. Always remember to check carefully their origins and currency. Many are designed to sell their own services! The list of resources below will direct you to accredited academic sources.

Where to look

UK

Admissions

UCAS

> **www.ucas.ac.uk**
> Organization which administers UK's centralized undergraduate admissions service. Its website offers a course database plus official advice for students and parents on when and how to apply for undergraduate study.

UKPASS

> **www.ukpass.ac.uk**
> Online application service for UK postgraduate courses which is administered by UCAS. Note that some universities continue to accept applications directly, so advice should be sought from the individual institution before applying. Site includes advice on the process and funding of postgraduate study, plus a searchable database of courses.

COURSES

Directories

Complete University Guide

www.thecompleteuniversityguide.co.uk

Comprehensive site managed by Robinson Digital Publishing in collaboration with Mayfield University Consultants and the University of Sheffield. Takes potential students through the university application process, helping them decide what subject to study, what university to go to and how to apply. Site includes rankings/league tables of UK universities. Strong coverage of undergraduate courses.

Hotcourses.com

www.hotcourses.com

Free access to a searchable database of over 1 million references. Covers evening classes, part-time, full-time and distance learning at all levels from vocational to postgraduate study. Entries include descriptions of individual courses and student reviews.

International Centre for Distance Learning (ICDL)

icdl.open.ac.uk

Provides free access to a directory of courses and websites covering UK distance-learning courses as well as links to examples from overseas.

The Virgin Guide to British Universities, Virgin Books. Annual

In addition to facts about universities and rankings of courses, this guide also aims to provide a student perspective on what it is like to study at individual universities. Covers undergraduate and postgraduate courses.

Times Good University Guide, Times Books. Annual

Well regarded annual guide. Includes league tables of UK universities, subject guides and advice on applications. The *Sunday Times* has a free associated website, **www.timesonline.co.uk/tol/life_and_style/education/sunday_times_university_guide**, where you can view and compare the rankings. Covers undergraduate and postgraduate courses.

Unistats

unistats.direct.gov.uk

Official site maintained by UCAS. It enables you to search and compare information about universities and colleges in the UK, and the subjects they offer. It includes results from the *National Student Survey*, which measures levels of student satisfaction.

International

Hotcourses Abroad

www.hotcoursesabroad.com

Site maintained by Hotcourses to offer advice to students wishing to study abroad. Includes a searchable database of courses, with student reviews. Main coverage is of universities and colleges in the USA, UK, Australia and Singapore.

World Higher Education Database (subscription required)

www.whed-online.com

Compiled by the International Association of Universities (IAU). Offers information on courses from thousands of colleges in over 180 nations worldwide.

Online learning courses

An increasing number of universities are starting to offer free access to course materials online for independent learners. This is often referred to as OpenCourseWare, or OCW. Many have online lectures and reading lists. Students should, however, check technical and prior knowledge requirements, learning objectives and the currency of courses. Good examples are:

MIT OpenCourseware

ocw.mit.edu/index.htm

Free access to lecture notes, exams and videos from MIT (Massachusetts Institute of Technology). No registration required. Strong coverage of science, information technology and management subject areas.

OER Commons

www.oercommons.org

Site maintained by ISKME (the Institute for the Study of Knowledge Management in Education) to provide information, news and links to resources associated with open access education on the internet. Its broad remit includes curriculum material produced by schools and advice for educational providers on producing online learning materials.

Open Courseware Consortium

www.ocwconsortium.org

An organization of universities committed to advancing OpenCourseWare. Get news and links to courses worldwide.

COURSES

OpenLearn OU
openlearn.open.ac.uk

Free access to Open University course materials covering all subject areas of the sciences, social sciences and humanities. Includes TV and audio content.

Online teaching and learning repositories

These websites store examples of online course notes, podcasts, tutorials and slides which lecturers can reuse in the classroom. They may be useful for finding ideas and inspiration when developing courses! However, do remember to check dates of creation, technical and copyright information. Also useful (for information skills teaching) are the resources listed in the **Information Literacy** section.

HumBox
humbox.ac.uk

Supports teachers in the humanities. Free acess to higher education (HE) materials covering Literature, Languages, Religious Studies and Philosophy.

Jorum
www.jorum.ac.uk

Resources created for and by the UK higher and further education community.

MERLOT – Multimedia Educational Resource for Learning and Online Teaching
www.merlot.org

Free access to an extensive collection of peer-reviewed online learning materials designed for use by faculty members worldwide. All subject areas covered. Site also includes news and events relating to digital learning.

National Digital learning Resources Ireland
www.ndlr.ie

CRIMINOLOGY AND CRIMINAL JUSTICE

Typical questions

- Where can I find journal articles on the link between poverty and crime?
- I need recent statistics on crime rates.

Points to consider

- Criminology can be wide ranging, encompassing forensic science, criminal justice systems, the sociology of crime, law and psychology. Try to identify if the user has a specific focus. This book has chapters on **Law, Science** and **Psychology** which may also help.

Where to look

Key organizations

Use these to identify specialist research groups, key academic journals and forthcoming conferences.

American Society of Criminology
> www.asc41.com
> Covers all branches of Criminology. Website includes sample syllabi, conference listings.

British Society of Criminology
> www.britsoccrim.org
> Covers academics and practitioners. Includes information on Criminology careers.

United Nations Office on Drugs and Crime (UNODC)
> www.unodc.org
> UN agency specializing in the fight against illegal drugs and organized crime. Its website includes examples of research on the causes of crime and crime prevention, international treaties relating to crime, forensic science and the fight against crime, and official statistics.

Criminal justice data

Students often need to locate statistics on crime. These are useful starting-points.

Home Office Research Development and Statistics (RDS)
> www.homeoffice.gov.uk/science-research/research-statistics

Free access to research reports and statistics covering crime prevention, policing and prisons. Very useful is the *British Crime Survey*, which conducts annual surveys into household experiences of and attitudes to crime.

International Crime Victims Survey
rechten.uvt.nl/icvs

Free access to surveys of householders' experience with crime, policing, crime prevention and feelings of unsafeness in a large number of countries.

National Archive of Criminal Justice Data (USA)
www.icpsr.umich.edu/NACJD

Searchable catalogue of data, some of which may be downloaded free of charge. Main emphasis on America, but also includes some international data. Topics include homicide, capital punishment, victims of crime.

United Nations Office on Drugs and Crime (UNODC)
www.unodc.org/unodc/data-and-analysis/Crime-Monitoring-Surveys. html

UNODC collects cross-national data for over 120 nations. These cover homicide, organized crime, policing responses etc.

Libraries

Use these to locate lists of books and guides to research sources.

Radzinowicz Library
www.crim.cam.ac.uk/library

Based in the Institute of Criminology, University of Cambridge. Houses the most comprehensive Criminology collection in the UK.

United Nations Interregional Crime and Justice Research Institute (UNICRI)
www.unicri.it/institute

Website offers free access to the catalogue and criminology thesaurus and a calendar of criminal justice events. Strong coverage of United Nations, international agency and grey literature resources.

Dictionaries and encyclopedias

Maguire, M., Morgan, R. and Reiner, R. (2007), *The Oxford Handbook of Criminology*, 4th edn, Oxford University Press

Well respected student textbook. Associated website, **www.oup.com/uk/orc/bin/9780199205431**, contains sample chapters, advice on answering essay questions and web links.

McLaughlin, E. (ed.) (2005) *The SAGE Dictionary of Criminology*, 2nd edn, Sage

Accessible introduction to key theories, concepts and topics for students.

Journal article indexes

Criminal Justice Abstracts (subscription required)

www.ebscohost.com/academic/criminal-justice-abstracts

Prepared in co-operation with the Don M. Gottfredson Library of Criminal Justice at Rutgers University Law Library, covers all fields of Criminology from 1968 onwards.

National Criminal Justice Reference Service (NCJRS) Abstracts Database

www.ncjrs.gov/App/AbstractDB/AbstractDBSearch.aspx

Free access to the database published by the US Department of Justice's National Criminal Justice Reference Service. Summaries of English-language materials about crime and policing. Includes US federal and state government documents and journal articles from 1975 onwards.

Internet gateways and portals

Crimlinks

www.crimlinks.com

Maintained by criminologist Michael Teague, aims to direct to all key Criminology websites. Also includes links to archived news stories from 1994 onwards.

World Criminal Justice Library Electronic Network

andromeda.rutgers.edu/~wcjlen/WCJ/index.htm

Maintained by a network of specialist libraries. Excellent annotated links to Criminology organizations, journal indexes and lists of criminal justice agencies worldwide.

CURRENT AWARENESS TOOLS

Typical questions

- How can I keep up to date with the latest publications in my field?
- Where can I get information on the most recent articles published in my favourite journals?
- Where can I sign up for tables of contents alerts?

Points to consider

- It is very important for all researchers to keep up to date with the latest developments in their subject field. These can include conference listings, new journal articles, books and other research publications. Many scholars are short of time and need assistance on how to quickly identify the most relevant publications.
- Professional organizations are a key starting-point. Most have websites which provide blog feeds, twitter channels and newsletters. Important examples are highlighted in the subject sections of this book. Other related services are conference alerts (see the **Conferences** section) and news alerts (see **Newspapers**). This section is intended to offer general guidance which will supplement these.
- As technology changes rapidly, further new tools will evolve. A good starting-point for keeping up to date with these is **Phil Bradley's blog** (which is designed specifically for information professionals), **www.philbradley.typepad.com**.

Where to look

E-mail forums/discussion lists

Remain useful for receiving updates on forthcoming events and new publications. These websites contain directories of hundreds of academic lists covering all subject areas. View the archives to see the typical content and volume of messages before signing up!

H-NET – Humanities and Social Sciences online
   www.h-net.org
   Hosted by Michigan State University and used by an international community. Includes an announcements section, **www.h-net.org/announce**, which highlights forthcoming conferences, calls for papers and new academic websites.

JISCMail
> **www.jiscmail.ac.uk**
> National service for the UK academic community.

RSS alerts

RSS stands for Really Simple Syndication. It enables researchers to keep up to date with new items posted on a specific website. Many journal home pages, publishers and news services offer this. Look for the orange RSS icon.

In order to subscribe, users must have a newsreader. Common examples are available via personalized home pages such as **MyYahoo, my.yahoo.com** and **iGoogle, www.google.com/ig**.

Tables of contents (TOC) alerts

Many publishers have websites which enable users to receive the latest tables of contents from selected journals via e-mail and/or RSS feeds. However, there are a number of services which are broader in scope, offering the facility to sign up to alerts from thousands of titles from many different publishers. Note that while access to the contents pages is often free, full-text articles are usually limited to subscribers only.

Remember that TOC services are of greatest value if researchers can identify key journals because most (apart from Zetoc) do not enable feeds to be tailored to keywords within individual articles. Therefore it is a good idea to recommend that researchers also explore the alert functions offered by major journal indexing services such as Scopus and ISI Web of Knowledge, which will send messages when individual articles matching their search terms (either by subject keyword or author) are entered into the database. Further details of these are in the **Journal Article Indexes** section.

JournalTocs
> **www.journaltocs.ac.uk/index.php**
> Free service developed by Heriot Watt University. Contains searchable tables of contents from over 16,000 academic journal titles (including open access titles). It is possible to sign up to receive alerts via e-mail or RSS. Very strong coverage of medical and scientific subject areas, although the social sciences are also well represented.

CURRENT AWARENESS TOOLS

Sign@l: Signalement des contenus de périodiques en sciences humaines et sociales
doc.sciencespo-lyon.fr/Signal
Maintained by Sciences Po Lyon in collaboration with other French research centres, this service provides free access to the tables of contents of 160 French-language journals in the humanities and social sciences. The website contains a database of bibliographic references (dating back to 1983) plus the facility to sign up to receive RSS feeds of the latest tables of contents.

ticTOCs Journal Tables of Contents service
www.tictocs.ac.uk
Free service created by a consortium of UK universities. The website also has a searchable database of tables of contents of over 14,000 journal titles covering all subject areas. It is possible to sign up to RSS feeds from individual journals.

Zetoc (subscription required)
zetoc.mimas.ac.uk/alertguide.html
Widely available in UK academic libraries. Provides access to the British Library's Electronic Table of Contents service, which contains references to articles from around 20,000 journals covering all subject areas. It also offers alerts to thousands of conference proceedings. It is possible to sign up to receive tables of contents lists from specific journals or to set up alerts for new articles covering a specific subject area.

DEVELOPMENT STUDIES

Typical questions

- Does the British government still fund aid programmes in India?
- Where can I find recent research on ICT and development?
- I need statistics on trends in foreign aid to DRC Congo.

Points to consider

- Development studies students often need access to financial data on foreign aid. This section has a statistical data sub-section to guide you to key resources.
- Increasing numbers of development organizations (including charities) are publishing full-text reports on the web. As a result, some libraries have discontinued purchasing print copies. Students are advised to explore the internet portals sub-section to locate recent references.
- Researchers focusing on specific regions of the world may also benefit from consulting the appropriate area studies sections of this book. Additionally, many of the journal indexes in the **Economics** section cover economic development issues.

Where to look

Key organizations

Scholarly

Use these websites to trace key publications, conference listings and information on cutting-edge research.

Development Studies Association
www.devstud.org.uk
Seeks to connect academic and NGO research organizations in the UK and Ireland.

European Association of Development Research and Training Institutes (EADI)
www.eadi.org
Professional network for Development Studies scholars and organizations in Europe.

Inter-regional Coordinating Committee of Development Associations (CCDA)
www.iccda.net

Umbrella network for a number of regional Development Studies organizations. Established in 1976 and renowned for its efforts in encouraging co-operation between North/South researchers. The website is good for tracing links to key bodies outside Europe and North America.

Society for International Development Forum
www.sidint.net
Founded in 1957, SID is a well established network of Development Studies researchers and organizations. Website is a good source of news stories plus links to organizations worldwide.

Charities

Many charities now possess websites where they post full-text news stories about their projects, plus comment on government development aid projects.

A leading example is:

Oxfam
www.oxfam.org.uk
For advice on tracing other examples see the **Charities** section.

Government departments

Useful for information on aid projects, policy and budgets. Remember that government departments often change their names/remits. Further advice on tracing official publications is given in the **Government Publications** section.

Department for International Development (DFID)
www.dfid.gov.uk
Body of UK government with current responsibility for managing foreign aid. Its website provides free access to **Research4Development (R4D)**, **www.dfid.gov.uk/r4d/AboutR4D.asp**, a database containing information about research programmes supported by DFID. It contains many in-depth case studies and evidence-based reviews.

International Development Committee
www.parliament.uk/business/committees/committees-a-z/
commons-select/international-development-committee
Select Committee of the House of Commons which critically reviews the policy and performance of the Department for International Development.

United Nations Development Programme (UNDP)
www.undp.org
Body of the United Nations responsible for global development. Publishes

the influential *Human Development Reports* which provide regular surveys of global, regional and national human development worldwide. Website provides free access to reports and statistics. They include indicators relating to the Millennium Development Goals.

United States Agency for International Development (USAID)
www.usaid.gov
Independent US federal government agency. Its website contains the USAID **Development Experience Clearinghouse, dec.usaid.gov/index.cfm**, which provides free access to over 134,000 technical and other reports relating to USAID-funded projects.

Libraries

British Library of Development Studies (BLDS)
blds.ids.ac.uk
Holds the largest specialist collection of economic and social development materials in Europe. Website has excellent country profiles and subject-based research guides. Library catalogue includes references to many journal articles indexed by BLDS staff.

Eland: Research for Development
www.1site-europe.net/eland/04/index.html
Cross-search the library catalogues of a growing number of specialist Development Studies institutions in Europe. They include the Institute of Development Studies (IDS), European Centre for Development Policy Management and CIDOB library database. Many of these contain references to journal articles as well as publications. Major European languages are covered.

School of Oriental and African Studies (SOAS)
www.soas.ac.uk/library
Part of the University of London. Specialist library holdings covering economic, social and cultural development in nations of Asia, Africa and the Middle East. Archives include materials from major humanitarian aid organizations such as Christian Aid and War on Want.

Dictionaries and encyclopedias

Desai, V. and Potter, R. (eds) (2008) *The Companion to Development Studies,* **2nd edn, Hodder Education**
A collection of essays by leading writers which provides an introduction to key concepts of development theory and practice.

DEVELOPMENT STUDIES

Forsyth, T. (ed.) (2005) *Encyclopedia of International Development,*
Routledge
Over 600 entries covering all aspects of development theory and practice,
ranging from international aid to human rights.

Journal article indexes

British Library of Development Studies Library Catalogue
blds.ids.ac.uk/articles.html
Provides free access to references to articles from over 150 journals taken by
the library. The full list can be viewed on the website, which also offers
options for obtaining access to materials via interlibrary loan.

Rural Development Abstracts
www.cabi.org
CABI produces a number of databases of relevance to development issues.
Rural Development Abstracts covers economic, social and health development literature from 1973 onwards.

News services

These are specialist news wires which offer in-depth coverage of development
issues. Other good sources of headlines are aid agencies and the United Nations
website.

AlertNet
www.trust.org/alertnet
Free news service run by Thomson Reuters Foundation. Although focusing
primarily on disasters and humanitarian aid, it covers many issues relating
to development, such as foreign aid.

OneWorld
www.oneworldgroup.org
Online portal of news from civil society organizations campaigning for
human rights, social justice and sustainable development. Get daily
headlines, events listings and analysis.

Statistical data

This section highlights major series. Other sources of development-related data
can be traced by browsing the resources in the internet portals sub-section.

Global Development Finance
data.worldbank.org/data-catalog/global-development-finance

Focuses on financial flows and trends in external debt for developing countries. Includes over 200 time-series indicators from 1970 onwards. A more recent tool which is under development using World Bank data and OECD data is the **Aidflows website, siteresources.worldbank. org/CFPEXT/Resources/299947-1266002444164/index.html.** Users can focus on countries receiving aid or on donor nations and track data on amounts, sources and use of aid.

OECD
www.oecd.org/dac/stats

OECD produces a number of key series relating to development aid. These include: *International Development Statistics* and *Development Aid at a Glance*. Indicators available include aggregate aid by donor, type of aid and flow. The data focuses on flows from member countries and the EU and generally covers the period from 1960 onwards. Note that some materials are offered to subscribers only.

Increasingly, many of the data sets are being made freely available on the **AidData Portal, www.aiddata.org,** a project of Brigham Young University, the College of William and Mary and Development Gateway. In addition to OECD data it is also adding materials supplied by other aid agencies.

United Nations Development Programme (UNDP)
hdr.undp.org

Influential series include the *Human Development Reports*. These are online from 1990 onwards and enable users to consult rankings of nations for a variety of human, social, economic and political development indicators and to generate and download their own charts.

World Bank
Some key series are now available free online. They include:
World Development Indicators, data.worldbank.org/data-catalog/ world-development-indicators.

Contains more than 900 indicators of development. These are sub-divided into themes which include: people, environment, economy, states and markets. Currently the website offers free access to material from 2005 onwards.

Historical datasets are offered to subscribers via print or online subscription-based services such as **ESDS, www.esds.ac.uk/ international/ access/dataset_overview.asp**.

DEVELOPMENT STUDIES

Internet gateways and portals

Advise users to explore these resources to trace references (and in many cases full-text copies) of the latest reports, comment and analysis from charities, international organizations and campaign groups.

Eldis

www.eldis.org

Maintained by the Institute of Development Studies, Sussex. Provides references to thousands of high-quality resources covering Development Studies research and practice. Includes many working papers and evidence-based reports which are often difficult to trace elsewhere. Sign up to receive e-mail alerts, or browse the country profiles and subject indexes. The site also has excellent directories of links to development research organizations, a large number of which are based in nations of the developing world.

Global Development Network

cloud2.gdnet.org

International organization of development research and policy institutes, including the Institute for Development Studies, World Institute for Development Economics Research and the German Development Institute. Website contains an extensive directory of links to development organizations worldwide, plus free access to online working papers and discussion from member institutions.

Governance and Social Development Resource Centre (GSDRC)

www.gsdrc.org

Established by the UK Department for International Development (DFID) in 2005 to provide high-quality, timely information to support international development project and programme planning. Its website has a large resource library of documents relating to governance, conflict and social development issues.

DICTIONARIES

Typical questions

- When was the term 'dole queue' first used?
- Where can I get a definition of the term 'carbon footprint'?

Points to consider

- Many dictionaries are now available online. However, those which are offered free of charge on the internet may be limited. Always check the date and number of words covered.
- Most libraries subscribe to reference e-book packages which contain excellent dictionaries. Therefore students should be directed to search local library catalogues/electronic libraries first. Remind them that searches via Google may not retrieve the correct login page for library subscriptions.
- This section highlights recommended general English-language dictionaries. The subject sections cover specialist reference resources.

Where to look

Subscription services

A number of packages are offered by different suppliers. These are only a few well known examples. Check access locally.

Credo Reference
 corp.credoreference.com
 Package of encyclopedias and dictionaries from a range of publishers.

Oxford English Dictionary (OED)
 www.oed.com
 Widely regarded as an authoritative guide to the English language. Access definitions plus information on the history of specific words. Website offers free access to 'the word of the day'.

Oxford Reference Online
 www.oxfordreference.com
 Includes English, foreign language and subject-based dictionaries published by Oxford University Press.

Free websites

Cambridge Dictionaries Online
 dictionary.cambridge.org

DICTIONARIES

Specializes in dictionaries for learners of English. Site includes pronunciation guide.

Merriam-Webster
www.merriam-webster.com
Website includes some free access to an English-language, medical and visual dictionary plus a thesaurus.

YourDictionary.com
www.yourdictionary.com
Directory of links to thousands of dictionaries available online.

DIPLOMATIC, CONSULAR AND FOREIGN SERVICE LISTS

Typical questions

- Where is the Indian embassy in London?
- Does Britain have an ambassador in Cuba?

Points to consider

- Diplomatic lists usually refer to publications by the 'host nation' that contain the names of resident diplomats and diplomatic missions. Many current diplomatic lists can now be located by browsing the Foreign Office website of the nation concerned. Often these also contain lists of other Foreign Office officials.
- International organizations, such as the United Nations, have sections on their websites listing their members and these may also have information on diplomatic and foreign service staff.
- Always check how up to date they are.
- Some lists are not comprehensive; they may only cover the head staff.
- For information on job titles, definitions and the content of lists try Berridge, G. R. and James, A. (2000) *The Dictionary of Diplomacy*, Macmillan.

Where to look

UK

Diplomatic Archive
www2.le.ac.uk/library/find/rarebooksandarchives/specialcollections/diplomaticarchive
Catalogue of the archive of diplomatic, consular, foreign service and foreign ministry lists dating from the 1950s to the 1990s held at the University of Leicester.

Foreign and Commonwealth Office (FCO)
www.fco.gov.uk/en/about-us/what-we-do/public-diplomacy/
Maintains lists of current senior staff and addresses.

London Diplomatic List, incorporating Directory of International Organizations, The Stationery Office, www.tsoshop.co.uk. Annual
An alphabetical list of all the representatives of foreign states and Commonwealth countries in London. Some of its information is offered free of charge via the Diplomatic and Consulate Yearbook website, **www.diplomaticandconsular.com**, which includes links to individual embassy websites.

International

Diplomatic List (US State Department)

www.state.gov/s/cpr/rls/dpl

Listing of foreign embassies and missions staff based in the USA. Prepared quarterly. Entries include the names and addresses of all current diplomatic staff. Previous editions from 1993 onwards can be accessed on the website.

EmbassyWorld

www.embassyworld.com

Free directory of addresses and links to embassies and consulates in many nations.

Statesman's Yearbook (subscription required)

www.statesmansyearbook.com

Online or in print, the annual publication lists key diplomatic representatives of individual nations. Online version covers the full archive from 1860 onwards.

Worldwide Diplomatic Archives Index

history.state.gov/countries/archives

Maintained by the US Department of State, Office of the Historian. Free access to a searchable database of information about the location and content of national diplomatic archives. These cover all forms of diplomatic documents produced but are likely also to include lists of key officials.

DISABLED STUDENTS

Typical questions

- Where can I get advice on voice recognition software?
- Are there any financial allowances for disabled students?

Points to consider

- All universities should provide local support for students with special needs. Advise students to contact local student unions and learning support services first.
- Lecturers may need advice in adapting courses. This frequently includes information about assistive or adaptive technology. Again, check first with local IT /learning support services.
- The resources below will provide further starting-points for advice. Additionally, the main charities dealing with specific types of disability (e.g. RNIB) may offer support to students.

Where to look

UK

JISC TechDis Service
   www.techdis.ac.uk
   National advisory service on disability and technology in UK education. Get news, advice and training on creation of learning materials, web accessibility and technology suitable for students with visual disabilities, hearing disabilities, learning difficulties, mobility and motor disabilities, language and communication issues, mental health issues.

National Union of Students (NUS)
   www.nus.org.uk/Campaigns/Disability
   Runs a special disability campaign to improve awareness and facilities for disabled students in the UK. Website has materials and reports which can be downloaded.

Skill: National Bureau for Students with Disabilities
   www.skill.org.uk
   UK charity promoting the rights of disabled adults in post-16 education and training. Website offers free access to factsheets for potential students covering entry into higher education, grants and student support. A section for practitioners has guidance on statutory obligations and good practice in adapting courses. The organization also publishes a number of guides

which can be purchased. These include the annual guide *Into Higher Education*, which covers where to study, how to apply for courses and financial allowances.

International
HEATH Resource Center
www.heath.gwu.edu

Official resource website of the HSC Foundation's National Youth Transitions Center. Serves as a national clearing house (for the USA) on post-secondary education for individuals with disabilities. Free access to factsheets, reports, online learning modules and calendars of forthcoming events. Covers access, financial support and assistive technology. Many contain good general advice applicable outside the USA.

United Nations Educational, Scientific and Cultural Organization (UNESCO)
www.unesco.org/new/en/education

Mandate includes facilitating access to higher education worldwide. While not specifically concerned with disability, its website does have reports, statistics and guidelines covering equal access to universities and colleges.

E-BOOKS

Typical questions

- Is this book available electronically?
- Can I get a list of all the books digitized by Google?

Points to consider

- Many libraries subscribe to e-book packages. These offer access to textbooks which are not available free via the internet. Therefore students should be directed to search local library catalogues/electronic libraries first. Remind users that searches via Google may not retrieve the correct login page, so it is always safer to go via their own institutional catalogues/web pages.
- Many governments, charities and think-tanks now publish pamphlets and reports in e-format only. Many libraries do not create individual records for these items in their catalogues. They can usually be located by searching for the title of the publication or the organization on an internet search engine.
- Some free e-book websites are of low quality. Advise students to check publication dates and details carefully before use.

Where to look

This section highlights major free collections suitable for academic use.

Europeana

www.europeana.eu

European Commission-funded portal which is working to build a virtual European library offering free access to Europe's cultural resources. It includes millions of texts (manuscripts, papers, e-books), images (photographs, maps), films (moving images, videos, film clips, TV broadcasts) and sound recordings from Europe's main research libraries, archives and galleries.

Gallica

gallica.bnf.fr

Electronic library of the Bibliothèque Nationale de France. Provides free access to thousands of full-text historic French-language books, journals and newspapers from the library, covering all subject areas.

Google books

books.google.com

Go directly to this site to search for e-books. The help screens and blog provide useful updates on library collections that have been scanned by

Google. Use the advanced search form to restrict your search to full-text only.

HathiTrust Digital Library
www.hathitrust.org
Consortium of research libraries (mostly American based) that are creating a digital archive of their major research materials. This includes the full texts of books and pamphlets out of copyright. All subject areas of the arts and humanities, sciences and social sciences are covered. There is particularly strong coverage of American political, social and economic history.

Online Books Page
onlinebooks.library.upenn.edu
Excellent index to free e-books maintained by Penn University. Highlights individual titles and large e-book directories. Over 1 million titles currently listed. Covers all subject areas.

ECONOMIC HISTORY

Typical questions

- Where can I find information on the economic history of the slave trade?
- What would 10 shillings in 1950 be worth today?

Points to consider

- This section should be used in conjunction with the resources listed in the **Economics** section. In particular, students should be advised to use the journal article indexes and working paper series listed there.
- This section has specialist sub-sections for business history and economic history data (covering old prices), as these are frequently encountered queries.

Where to look

Key organizations

These websites are maintained by scholarly societies. Use them to trace examples of recent publications, conference listings and research projects.

British Agricultural History Society
> www.bahs.org.uk

Economic History Association
> www.eh.net/eha
> Major American body. Read recent issues of its newsletter and search the directory of members. Extensive collections of links to Economics websites on its **EH.Net** website, **www.eh.net**.

Economic History Society
> www.ehs.org.uk
> Key UK society founded in 1926. Website provides access to recent podcasts, plus tables of contents and some papers from its journal *Economic History Review*.

International Economic History Association (IEHA)
> www.uni-tuebingen.de/ieha
> Key international body. Its website is useful for tracing national Economic History organizations worldwide.

Archives

Economists' Papers

www.economistspapers.org.uk

Project to create an online guide to manuscript collections containing the private papers of English and Irish economists 1750–2000.

Goldsmiths' Library of Economic Literature

www.shl.lon.ac.uk/specialcollections/goldsmiths/index.shtml

World-famous collection of over 70,000 printed books, pamphlets, periodicals, and manuscripts covering economic and social history. Based in the Senate House Library. Selections from the library are available online to subscribers as *The Making of the Modern World: The Goldsmiths'-Kress Library of Economic Literature 1450–1850*, **www.rdsinc.com/DigitalCollections/ products/ModernWorld.**

Statistical data

In addition to the specialist resources listed below, all the national data archives listed in the Statistical Data section have holdings relating to Economic History.

Current Value of Old Money

projects.exeter.ac.uk/RDavies/arian/current/howmuch.html

Maintained by Roy Davies. Provides an extensive collection of links to websites that answer the question 'how much would this sum be worth today?'

European State Finance Database

esfdb.websites.bta.com/Default.aspx

International collaborative research project contains data on fiscal history from European states in the medieval and early modern periods.

How Much Is That?

eh.net/hmit

Site maintained by EH.Net. Historic price data covering a range of nations, including the UK, the USA and Japan.

Montevideo Oxford Latin American Economic History Database (MOxLAD)

oxlad.qeh.ox.ac.uk

Contains statistical series for a wide range of economic and social indicators covering 20 countries from 1900 to 2000.

National Archives Currency Converter (UK)

www.nationalarchives.gov.uk/currency

Find out how much yesterday's prices would be worth today using this handy tool. Covers purchasing-power comparisons.

Internet gateways and portals

EH.net
> eh.net
>
> Not-to-be-missed site maintained by the Economic History Association in association with other scholarly societies. Key features include an extensive collection of book reviews, an encyclopedia which provides guidance on researching a wide range of Economic History topics and extensive online links to dataset collections.

McMaster University Archive for the History of Economic Thought
> socserv.mcmaster.ca/econ/ugcm/3ll3
>
> Online collection of 'classic economics texts'. Covers all fields of thinking from Adam Smith to Robert Owen.

Business history

Key organizations

Use these sites to locate news, events and publications.

Association of Business Historians
> www.abh-net.org
>
> Leading UK scholarly society. Its website maintains a good listing of UK-based business archives.

Business History Conference
> www2.h-net.msu.edu/~business/bhcweb/index.html
>
> International organization based in the USA. Website provides free access to *Business and Economic History* online. This contains full-text papers from its recent annual conferences.

European Association for Banking and Financial History
> www.eabh.info

European Business History Association
> www.ebha.org
>
> Website includes details of annual conferences plus access to some full-text papers.

Historical company information

Use these in conjunction with the resources listed in the **Business Studies** section. Also useful are back files of the major news services listed in the **Economics** section such as the *Wall Street Journal*, *Financial Times* and *Economist*.

Historic Annual Reports (subscription required)
www.proquest.co.uk/en-UK/catalogs/databases/detail/pq_hist_
annual_repts.shtml
Historic reports from over 800 influential American companies. Materials date from 1844 onwards.

Historical Directories
www.historicaldirectories.org
Digital library of local and trade directories for England and Wales 1750 to 1919. Useful for tracing the types of businesses in a specific location.

International Directory of Company Histories (subscription required)
www.gale.cengage.com/pdf/facts/CompanyHist.pdf
Multi-volume work. Contains histories of companies worldwide. Entries include facts and figures on foundation, mergers and business history using information from company reports, journals articles and newspapers. Available in print or online.

ECONOMICS

Typical questions

- Where can I find an explanation of cyclical unemployment?
- How can I search for literature on the causes of the recent financial crisis?
- I want the UK GDP for the past five years.

Points to consider

- This section focuses on academic resources for the study of economic theory and policy. The separate sections for **Banking, Business Studies, Company Information** and **Economic History** may also be relevant.
- Scholarly publishing in economics often takes the form of working papers. Therefore, when conducting a literature search students are advised to use the resources listed in both the journal article indexes and working papers sub-sections.
- Economic data is also significant. This section lists resources useful for tracing basic economic indicators.

Where to look

Key organizations

Use these to locate news, publication and conference alerts.

American Economic Association
www.aeaweb.org/index.php
World-famous scholarly association established in 1885. Free access to some webcasts and papers from its influential conferences covering all aspects of economics.

European Economic Association
www.eeassoc.org
Supports Economics research in Europe. Website has useful directory of links to member websites.

Higher Education Academy
www.heacademy.ac.uk
Aims to support teaching and learning in UK higher education. Includes subject coverage of Economics. Website offers free access to learning materials. It has produced the **Why Study Economics** website, **www.whystudyeconomics.ac.uk**, which has guidance on choosing courses for prospective students and the **Studying Economics** website, **studyingeconomics.ac.uk**, which has advice for undergraduates.

International Economic Association (IEA)
www.iea-world.com
Federated member of the International Social Science Council. In addition to news, its website can be effectively used to locate lists of national and regional Economics associations and research bodies.

Royal Economic Society
www.res.org.uk
The major UK scholarly society.

Libraries

British Library
www.bl.uk/reshelp/findhelpsubject/socsci/economics/ economicspage.html
Extensive collection of current and historic materials relating to economic theory and policy. Coverage of UK is comprehensive; also strong are English-language collections from Europe, Australia and North America. The website has a collection guide which lists useful databases and websites.

LSE Library
www2.lse.ac.uk/library/subjectGuides/Home.aspx
Library of the London School of Economics. Has extensive current and historic holdings of economics books, pamphlets and journals. The archives holds collections from a number of influential organizations, including the Royal Economic Society.

Dictionaries and encyclopedias

Black, J., Hashimzade, N. and Myles, G. (2009) *A Dictionary of Economics*, 3rd edn, Oxford University Press
Available in print or online. Over 2500 entries covering all aspects of Economics, including international economic institutions. Appendices include lists of Nobel Prize winners and major economics acronyms. Companion website has links to recommended internet resources: **www.oup.com/uk/ booksites/content/9780199237043**.

New Palgrave Dictionary of Economics (subscription required)
www.dictionaryofeconomics.com
Widely regarded as the definitive dictionary for economists, with over 1700 articles covering all aspects of Economics and economic theory. Online version is based on the *New Palgrave Dictionary of Economics*, 2nd edn,

edited by Steven N. Durlauf and Lawrence E. Blume, published by Palgrave in 2008. Continuously updated with new materials and an online news blog. Each article has a bibliography to guide further reading.

Journal article indexes

EconLit (subscription required)
> **www.aeaweb.org/econlit/index.php**
> Produced by the American Economic Association. Comprehensive index of Economics articles, papers, reports and dissertations from 1969 onwards.

International Bibliography of the Social Sciences (IBSS)
> **www.proquest.co.uk/en-UK/catalogs/databases/detail/ibss-set-c.shtml**
> Cross-disciplinary social sciences database which includes in-depth coverage of Economics articles and book chapters. Extensive coverage of European-language materials dating from the early 1950s to the present day.

News services

These are specialist services which can be used to supplement coverage of the economy in the main daily newspapers.

Economist (subscription required)
> **www.economist.com**
> Influential weekly magazine covering world economics, finance and politics. Available in print or online. Website also features interactive guides to topics and blogs containing discussion and comment. Back files plus some articles offered to subscribers only.

Financial Times
> **www.ft.com**
> World-famous newspaper offering daily economic, political and financial news and analysis. Available in print or online. Website has archives and some special reports restricted to subscribers only.

Wall Street Journal
> **online.wsj.com**
> **europe.wsj.com/home-page (Europe edition)**
> Check the latest news, stock market data and analysis. Also available are blogs, discussion and special reports. Premier e-services for subscribers only.

ECONOMICS

Statistical data

These sites all contain economic indicators. More sources with regional data can be found in the areas studies sections of this book. Remember to remind students to check the pages which explain the coverage and methodology used for compilation. They should also verify if their institution has access to any of the subscription databases via any national data archive services or other suppliers.

UK
Bank of England
www.bankofengland.co.uk

Key publications that can be downloaded from the website include: monthly inflation reports, Monetary Policy Committee minutes, Financial Stability report, trends in lending to UK businesses and individuals. Online data is generally from 1997 onwards.

HM Treasury
www.hm-treasury.gov.uk

Official website of the UK government ministry responsible for UK economics and finance. In addition to government documents and reports (including extensive coverage of the budget), the website provides free access to several major statistical series. These include: weekly UK economic forecasts, public sector finance statistics and local authority spending. More detailed datasets are available on the National Statistics website.

National Statistics
www.statistics.gov.uk/default.asp

Contains a detailed section on the economy. One of the most important resources is the *UK Economic Accounts* (*UKEA*) or Blue Book. This has detailed estimates of income and expenditure for the UK. It contains tables showing the main aggregates of gross domestic product (GDP) and balance of payments (BoP), plus financial balance sheets by sector. Also valuable is the annual *United Kingdom Balance of Payments* or Pink Book. Other specialist services include retail price indexes, regional accounts, tax revenues and household expenditure. Dates of coverage differ. Earlier editions of data can usually be obtained in major national and university libraries, including those listed in the Libraries sub-section.

In addition to these official statistics, other common indexes used to measure the state of the UK economy include:

British Retail Consortium Sales Monitor
www.brc.org.uk/brc_home.asp
Monthly spending on the high street.

Council of Mortgage Lenders
www.cml.org.uk/cml/statistics
Data on mortgage lending, repossessions and buy-to-let markets.

Hometrack House Price Survey
www.hometrack.co.uk/commentary-and-analysis/house-price-survey/about.cfm

Nationwide House Price Index
www.nationwide.co.uk/hpi/default.asp

United States

Federal Reserve System
www.federalreserve.gov/econresdata/default.htm
Central bank of the US government. Free access to working papers, policy reports and data. Key series include consumer credit, interest rates, exchange rates, money stock and reserves.

FRED – Federal Reserve Economic Data
research.stlouisfed.org/fred2
Maintained by the Federal Reserve Bank of St. Louis. Provides free access to over 27,000 economic data time series covering all aspects of economic and financial policy.

US Bureau of Economic Analysis
www.bea.gov
Free access to national and regional accounts covering all aspects of the US economy, plus US international transactions. Some files go back as far as the 1960s.

International

Annual Macro-Economic Database (AMECO)
ec.europa.eu/economy_finance/db_indicators/ameco/index_en.htm
Database of the European Commission's Directorate General for Economic and Financial Affairs (DG ECFIN). Contains statistics for the Euro area, EU Member States, candidate countries and other OECD countries.

European Economy

ec.europa.eu/economy_finance/publications/european_economy/
index_en.htm

Has reports on the EU economy and euro area.

Eurostat

epp.eurostat.ec.europa.eu/portal/page/portal/eurostat/home

Statistical office of the European Union. Provides free access to a range of economic indicators. They include European national accounts.

International Monetary Fund (IMF)

www.imf.org/external/about.htm

Major financial organization. Its website provides access to time series data on IMF lending, exchange rates and other economic and financial indicators. Some titles are offered free of charge, others are limited to subscribers only.

Key series are:

- *International Financial Statistics (IFS).* The IMF's principal statistical publication containing approximately 32,000 time series covering more than 200 countries, some dating back to 1948.
- *World Economic Outlook.* Data on national accounts, inflation, unemployment rates, balance of payments, fiscal indicators, trade for countries and country groups and commodity prices whose data are reported by the IMF.
- *Balance of Payments Statistics (BOPS).*
- *Direction of Trade Statistics (DOTS).* Information on imports and exports for specific countries.
- *Government Finance Statistics.*
- *Financial Access Survey (FAS).* Provides annual geographic and demographic data on access to basic consumer financial services worldwide.

Increasing numbers of recent datasets are being made available via the **IMF DataMapper** site, **www.imf.org/external/datamapper/index.php,** which is well designed and enables easy downloading.

OECD

www.oecd.org/topic/0,3699,en_2649_37443_1_1_1_1_37443,00.html

Extensive coverage of economic issues in OECD and other major economies. The website provides free access to some reports and headline statistics. Some more detailed datasets are offered to subscribers only. Key publications include **Economic Outlook, www.oecd.org/oecdeconomicoutlook,** which has general assessments of the macroeconomic situation, country surveys and future predictions.

UN Comtrade
comtrade.un.org
Service of the United Nations Statistics Division. Provides access to International Merchandise Trade Statistics (IMTS). Offers free access to more than 1.7 billion trade records from 1962 onwards. Covers nations, regions and commodities. Includes the *International Trade Yearbook* statistics.

United Nations Conference on Trade and Development (UNCTAD)
unctadstat.unctad.org
Publishes the influential annual *World Investment Report*, which contains data on foreign direct investment, international mergers and transnational corporations. Has an online statistical database, *UNCTADstat*. This contains data on international trade, foreign direct investment (FDI) and commodity prices.

World Bank
www.worldbank.org
data.worldbank.org
Provides financial and statistical assistance to developing nations. Its website has a specialist data section which includes free access to the *Global Economic Monitor*, which offers daily updates on developments in markets and other economic trends. It covers both developed and developing nations.

World Economic Forum
www.weforum.org
Independent organization committed to promoting sustained economic growth and social justice. Publishes the influential *Global Competitiveness Report*, which provides country profiles and ranks nations according to a number of factors including economic competitiveness.

World Trade Organization (WTO)
www.wto.org/index.htm
International organization regulating rules of trade between nations. The statistics section of the website has international trade statistics from 2000 onwards, tariff data (customs duties and rates) and country trade profiles.

Working papers
Economists Online
www.economistsonline.org/home
Site created by the Nereus Consortium of major universities and research

bodies. It aims to provide references (and, where copyright allows) free access to the output (journal articles, working papers, data and reports) from the world's leading economists. This includes materials from staff at the London School of Economics (LSE), Sciences Po, Columbia University and Kiel Institute for the World Economy. Coverage strongest in terms of European universities. Content is also integrated with RePEc archives.

NBER Working Papers (subscription required)
www.nber.org/papers.html

Founded in 1920, the National Bureau of Economic Research (NBER) is America's largest non-profit economic research organization. Working papers cover the full range of economic theory and policy, ranging from environmental economics to corporate finance. Online versions date from approximately 2002 onwards.

RePEc (Research Papers in Economics)
www.repec.org

Vast site created by volunteer effort which provides free access to thousands of high-quality resources covering all aspects of Economics. It has close links with publishers and collaborates with *Economists Online* and the American Economics Association.

A number of services are offered. These include:

- **EconPapers, econpapers.repec.org**. Provides access to online working papers, journal articles and software.
- **New Economics Papers, nep.repec.org**. Free service providing e-mail alerts when new content is added to specific subject sections of the website.

Social Science Research Network (SSRN) (subscription required)
www.ssrn.com

Comprised of a number of specialist networks which publish cutting-edge social science research. These include general economics, health and financial economics. Users may search the abstracts database free of charge; access to the full text of most requires a subscription.

Vox.eu
www.voxeu.org

Maintained by the Centre for Economic Policy Research in collaboration with other European research institutes. Provides free access to their latest writings, covering the full range of Economics topics.

Internet gateways and portals

EDIRC

edirc.repec.org

Directory of links to the websites of Economics departments, institutes and research centres worldwide which is maintained by Christian Zimmermann and can be accessed via the RePEc website. Resources can be searched by country or specialism. Also provided are useful lists of links to national Economics associations worldwide.

RFE: Resources for Economists on the internet

rfe.org

Well regarded resource maintained by Bill Goffe and sponsored by the American Economics Association. Access to links to over 2000 items categorised into 97 sections.

EDUCATION

Typical questions

- Where can I get information on the education system of Zambia?
- I want to get statistics on educational expenditure in Russia.
- Can you help me find some articles about the educational attainment of girls in maths?

Points to consider

- This section focuses on general resources for educational research. There are separate sections for **Higher Education** and **Further Education**.
- Many students may be training as teachers. They should explore the professional organizations listed and the internet gateways to find more links relating specifically to teaching practice. They may also find it useful to check the **Sociology** and **Psychology** (to find materials relating to child development) sections.

Where to look

Key organizations

Government departments

Recent government reports are often online. Earlier ones can often be located in paper in major libraries, including those listed in the **Education** section of this book. Departmental names often change, so remember to check details as carefully as possible.

UK

Department for Education
   www.education.gov.uk
   Currently responsible for nursery, primary and secondary education policy. Use the website to trace news, circulars, government papers and official statistics. It includes free access to school performance tables and links to materials relating to the National Curriculum.

House of Commons Education Select Committee
   **www.parliament.uk/business/committees/committees-a-z/
   commons-select/education-committee**
   Access minutes and reports from this influential parliamentary body which monitors the policy, administration and spending of the Department for Education.

Ofsted

www.ofsted.gov.uk

Office for Standards in Education, Children's Services and Skills. Responsible for inspection and regulation of quality and standards. Use the website to access inspection reports covering nursery education, primary, secondary and adult education nationally and at local authority level.

International

World Education Services

www.wes.org

Useful directory of links to education system information for many nations worldwide. Covers all levels. Links to key government departments, funding bodies and agencies.

Research organizations

American Educational Research Association (AERA)

www.aera.net

Founded in 1916, major organization supporting research. The website provides free access to many presidential addresses and lectures, plus contents pages from its academic journals and news about conferences and publications.

British Educational Research Association (BERA)

www.bera.ac.uk

Organization which supports policy- and practice-related research. Website is useful for tracing information about on-going research projects and recent and forthcoming conferences.

Educational Research Association (EERA)

www.eera-ecer.eu

Network of national and regional educational research organizations based in Europe. Get details of projects, publications and events. Plus links to the websites of its members.

National Foundation for Educational Research (NFER)

www.nfer.ac.uk

Independent provider of research relating to education, training and children's services. Main focus is on the UK. Website provides free access to project information and many of its full-text reports. It also publishes a very useful free current awareness service, **NFER OntheWeb, www.nfer. ac.uk/what-we-offer/information/ontheweb**, which indexes the latest reports and publications relating to all aspects of education and teaching. Current and past issues can be viewed via the website.

World Education Research Association (WERA)
www.weraonline.org
Established in 2009. Aims to co-ordinate educational research activities worldwide. Its website has a good directory of national and regional research organizations.

Professional organizations/trade unions

Use these sites to trace information on training and professional development, salaries and conditions for practitioners, and comment on government educational policy.

UK

ATL Association of Teachers and Lecturers
www.atl.org.uk

Educational Institute of Scotland (EIS)
www.eis.org.uk
Biggest teaching union in Scotland, representing professionals in nursery, primary, special and secondary education, as well as further and higher education.

National Association of Schoolmasters/Union of Women Teachers (NASUWT)
www.nasuwt.org.uk

National Union of Teachers (NUT)
www.teachers.org.uk

International

Association for Teacher Education in Europe (ATEE)
www.atee1.org
Supports teaching professionals in European nations. Website has links to many national organizations.

Association of Teacher Educators (ATE)
www.ate1.org/pubs/home.cfm

World Federation of Associations of Teacher Education
www.wfate.org

Global network of teacher associations. Website includes materials relating to teaching in developing nations. Also gives free access to news and conference papers.

Libraries

British Library
www.bl.uk/reshelp/findhelpsubject/socsci/education/educationpage.html
Extensive collection of books and journals (current and historic). Strongest in terms of English-language material published in the UK and North America.

Institute of Education Library
www.ioe.ac.uk/services/4389.html
Specialist college of the University of London. Its library offers comprehensive coverage of all areas of education. This includes a teaching practice collection, plus materials relating to international and comparative education. Website has excellent guides on researching educational topics.

Dictionaries and encyclopedias

Peterson, P. (ed.) (2010) *International Encyclopedia of Education*, **Elsevier**
Major eight-volume work available in print or online. Contains articles on all aspects of the history, politics and practice of education.

Wallace, S. (2009) *A Dictionary of Education*, **Oxford University Press**
Contains definitions of over 1200 terms covering all levels of education from primary to university, as well as specialist teaching and theory concepts. Useful appendix of key British educational legislation since 1945. Associated website has a directory of web links: **www.oup.com/uk/booksites/content/9780199212071**.

Journal article indexes

Australian Education Index (subscription required)
www.acer.edu.au/library/aei
Produced by Cunningham Library at the Australian Council for Educational Research. Indexes hundreds of leading Education journal titles from Australia and New Zealand. Coverage from 1979 onwards.

British Education Index (subscription required)
www.leeds.ac.uk/bei/index.html
Indexes major British Education journal titles and doctoral theses. Coverage from 1975 onwards. Free access to some records via the website.

EDUCATION

Educational Research Abstracts Online (subscription required)
www.informaworld.com/smpp/title~content=t713417651~db=all

Indexes over 700 titles from 1995 onwards. Key topics covered are: child development, educational management, educational technology, health education, higher education, literacy, multicultural education, sociology of education, special needs and technical education and training.

ERIC – the Education Resources Information Center
eric.ed.gov

Online digital library of Education research and information sponsored by the US Department of Education. Provides free access to more than 1.3 million references to journal articles, book chapters, reports and other documents covering all aspects of education. Coverage from 1966 onwards. Site also has a *What Works Clearinghouse*, which highlights case studies of useful intervention techniques.

Teacher Reference Center
www.ebscohost.com/us-elementary-schools/teacher-reference-center

Journal index currently offered free to UK educational establishments. Indexes over 270 well regarded journals covering education and teaching. These include the *Times Higher Education Supplement*.

News services

Most national newspapers cover news stories relating to education and schools. These are specialist services.

Guardian
www.guardian.co.uk/education

Latest stories from the well regarded Education section. Includes school rankings and job advertisements.

Teachers College Record
www.tcrecord.org

Published since 1900 by Teachers College, Columbia University. Offers free access to the latest news, analysis and job listings. Covers all levels of education, plus use of educational technology.

TES Connect (Times Educational Supplement)
www.tes.co.uk

Free access to recent articles from the *Times Educational Supplement*, plus job listings, blogs and discussion networks. The website also has an extensive resources section with lesson plans and curriculum materials for teachers.

Statistical data

Education, Audiovisual and Culture Executive Agency (EACE)

eacea.ec.europa.eu

Responsible for the management of certain parts of the EU's programmes in the fields of education and culture. Website offers free access to the *Eurydice Network*, which contains statistical data on education in European nations as well as profiles of their educational systems.

OECD

www.oecd.org

Produces a number of key statistical series relating to education. The annual *Education at a Glance* contains statistical indicators on all aspects of educational systems in OECD nations. Full text offered to subscribers only. Another key initiative is the **Programme for International Student Assessment (PISA), www.pisa.oecd.org**, which compares student/school attainments in different countries. Some rankings and reports can be downloaded from the website.

Office of National Statistics

www.statistics.gov.uk/hub/index.html

Provides free access to official statistics covering all aspects of education. Browse the topic guides to view major series. Older versions can usually be obtained in print via major academic libraries.

UNESCO

www.ibe.unesco.org/en.html

Maintains a specialist International Bureau of Education (IBE). The website provides some access to *World Data on Education*, which contains profiles of the education systems and curriculums of over 160 countries worldwide. UNESCO data on education can also be found on the free **World Bank** website, **data.worldbank.org/topic/education**, and on the **Global Education Database (GED), ged.eads.usaidallnet.gov**. The latter is a repository of international education statistics compiled from the UNESCO Institute for Statistics and the Demographic and Health Surveys (DHS), sponsored by USAID's Office of Education.

Internet gateways and portals

Educator's Reference Desk

www.eduref.org

Site maintained by the Information Institute of Syracuse (USA), which offers free access to a directory of over 3000 links to educational websites (including journals, organizations and curriculum materials), plus an online library of several thousand lesson plans written and submitted by teachers.

Fachportal Pädagogik – German Education Portal
www.fachportal-paedagogik.de/start.html
Site co-ordinated by the German Institute for International Educational Research (DIPF) which provides free access to a number of databases where you can trace online articles. These include the *German Education Index* – a searchable index to journal articles, book chapters, reports and other grey literature covering all aspects of education policy, practice and theory. Over 400 journal titles are indexed. These are primarily German-language materials. Coverage from approximately 1980 onwards.

ELECTION RESULTS

Typical questions

- How many seats did the Labour Party win in the last election?
- Where can I get the results of the last US presidential election?

Points to consider

- Many websites post election results. Always check the validity/currency of the source. Good starting-points are national parliaments and/or election commissions, which usually have official results. However, do note that some nations (especially developing nations) may not update their websites regularly. In these cases an excellent source is the **IFES election guide, www.ifes.org/Content/Projects/Applied-Research-Center/Cross-Cutting/Election-Guide.aspx**. In addition, many nations also sponsor election surveys, which are useful sources of research on voter behaviour.

Where to look

UK

Britain Votes

Series of volumes containing full election results, plus scholarly essays analysing key themes. Volume 1 edited by F. W. S. Craig and published by Parliamentary Research Services in 1977 covered the general elections of 1974; subsequent volumes (compiled by different editors) covered the succeeding elections. The full series (plus holding libraries) can be traced via the **Copac** catalogue, **copac.ac.uk**.

British Election Study
www.essex.ac.uk/bes
Long established study of the attitudes and behaviour of the electorate. Covers general elections from 1963 onwards. Information, research papers and some quantitative data can be downloaded from the website. Earlier data sets can be obtained via the **ESDS** data service, **www.esds.ac.uk/findingData/besTitles.asp**.

Craig, F. W. S., *British Parliamentary Election results*, **Parliamentary Research Services**
Key printed series covering results by constituency from 1832 to 1984. Five volumes published between 1989 and 1984.

Elections Centre at the University of Plymouth
www.plymouth.ac.uk/elections

Collates and analyses electoral data, with a particular emphasis on local elections. Some results online. Also produces the *Local Elections Handbook*, published annually since the 1980s, which is a comprehensive source of voting and electoral statistics for every local authority in Great Britain.

Electoral Commission

www.electoralcommission.org.uk/elections

Independent body established by the UK Parliament. Website provides access to local, national, devolved assembly and European Parliament elections since 2005. Also available is data on political spending and analysis of the election campaigns.

House of Commons Library Research Papers

www.parliament.uk/business/publications/research/research-papers

Produced by staff of the House of Commons Library to brief MPs, these regularly cover by-elections, general elections and devolved assembly elections, providing facts and figures on seats, votes cast and party representation.

Thrasher, M. and Rallings, C. (2007), *British Electoral Facts 1832–2007*, Ashgate

Detailed historical analysis of national, local and European elections. Includes boundary changes, analysis and trivia.

Times Guide to the House of Commons

Long established series, written by *Times* political journalists. Editions cover most general elections since 1885, offering election results, analysis, manifestos since 1950 and biographies of candidates.

United States

America Votes, Congressional Quarterly

Published biennially since the 1950s. Provides official election returns and key data by county and by district for the House, Senate and gubernatorial elections. Congressional Quarterly Press also provides access to a range of subscription election products via its website, **www.cqpress.com**.

Clerk of the House

clerk.house.gov/member_info/electionInfo/index.aspx

Provides free access to the official US election statistics from 1920 to the current day. These include the counts for each state, information on the votes obtained by specific parties and candidates and some data on voter turnout levels.

Presidential elections 1789–

nationalatlas.gov/printable/elections.html

The National Atlas of the United States provides free access to printable maps covering all US presidential elections from 1789 onwards. These election atlases clearly show the distribution of votes for particular parties and candidates across the USA, enabling historical trends to be traced.

International

ACE Electoral Knowledge Network

aceproject.org

Free access to a wealth of election information about many nations worldwide. Maintained by a collaboration of authoritative institutions including International Institute for Democracy and Electoral Assistance (International IDEA) and the International Foundation for Election Systems (IFES). It contains an encyclopedia, election calendars and extensive country-level information. The latter includes information on electoral systems, results, analyses and examples of electoral materials produced by the nation.

Constituency-Level Elections Archive (CLEA)

www.electiondataarchive.org

Project led by Professor Ken Kollman of the University of Michigan. It aims to create a public repository of election results by constituency for parliamentary (lower-house legislature) elections worldwide. Data includes results, votes cast, votes received by individual candidates and parties.

Election Guide

www.electionguide.org

Compiled by the International Foundation for Election Systems. A key starting-point for research. Free access to authoritative national and presidential election data since 1998. Also offered are expert analysis, links to national electoral commission websites and a calendar of forthcoming events.

Lijphart Elections Archive

libraries.ucsd.edu/locations/sshl/data-gov-info-gis/ssds/guides/lij

Research collection of district-level election results for national legislative elections in 26 countries worldwide which is based at the University of California, San Diego. Covers the period before 2004. The website can be useful for tracing printed sources containing election results.

ELECTION RESULTS

Psephos Adam Carr's Election Archive
psephos.adam-carr.net
Extensive online archive of recent and historical election results maintained by Dr Adam Carr. It contains entries for over 160 nations worldwide, offering election results and statistics for national and local elections. Dates differ according to individual nation, but in some cases (such as Britain and Australia) extend back beyond 1900.

ELECTRONIC JOURNALS

Typical questions

* Is *The Economist* online?
* The journal home page asked me to pay for this article – is that right?
* Where can I get hold of the latest issue of *Media History*?

Points to consider

* Most academic libraries subscribe to electronic journals. These usually contain full-text articles which are not available free on the internet. Access to them is often via e-journal databases rather than the individual e-journal home pages. This can be confusing to students who search for titles via Google and are then unable to log in! Therefore it is advisable to direct them to search local library catalogues/electronic journals pages first. They should also be reminded to check the catalogue records carefully because the institution may subscribe only to certain years, or different years may be held on different databases.
* Some e-journals (particularly historic titles) have been digitized and placed on free open access; examples of academic directories are listed in the sources below. Other examples may be of variable quality and users should be advised to check whether items are peer reviewed.
* Finally, remember to remind students about journal article indexes (consult the separate section). Many prefer to download full-text articles immediately, and fail to realize that abstracting services usually index a broader range of publications and are therefore more suitable for academic literature searching. Other specialist journal indexes are listed in the subject sections of this book.

Where to look

This section highlights free open access initiatives. Use them to supplement subscription databases offered by your local library.

Directories and gateways

Directory of Open Access Journals (DOAJ)

    www.doaj.org

    Maintained by Lund University Library. A key starting-point for tracing and accessing thousands of academic e-journals covering all subject areas.

ELECTRONIC JOURNALS

Major online collections

These digitization projects provide free access to collections of journals. Other examples can be traced via the DOAJ.

African Journal Archive

www.sabinet.co.za/?page=african-journal-archive

Project hosted by Sabinet Gateway. Offers free access to historic back files of scientific, social science and humanities journals published in Africa. Recent issues are not available in full text; links are provided to publishers' websites.

Biomed Central

www.biomedcentral.com

Well regarded website specializing in open access publishing. Access current and historic issues of several hundred peer-reviewed scientific, technical and medical titles free of charge.

Note that students interested in medicine might also consult:

PubMed Central

www.pubmedcentral.nih.gov

US National Library of Medicine's free digital library of biomedical and life sciences journal literature; and its UK version, **UK PubMed Central**, **ukpmc.ac.uk**. Note that some titles do not provide free access to the most recent issues.

Revues.org

www.revues.org

Open access French-language e-journals site maintained by Le Centre pour l'Édition Électronique Ouverte. Covers growing numbers of French social sciences and humanities journals. Check the date coverage of individual titles.

SciELO – Scientific Electronic Library Online

www.scielo.cl

Project involving a number of Latin American research institutions, including FAPESP (Fundação de Amparo à Pesquisa do Estado de São Paulo) and BIREME (Centro Latinoamericano y del Caribe de Información en Ciencias de la Salud). Provides free access to scientific journal titles from Latin America.

There is also a **Social Sciences SciELO** website, **socialsciences.scielo. org**, which offers access to ejournals covering subject areas from the social sciences including economics, politics and sociology.

Organizations

UKSG (United Kingdom Serials Group)

www.uksg.org

Professional organization of UK Library staff. Offers support in issues relating to purchasing, licences and copyright regarding printed and electronic journals.

ENCYCLOPEDIAS

Typical questions
- When was the Battle of Slankamen?
- Are there any free encyclopedias online?

Points to consider
- Most students use Wikipedia, **www.wikipedia.org**. This can be excellent, but they should be encouraged to evaluate the age, source and validity of the information offered. One valuable use is to explore the bibliographies and/or external links contained within individual articles, as these often lead directly to original sources.
- This section aims to offer a few suggestions of other general academic resources that students can explore. Specialist subject encylopedias are listed in the relevant subject sections of this book.
- Note that many libraries subscribe to packages of reference works online which contain encyclopedias. Examples of these are listed in the **Dictionaries** section.
- Another good starting-point is the resources listed in the **Country Information** section, which have facts about specific nations.

Where to look
Britannica Online (subscription required for full access)
> www.britannica.com
> Search content from the world-famous *Encyclopaedia Britannica*. Some free articles offering basic definitions. Subscribers can also access timelines, multimedia content and statistics from the *Britannica Year in Review*.

Encyclopedia.com
> www.encyclopedia.com
> Owned and operated by HighBeam Research. Provides free access to word definitions, facts and basic statistics from over 100 credited resources, including *The Columbia Encyclopedia*, *Oxford's World Encyclopedia* and the *Encyclopedia of World Biography*.

How Stuff Works
> www.howstuffworks.com
> Founded by North Carolina State University Professor Marshall Brain in 1998, this website is well regarded for its free basic explanations of technical and scientific topics.

ENGINEERING

Typical questions
- Where can I get recent articles on civil engineering?
- Can you recommend any websites on hydraulic engineering?

Points to consider
- The term 'engineering' can cover a wide range of different subject areas. Those interested in chemical engineering may benefit from consulting the **Science** section, electrical engineers the **Computer Science** section and civil engineers the sections on **Legislation** and **Standards**.
- The complexity of the subject area means that this section can only offer a brief introduction. Users should explore the resources to find more detailed guides to specific sub-fields of engineering.

Where to look

Key organizations

Professional associations

Use these websites to trace essential information about the specific sub-field. Each has careers advice for students, plus lists of forthcoming events, training courses and conferences. The organizations also possess specialist libraries where you can find information on books and journals.

Institute of Civil Engineers
www.ice.org.uk

Institution of Chemical Engineers (IChemE)
www.icheme.org/resources.aspx
International professional membership association. Site includes links to related national organizations.

Institution of Engineering and Technology (IET)
www.theiet.org
Leading international organization; coverage includes Electrical Engineering.

Institution of Mechanical Engineers
www.imeche.org.

Institution of Structural Engineers
www.istructe.org

World's largest membership organization dedicated to the art and science of structural engineering.

Research bodies

Engineering and Physical Sciences Research Council (EPSRC)
www.epsrc.ac.uk

UK government agency for funding research and training in Engineering and the physical sciences. Find information on how to obtain grants and get information on recent awards and on-going projects.

Teaching and learning organizations

American Society for Engineering Education (ASEE)
www.asee.org

Access newsletters and blogs designed for Engineering students and lecturers. The website also has some abstracts of conference papers.

Higher Education Academy
www.heacademy.ac.uk

Aims to support UK-based teaching and learning. Includes coverage of Engineering. Website has lists of training events, conferences and support guides for teachers.

Royal Academy of Engineering
www.raeng.org.uk

UK-based scholarly society. Covers all branches of Engineering. Website includes news, plus free access to some webcasts of Academy lectures and other events.

Libraries

Institute of Civil Engineers Library
www.ice.org.uk/Information-resources/library

World's largest Civil Engineering library. Find references to books, journals and recommended websites.

Institution of Mechanical Engineers
www.imeche.org/knowledge/library

Maintains one of the largest Engineering library collections in the world. In addition to its catalogue, the library website has an extensive directory of links to specialist Engineering websites.

Handbooks and directories

McGraw-Hill Dictionary of Scientific and Technical Terms (2003) 6th edn,
McGraw-Hill

Long established reference source, includes definitions, calculations and
conversion tables used by engineers.

Macleod, R. and Corlett, J. (eds) (2005) *Information Sources in Engineering,*
4th edn, K. G. Saur Verlag

Specialist guidance on how to find primary and secondary sources for all
the main sub-fields of Engineering.

Journal article indexes

Compendex (subscription required)

www.ei.org/compendex

Extensive coverage of Chemical Engineering, Civil Engineering, Electrical
Engineering, Mechanical Engineering, Mining Engineering. Materials
from 1970 onwards.

InSPEC (subscription required)

www.theiet.org/publishing/inspec

Offers over 11 million bibliographic abstracts and indexing to journal articles,
conference proceedings, technical reports and other literature in the fields of
science and technology. Extensive coverage of Electrical Engineering.

Internet gateways and portals

Use these to locate databases of full-text articles, working papers and links to key
Engineering organizations.

GlobalSpec

www.globalspec.com

Specialist news service and search engines for the Engineering community.
Includes updates on products.

iCivilEngineer.com

www.icivilengineer.com

Links to news, careers resources and websites covering Civil Engineering.

TechXtra

www.techxtra.ac.uk

Specialist search engine for Engineering, Mathematics and Computing
created by Heriot Watt University. Quickly find academic working papers,
news, technical reports and announcements. Many have links to full text.

ENVIRONMENT

Typical questions
- Where can I get recent data on carbon emissions for EU nations?
- How can I get information on environmental accounting?
- Where can I search for articles on climate change?

Points to consider
- Environmental Studies, the academic study of human interaction with the environment, is a large interdisciplinary topic. Students studying ecology may also benefit from consulting the **Science** section; environmental regulation, the **Law** section; and physical phenomena of climate change, the **Geography** section.
- Many websites relating to the environment are created by activists or lobby groups. These can give useful viewpoints but should be evaluated carefully, taking into consideration any lack of objectivity. This section directs users to recommended academic resources.
- Environmental statistics/indicators are often of key importance and these are highlighted in their own sub-section.

Where to look
Key organizations
Scholarly associations

UK

Use these to locate news, publication reviews, conference listings and details of on-going research.

CHES (Committee of Heads of Environmental Sciences)
www.ches.org.uk
Represents higher education and further education departments in the UK. Website has news on educational policy and continuing professional development events.

Higher Education Academy
www.heacademy.ac.uk
Supports good-practice teaching and learning in the UK higher education sector. Includes subject coverage of Geography, Geology and Earth Sciences. Website has case studies plus information on projects, many of which involve technology in teaching.

United States
American Geophysical Union
www.agu.org

Long-established body which has a reputation for promoting scientific research in the earth sciences. This covers environmental issues from a scientific angle. Website has science policy and legislation alerts relating to the United States.

Association for Environmental Studies and Sciences (AESS)
www.aess.info

Professional association representing scholars and lecturers in American higher education. Website covers syllabi, teaching and learning projects.

National Council for Science and the Environment (NCSE)
ncseonline.org

Leading non-profit body which seeks to promote scientific research about the environment. Its website also has a large section on its support for education and careers.

International
Environmental Studies Section (ESS) of the International Studies Association (ISA)
environmental-studies.org

Good starting-point for finding out about the latest events, publications and research in environmental politics.

International Society for Environmental Ethics (ISEE)
iseethics.org

Aims to promote research in environmental philosophy and sustainable development. Website provides free access to some online bibliographies which have references to books, articles and reports covering the relationship between humans and the environment.

International Union for Conservation of Nature (IUCN)
iucn.org/knowledge

World's oldest global environmental network covering all aspects of environmental protection. Website provides free access to many of its publications and databases. These include the influential *Red List* of endangered species; *Ecolex*, a database of environmental laws; and the *World Database on Protected Areas*.

ENVIRONMENT

Government bodies

Use these to locate policy documents, legislation and statistics. Remember that responsibilities and departmental names have a tendency to change. For further advice see the **Government Publications** section.

Department of Environment, Food, Rural affairs (DEFRA)
www.defra.gov.uk
UK government body with current responsibility for the environment. Has conducted regular public surveys on attitudes towards the environment.

Environment Agency
www.environment-agency.gov.uk
Key UK government public body responsible for promoting and implementing UK environmental policy and sustainable development. Website has coverage of on-going projects.

European Environment Agency (EEA)
www.eea.europa.eu
Official body of the EU covering all aspects of the environment. Its website has extensive information, policy documents and statistics on the current state of the environment and environmental policy in Europe. The EEA also co-ordinates the *European Environment Information and Observation Network (Eionet)*. Its website supports the collection and dissemination of environmental data.

United Nations Environment Program (UNEP)
www.unep.org
Specialist environmental section of the UN with a wide remit covering climate change, sustainable development, environmental governance and ecosystems management. Access reports, documents, multimedia and statistics.

United States Environmental Protection Agency
www.epa.gov
Website includes a section for researchers containing news, legislation and research findings. It also maintains the **Health and Environmental Research Online (HERO)** database, **hero.epa.gov**, which offers open access to hundreds of thousands of references to scientific literature used by the government in its policy making and risk assessments. Topics covered include chemical risk, occupational health, pollution, air quality and waste. In many cases full-text articles can be downloaded free of charge.

Charities

Don't forget to check charity sites, because they can contain useful surveys of the state of the environment and critical comment on government policy. Good examples include:

Friends of the Earth
www.foe.co.uk

Greenpeace
www.greenpeace.org.uk
Others can be located by browsing the internet portals sub-section or using the directories in the **Charities** chapter.

Trade and professional organizations

These resources will direct users to information about practitioners working in trade and industry.

ENDS Directory
www.endsdirectory.com
Free access to the famous searchable directory of environmental consultants. Worldwide coverage. Search by location, type of contract and specialism. All areas of environmental work are covered. Entries give profiles and links to websites.

European Network of Environmental Professionals (ENEP)
www.efaep.org
Brings together professionals from various European nations who are working in the field of environmental protection. Website has a directory of links to national members.

Society for the Environment
www.socenv.org.uk
Leading UK body which works to promote sustainable development through environmental professionalism. Awards the Chartered Environmentalist qualification. Website has details of its member organizations (all of whom focus on specific environmental areas, such as town planning and agricultural management), plus guidance on environmental careers and professional development.

Libraries

Search the library catalogues and read the online research guides.

ENVIRONMENT

British Library
www.bl.uk/reshelp/experthelp/science
Holds extensive collections of books, journals and government reports covering all aspects of the scientific and social science aspects of the environment. Coverage strongest in terms of the UK and Europe.

Radcliffe Science Library
www.bodleian.ox.ac.uk/science
Part of the University of Oxford Libraries. Large holdings of books and journals covering scientific aspects of Geography and the environment.

Dictionaries and encyclopedias

Park, C. (2008) *Dictionary of Environment and Conservation*, **Oxford University Press**
Designed for use by students. Contains over 8500 entries covering both scientific concepts and social science theories relating to the environment and conservation. Useful appendixes include international environmental treaties and online sources of environmental information.

Robbins, P. (2007) *Encyclopedia of the Environment and Society*, **Sage**
Five volumes covering environmental science concepts, theories and practice. Entries contain bibliographies to guide further reading.

Journal article indexes

Use these in conjunction with those suggested in the **Geography** section to trace references to articles, book chapters and reports.

Environmental Impact (subscription required)
www.cabi.org
Database maintained by CABI. Provides access to bibliographic information (dating back to the early 20th century) about human impact on the environment. Extensive coverage of climate change materials.

Environment Index (subscription required)
www.ebscohost.com/academic/environment-index
Originally known as *Environmental Knowledgebase Online* and created by the International Academy at Santa Barbara. Provides references to articles covering all aspects of environmental science dating back to 1888. This includes coverage of the scientific, economic and legal aspects of environmental management.

GreenFile (subscription required)

www.ebscohost.com/academic/greenfile

Indexes thousands of articles and government reports covering all aspects of the human impact on the environment. Topics include recycling, renewable energy, climate change and pollution.

News services

These specialist services can be used to supplement the general environmental coverage offered by most quality national newspapers.

Earth Times

www.earthtimes.org

Free access to online news service focusing on green/conservation and environmental topics worldwide.

ENDS Report

www.endsreport.com

www.endseurope.com (Ends Europe)

News service designed to keep environmental professionals up to date with UK and EU policy and legislation relating to the environment, low-carbon economy and sustainable development. Free access to some features of the site, including blogs and the specialist jobs-search service, **www.endsjobsearch.co.uk**. Access to the full-text journal *Ends Report* requires a subscription.

Environment News Service (ENS)

www.ens-newswire.com

International daily newswire offering free access to the latest press releases covering environmental politics, policy, legislation and events. Website has archives dating back to 2002.

New Scientist

www.newscientist.com

Well regarded weekly science and technology news magazine. Covers a wide range of scientific issues, including climate change and the environment, for the public and research community. Free access to selected articles and job listings. Back files and other features offered to subscribers only.

Statistical data

European Environmental Agency data

www.eea.europa.eu

Includes access to the European Union Emissions Trading System, air pollution emissions data, greenhouse gas data. Most of these date from 1990 onwards, offering regular updates on trends in EU nations. Many datasets and graphs can be downloaded from the site.

National Statistics Online
www.statistics.gov.uk

Provides free access to recent statistics relating to the environment. These include the *United Kingdom Environmental Accounts*, which contain data on the environmental impact of UK economic activity. Topics covered include emissions, waste and energy consumption. Older materials may be offered in print only. Good sources for tracing these include the major libraries listed in the sub-section above.

OECD
www.oecd.org/department/0,3355,en_2649_34283_1_1_1_1_1,00.html

Publishes an *Environment Outlook*, which offers key statistical indicators and predictions for OECD nations and other major economies. Key topics include emissions, waste management and pollution. Detailed data offered to subscribers only.

UNEP World Conservation Monitoring Center
www.unep-wcmc.org/species/dbases/about.cfm

Maintains databases of information and statistics on endangered species (plant, animal marine), biodiversity and CITES trade in endangered species. The latter is a useful complement to the **IUCN Red List, www.iucnredlist. org**, which is often regarded as the world's most comprehensive inventory of endangered plant and animal species.

United Nations
unstats.un.org/unsd/environment/default.htm

Has a specialist environmental statistics division which produces country snapshots and the *UNSD Environmental Indicators*. The latter cover a range of topics, including environmental governance, waste management, land management, biodiversity, climate and air quality. Recent data can be downloaded free of charge. The site also has an excellent directory of links to national environmental agencies worldwide. Additionally, the United Nations Environment Programme (UNEP) maintains the specialist **Geo Data Portal, geodata.grid.unep.ch** for subscribers. This uses data from its influential *World Environmental Outlook* to enable users to create charts/graphs of more than 500 variables covering all aspects of the environment at international, national and sub-national levels.

World Bank Environmental Data

www.worldbank.org/environment/data

Offers free access to country fact files and the annual *Little Green Data Book*, which has basic indicators on over 200 nations worldwide.

Internet gateways and portals

These include digital libraries of full-text publications as well as links to high-quality websites covering specialist environmental areas such as land, sea and air pollution.

Earth Portal

www.earthportal.org

Developed by the Environmental Information Coalition (EIC). Provides free access to environmental news, discussion forums and the **Encyclopedia of Earth (EoE), www.eoearth.org**, an encyclopedia-type resource written collaboratively by scholars for the public which contains articles on the Earth and human interaction with the environment.

EarthTrends

earthtrends.wri.org

Maintained by the World Resources Institute to offer the public an easily accessible source of information. Country and topic profiles cover the full range of physical, social and economic aspects of the environment.

EnviroLink

www.envirolink.org

Non-profit organization whose website provides free access to thousands of links covering environmental issues. These include organizations, news services, e-mail listings and online articles.

EUROPEAN UNION

Typical questions
- Where can I access the Treaty of Rome?
- What does the Committee of the Regions do?
- How can I trace COM documents?

Points to consider
- Increasing amounts of information by and about the EU are now available on the internet. However, many websites are created by organizations lobbying for or against integration, so remind students to evaluate resources carefully. This section will guide you to recommended academic resources. These include primary sources (laws, treaties, documents) produced by the EU and secondary materials (commentary in articles and books about the EU)
- Remember that the Council of Europe is different from the EU and not all European nations are members of the EU!

Where to look

Key organizations

Government

Europa

    europa.eu

    Official website of the European Union. Can be difficult to navigate, so it is worth time exploring. Key features include:

- **CORDIS, cordis.europa.eu.** Research and development gateway. Has the latest news, advice and documents. Extensive coverage of researcher mobility in Europe.
- **Documents, europa.eu/documentation/official-docs/index_en.htm.** Access publications from key bodies, including the Parliament, Committee of the Regions.
- **Eurobarometer, ec.europa.eu/public_opinion.** Access opinion polls conducted by the European Commission. Useful surveys of attitudes towards the EU and integration.
- **Euro, ec.europa.eu/euro.** Policy, papers and statistcs on the euro.
- **TED (Tenders Electronic Daily), ted.europa.eu.** Contains public procurement notices published in the *Official Journal of the European Union*, Supplement S.
- **Who is Who, europa.eu/whoiswho/whoiswho.html.** Official directory of key office holders. Search by name, organization.

European Commission Representation in the United Kingdom
ec.europa.eu/unitedkingdom
Official voice of the EU in the UK. Find information on the history of British involvement and current activities.

House of Commons European Scrutiny Committee
www.parliament.uk/business/committees/committees-archive/
european-scrutiny
Access reports and critical comment from British MPs on European policy and legislation.

Scholarly associations

Use these websites to locate news on publications, conferences and academic research.

European Policy Institutes Network (EPIN)
www.epin.org
Network of think-tanks and policy institutes focusing on current EU policy debates. Website provides free access to many working papers produced by members.

European Union Studies Association (EUSA)
www.eustudies.org
Major international organization covering all aspects of EU studies. Membership in North American and Europe. Access recent conference papers online.

University Association for Contemporary European Studies (UACES)
www.uaces.org
Largest association in Europe. Supports student forums. Website includes free access to articles from *JCER: Journal for Contemporary European Research* and a conference paper archive.

Libraries

EU information in member states is provided through a number of official networks. Use their websites to locate specialist support near you.

Enterprise Europe Network
www.enterprise-europe-network.ec.europa.eu/info/network_en.htm
Supports the business community.

Europe Direct
europa.eu/europedirect
Intended to support the general public.

Europe Documentation Centres

europa.eu/europedirect/meet_us/index_en.htm

Supports the academic and research community. Based in university libraries which have specialist current and historic EU document collections. Key examples in the UK are the **British Library, www.bl.uk** and the **LSE Library, www2.lse.ac.uk/library.**

Information and contact details for all sectors can be found on the **Europe in the UK, www.europe.org.uk** website which also has excellent news about grants, events and EU publications.

European Commission's Central Library

ec.europa.eu/libraries/doc/index_en.htm

Located in Brussels. Its website provides free access to the ECLAS library catalogue, which can be used to trace key publications. The site also has links to key EU resources.

European Information Association

www.eia.org.uk

Membership composed of UK library and information professionals. The website provides guidance on researching the EU and lists of training events.

News services

EurActiv

www.euractiv.com

Specialist European news service. Covers economics, politics and legislation.

EuropeanVoice.com

www.europeanvoice.com

Weekly newspaper published by the Economist Group since 1995. The website has articles, interviews and blogs. Some reports and past issues are for subscribers only.

Rapid

europa.eu/rapid

Official EU press service.

European Law

Use this in conjunction with the **Law** section. Many of the commercial databases described there also cover EU law.

EUR-Lex

eur-lex.europa.eu

Free access to full-text law. Includes all issues of the *Official Journal of the European Union*, **publications.europa.eu/official/imdex_en.htm**, which is published daily in two series: L (Legislation) and C (Information and Notices).

Also available are the founding and accession treaties, international agreements, European Parliament questions and case law from the European Court of Justice.

Other related legal databases are:

Legislative Observatory of the European Parliament OEIL

www.europarl.europa.eu/oeil

Tracks legislative progress in Parliament.

PreLex

ec.europa.eu/prelex

Trace the progress of Commission legislative proposals and Commission (COM) documents from origin until adoption or rejection.

Journal article indexes and working papers

Use these for literature searching in conjunction with the resources listed in the general **Journal Article Indexes** section.

Archive of European Integration

aei.pitt.edu

Maintained by the University of Pittsburgh. Includes EU documents, journal articles and research papers.

Centre Virtuel de la Connaissance sur l'Europe (CVCE)

www.cvce/eu

Digital library which aims to provide free access to documents and other sources tracing the history of European integration.

European Integration Online Portal

eiop.or.at

Service of the European Community Studies Association, Austria. Provides a single gateway to a wealth of resources. Key features include: *European Integration Online Papers* (a refereed e-journal); the *European Research Papers Archive*, providing access to full-text discussion papers from leading European universities; and *EuroInternet*, a collection of annotated links to key EU websites.

EUROPEAN UNION

European Sources Online (subscription required)
www.europeansources.info
Guides users to key articles (journal and newspaper), official documents and websites relating to all aspects of the EU. Also includes introductory information guides.

Statistical data

Eurostat

epp.eurostat.ec.europa.eu
Official website offering detailed statistics relating to EU and candidate nations. Covers all aspects of economic and social policy at European, regional and national levels. Includes the *Eurostat Yearbook* from 2002 onwards. Consult the website for details of coverage and methodology. Note that some datasets may be offered to subscribers only. Some of these may also be available via the national data centres listed in the **Statistical Data** section.

FILMS, DOCUMENTARIES AND MOVING IMAGES

Typical questions

- I want to find examples of Latin American soap operas.
- Can I use this YouTube clip in my course?
- Are any of the 1980s public information films about AIDS online?

Points to consider

- The internet has revolutionized access to film. However, many materials appear and disappear rapidly and their origins and copyright status may be uncertain.
- Most students have used YouTube, **www.youtube.com**. This section aims to offer a wider range of starting-points for academic research. It should also be used in conjunction with the **Copyright** section!

Where to look

Key organizations

Use these to get advice on finding and using films for educational purposes.

BFI British Film Institute
www.bfi.org.uk/filmtvinfo/researchers
Promotes knowledge and appreciation of film. Its website offers an extensive annotated directory of film links. You can also search the catalogue of its library and archives. Note that in most cases access to materials will be offered on site only.

JISC Digital Media
www.jiscdigitalmedia.ac.uk
Provides advice, guidance and training to the UK further and higher education community on still and moving images. Website has copyright guides and tips on tracing moving images on the internet.

Search engines

- Most general internet search engines claim to find films. However, unfortunately not all materials are archived online. If an item cannot be traced, try to find out the date of transmission and the station/publisher and contact it directly. If the item is a webcast of an event try searching the website of the hosting body because it may have an institutional archive.

- Note that if references to items are found in other library catalogues, the items may not be available to visitors for viewing or interlibrary loan. Always check.

Blinkx

> **www.blinkx.com**
>
> Recommended video search engine. Find all genres of TV and film online. Covers both academic and many non-academic resources worldwide.

Google video

> **video.google.co.uk**
>
> Use the advanced search feature to search for films by length. You can also restrict your search to a specific domain, e.g. YouTube.

Good general websites

These can be useful for tracing educational lectures and documentaries.

FORA.tv

> **fora.tv**
>
> Founded by Brian Gruber. Aims to provide an online forum for free access to lectures, webcasts and video films from independent producers, non-profit institutions and universities. Current partners include the Heritage Foundation, Chatham House, Cato Institution, the Brookings Institution.

Internet Archive

> **www.archive.org/details/movies**
>
> Contains thousands of digital movies uploaded by Internet Archive users. These range from classic full-length films to daily alternative news broadcasts, cartoons, concerts and historical public information films.

YouTube edu

> **www.youtube.com/edu**
>
> Special section of YouTube which contains a directory of videos, film clips and channels from universities, colleges and higher education establishments worldwide.

Historical film collections

The following are examples of large online collections.

BFI InView

> **www.bfi.org.uk/inview**
>
> Free access to over 2000 moving image clips taken from the archives of the British Film Institute (BFI). They include rare examples of government

films, newsreels, TV documentaries, parliamentary recordings. Themes covered include British economic history, education, the development of the National Health Service, law and order. Each section has essays by historians.

BFI Screenonline
www.screenonline.org.uk

Also maintained by the BFI. Contains thousands of video images, sound extracts, still photographs, time lines and essays relating to the history of British film and TV. Full access to the moving images is for registered users (UK schools, educational establishments).

FedFlix
www.archive.org/details/FedFlix

Collaboration between the National Technical Information Service and Public.Resource.Org. Provides free access to historic films from the American government.

JISCMedia Hub (subscription required)
jiscmediahub.ac.uk

Cross-search an extensive collection of still and moving image collections especially selected for UK academic use. Film collections include Paramount news, Channel 4 news and Imperial War Museum films. The site also has an extensive directory of links to recommended free websites.

Public Information Films from the UK National Archive
www.nationalarchives.gov.uk/films

Free access to a collection of 20th-century UK government films. They include public health promotion films.

Video Active
www.videoactive.eu/VideoActive/Home.do

Project funded by European Commission. Will provide access to 10,000 films from TV archives across Europe, offering a fascinating insight into the development of broadcasting and the social, economic and political history of European nations.

Wellcome Film Library
library.wellcome.ac.uk/wellcomefilm.htm

Free access to over 450 titles relating to 20th-century healthcare and medicine. They include public health promotion videos.

FILMS, DOCUMENTARIES & MOVING IMAGES

Newsreels

ITN Source

www.itnsource.com/compilations

Contains footage (both recent and historic) from Reuters, ITN, ITV Productions, Fox News and Fox Movietone, Asian News International and other specialist collections. Some compilations offered free of charge. Other services offered to subscribers only.

Newsplayer – 20th Century Captured on Film

www.newsplayer.com

Free access to a fascinating collection of historic 20th-century newsreels from the libraries of ITN, Reuters, Paramount, Gaumont, British Empire News, Visnews and French Pathé. Most footage is short newsclips.

FREEDOM OF INFORMATION REQUESTS

Typical questions

- How do I make a FOIA request?
- Can I get the government to release cabinet minutes?

Points to consider

- Freedom of information legislation (FOIA) ensures public access to government documents. Upon written request, agencies of certain governments are required to disclose certain categories of material. However, the rules relating to this may be complex. Students/researchers need guidance on what kinds of material can be obtained, the information they need to make a request and the time-scales.
- In addition to government departments, good starting-points for tracing this advice include the websites of national archives and pressure groups.
- Do advise students to check whether what they need is already in the public sphere. Many government websites have FOIA sections where recently requested documents can be consulted.

Where to look

UK

Information Commissioner's Office
> **www.ico.gov.uk**
> Independent organization. Offers guides for the public on the Freedom of Information Act and how to gain access to public documents.

The National Archives
> **www.nationalarchives.gov.uk/foi**
> Offers advice for researchers.

What do they know?
> **www.whatdotheyknow.com**
> Maintained by mySociety, a registered charity. Designed to help citizens make and access recent requests. Look at recent releases on the website.

United States

National Archives and Records Administration Freedom of Information Act (FOIA) Reference Guide
> **www.archives.gov/foia/foia-guide.html**

Clear guidance on all stages of the process. See also the FOIA reading room for examples of recent and frequently requested items.

National Security Archive – FOIA resources
www.gwu.edu/~nsarchiv/nsa/foia/resources.html
Directory of useful guides and websites covering all aspects of FOIA, compiled by the specialist unit based at George Washington University.

International

FreedomInfo
www.freedominfo.org
Global network. Find news stories, links to laws and advice covering requests to national governments and international organizations.

FURTHER EDUCATION

Typical questions
- Where can I get a list of FE colleges in Wales?
- How are FE colleges funded?

Points to consider
- This section focuses specifically on further education (FE) resources. Definitions of FE can be broad, encompassing vocational courses and many different forms of adult learning; therefore relevant general educational theory resources may also be found in the broader **Education** section. Also of value are the resources listed in the **Higher Education** section, as many cover both sectors.
- Frequent changes to the post-16 educational landscape, including amalgamations and name changes of colleges, mean that it can be difficult to trace information. The resources listed below are good starting-points.

Where to look

Key organizations

UK

Scholarly bodies

Further Education Research Association (FERA)
www.fera.uk.net
Disseminates research findings covering policy evaluation, teaching and good practice in the further education and training sector. Its website provides free access to abstracts from its journal *Research in Post-Compulsory Education*. It also offers a link to the *Lifelong Learning Network Research Database*.

Professional organizations
The following are influential organizations. Their websites are useful starting-points for tracing comment from the sector on government policy regarding such topics as research, curriculum content and student funding/tuition fees.

157 Group
www.157group.co.uk
Membership organization of over 20 influential further education colleges which seeks to influence UK government policy. Access case studies and reports on the website.

Association of Colleges

www.aoc.co.uk

Includes tertiary and further education colleges, sixth form colleges and specialist colleges in England and Northern Ireland.

CoFHE

www.cilip.org.uk/get-involved/special-interest-groups/c-of-he/pages/introduction.aspx

Special-interest group of library and information professionals working in colleges of further and higher education. Use the website to get insight into issues relating to library provision, student information literacy and training needs.

FEAlliance

fealliance.org.uk

Aims to act as a social network and forum for further education professional and teaching staff.

National Institute of Adult Continuing Education (NIACE)

www.niace.org.uk

Influential charity which seeks to promote adult learning. Website provides information on its campaigns and publications. Topics covered include widening participation, adult literacy, workplace learning, informal learning and online learning. Some of its publications and case studies can be downloaded from the website. These include statistics on participation rates and funding. The site also maintains a good directory of links to key further education websites.

UK Qualifications and Skills Team (UKQST)

www.excellencegateway.org.uk/page.aspx?o=320139

Responsible for professional development of staff in further education learning organizations. Access news and information on qualifications and training.

Workers' Educational Association

www.wea.org.uk

Founded in 1903, the UK's largest voluntary provider of adult education. Website contains free access to news, course listings and its policy and research reports.

International

European Association for the Education of Adults (EAEA)

www.eaea.org

Represents education providers in further education, vocational and lifelong learning. Website offers access to news, event listings and some information on further education provision and funding in member states.

INVETA (International Vocational Education and Training Association)

www.iveta.org

Worldwide network of vocational and workplace training educators and organizations. Get news and events listings.

Government bodies

Remember that most recent government documents can now be found online. However, frequent changes to the names and responsibilities of organizations in the further education sector can make tracing materials difficult. A recent initiative is the **Digital Education Resource Archive (DERA), dera.ioe.ac.uk,** which aims to web-archive resources from UK government departments. It includes coverage of post-16 education.

For earlier materials try to get as much information as possible (title/year/department) and consult the **Government Publications** section.

Skills Funding Agency

skillsfundingagency.bis.gov.uk

Formerly the Learning and Skills Council. Body currently responsible for funding and regulating adult further education and skills training in England. Find information on news, government reports and advice for learners relating to vocational qualifications, apprenticeship standards and further education in general.

News services

FENews.co.uk

www.fenews.co.uk

Largest online news site in the UK further education and skills sector. Get free newsfeeds, online interviews and access job listings.

Statistical data

Many of the resources listed in the **Education** and **Higher Education** statistics sub-sections also have some datasets relating to post-compulsory education.

FURTHER EDUCATION

Data Service

www.thedataservice.org.uk/statistics

Specialist independent organization supported by the UK government. Website provides free access to recent datasets covering post-16 learner participation, retention rates and qualifications at national and local authority levels.

GEOGRAPHY

Typical questions

- Where can I find recent research on the impact of hurricane Katrina?
- I need to get GIS data for Sri Lanka.
- Where can I find out what causes a tsunami?

Points to consider

- The subject area of geography can be wide ranging. Students of physical geography may need access to **Maps**; or information about the **Environment**; while those focusing on human geography may find the coverage of human societies in the **Sociology** section relevant. Materials relating to **Development Studies** may be useful for those studying the human geography of developing nations.
- An increasing demand is for geospatial data. This can also be called geographical information systems or GIS, and commonly refers to software that combines features of cartography and other databases to overlay reference information (such as number of people living in a specific location, or the extent of soil erosion in an area) on computer-generated maps.

Where to look

Key organizations

Use these to find information on the main scholarly journals and conferences. They also contain careers advice for students.

UK

British Geological Survey

    www.bgs.ac.uk

    UK's national centre for earth science information. Coverage includes geology, climate change and natural hazards.

Geographical Association

    www.geography.org.uk

    Specialist organization for UK teachers. Free access to hundreds of resources for primary and secondary classes. These include suggested lesson plans and links to recommended websites, many covering topical news stories.

Royal Geographical Society (RGS)
www.rgs.org

Established in 1830, the main professional organization for the UK. Website has detailed information on where to study Geography, and news about research grants. Its **Unlocking the Archives** section, **www.unlockingthearchives.rgs.org**, provides free access to historic images/documents and associated lesson plans for schools. Topics covered include the race to the South Pole. Other features of the site include a commercial picture library with access to photographs and prints of travel and exploration.

International

Association of American Geographers
www.aag.org

Main US body. Website includes information on cutting-edge projects which it has supported.

HERODOT – Network for Geography in Higher Education
www.herodot.net

Seeks to improve the quality of Geography teaching and learning in higher education in Europe. Website is a good starting-point for locating training, forthcoming conferences and links to innovative teaching and learning projects.

International Geographical Union (IGU)
igu-online.org

International organization of geographers. Website has a directory of links to national bodies and university departments worldwide.

Libraries and archives

Royal Geographical Society Library
www.rgs.org/OurWork/Collections/About+The+Collections

One of the world's largest collections with extensive holdings of books, journals, atlases, maps, photographs and other artefacts. Open free of charge to the public. Its catalogue can be searched online.

Dictionaries and encyclopedias

Douglas, I., Huggett, R. and Perkins, C. (eds) (2006) *Companion Encyclopedia of Geography*, 2nd edn, Routledge

Comprises 64 essays covering major topics in Physical and Human Geography.

Mayhew, S. (2009) *A Dictionary of Geography*, 4th edn, Oxford University Press

Over 6400 entries covering all aspects of Human and Physical Geography. Associated website, **www.oup.com/uk/booksites/content/9780199231805**, has links to recommended internet resources.

Geospatial data

Digimap (subscription required)

edina.ac.uk/digimap

Online maps and geospatial data covering the UK. Collections include current and historic maps as well as geological surveys.

ESRI

www.esri.com/about-esri

Specialist supplier of GIS products. Website offers news of new technology, plus free access to some GIS mapping tools and the GIS bibliography of references to journal articles and papers, **training.esri.com/library/index.cfm**.

Go-Geo!

www.gogeo.ac.uk

Collaborative project between the EDINA National Data Centre, University of Edinburgh, and the UK Data Archive, University of Essex, which aims to provide researchers with a place to locate and access geospatial data. Search a data catalogue, get links to key organizations, news, updates on training and some free case studies and articles to download.

Journal article indexes

Geobase (subscription required)

www.elsevier.com/wps/find/bibliographicdatabasedescription.cws_home/422597/description#description

Leading earth sciences database, indexing over 2000 journals covering Physical and Human Geography, Geology and Ecology. Coverage from 1973 onwards.

GreenFile (subscription required)

www.ebscohost.com/academic/greenfile

Multi-disciplinary database covering all aspects of human impact on the environment, including pollution, sustainable development and climate change.

Internet gateways and portals

Use these megasites to locate references to recommended web resources covering specialist fields of Geography.

Geoguide

www.geo-guide.de

Specialist gateway to scholarly websites in earth sciences, physical geography and mining maintained by the State and University Library, Göttingen and the University Library 'Georgius Agricola', Freiberg, Germany.

Geosource

www.library.uu.nl/geosource

Excellent directory covering all aspects of Physical and Human Geography maintained by the University of Utrecht. Includes indexes for material by type of source and geographical region.

GOVERNMENT PUBLICATIONS

Typical questions

- How can I find the Warnock Report?
- I need to trace recent UK government reports on banking.
- How can I keep up to date with the latest reports on social care?

Points to consider

- Government reports are often referred to as official publications. They may be underused by students who fail to recognize their importance as a primary source of information and find difficulty in tracing them in library catalogues. Other commonly requested forms of government publications are **Statistical Data** and **Legislation,** which are covered separately.
- A common problem is that many reports are known by the name of the chairperson of the reporting body rather than their official title. Searches for these in the library catalogue are often unsuccessful.
- Additionally, many libraries do not individually catalogue government documents. Instead they make single entries to series, such as House of Commons Papers, and file items within them numerically. The best advice is to check local cataloguing practices first. Then try to locate the document series and numbers by using the original source of the reference and/or the databases listed below. For example the Hutton Report has the official title *Report of the Inquiry into the Circumstances Surrounding the Death of Dr David Kelly* HC 247 session (2003–04). In many library catalogues it can be traced only by the full title or by searching for the HC or House of Commons papers series.

UK

Some common series are:

- Command papers, the numbers of which often appear in the formats Cm100, C100, Cd100, Cmnd100, Cmd100 alongside a session number relating to the year of publication.
- House of Commons Papers: HC, then a number and session year, e.g. HC 95 (2004–05).
- House of Lords Papers: HL.
- For more detailed advice see the key organizations below.

GOVERNMENT PUBLICATIONS

Where to look

Key organizations

Use these websites to contact specialist librarians.

British Library
    www.bl.uk/reshelp/findhelprestype/offpubs/ukofficalpub/ukpublications.html
    Maintains a comprehensive UK collection. Website has guidance on tracing British government documents using its collections.

Standing Committee on Official Publications (SCOOP)
    www.cilip.org.uk/get-involved/special-interest-groups/information-services/scoop/Pages/default.aspx
    Special-interest group of CILIP (Chartered Institute of Library and Information Professionals).

Current awareness resources

COI News Distribution Service
    nds.coi.gov.uk
    Official press releases from the UK government. Coverage includes new publications. It is possible to sign up for alerts.

Daily List
    www.tso.co.uk/daily_list/issues.htm
    Published by The Stationery Office (TSO). Although intended as the TSO's sales list of the most recent parliamentary publications, it is a useful current awareness alerting tool. Note that some items listed may be free on the web, so it is worth searching. Archived lists from 2001 onwards can be downloaded.

Info4local
    www.info4local.gov.uk
    Provides daily news and new publication alerts from over 70 government bodies. Note that while this includes all major sites it is not yet comprehensive.

Digital libraries

House of Commons Parliamentary Papers (HCPP)
    (subscription required)
    parlipapers.chadwyck.co.uk/marketing/guide.jsp
    Search for full-text parliamentary papers from 1715 onwards (with some

selected materials dating back to 1688). Includes Bills, Royal Commission reports, Command Papers, House of Commons and House of Lords Papers.

Official Documents
www.official-documents.gov.uk
Site maintained by The Stationery Office on behalf of the UK government. Provides free access to the full text of Command Papers, House of Commons Papers and key departmental papers from 2004 onwards. Older items can be traced in the British Library.

UK Government Web Archive
www.nationalarchives.gov.uk/webarchive
Maintained by The National Archives. Preserves regular snapshots of UK government central and departmental websites. These can be used to access documents which may have since disappeared. Some sites date as far back as 1997. The catalogue can be searched by keyword.

United States

FDsys: GPO's Federal Digital System
www.gpo.gov/fdsys
Replaces the former GPO Access. It is very user friendly and has the facility to browse and in many cases access current and historical documents free of charge. Includes: *Congressional Record*, congressional hearings and bills. Most items from at least 1993 onwards.

GODORT
www.ala.org/ala/mgrps/rts/godort/index.cfm
Government Documents Round Table of the American Library Association. Its website and wiki provide free access to detailed specialist advice on tracing US official publications.

International

Government Gazettes
www-personal.umich.edu/~graceyor/doctemp/gazettes/index.htm
Gazettes are official news services issued by national governments worldwide. They can be used successfully to trace the latest government publications. This useful directory, hosted by the University of Michigan, has links to a large number of them, alongside descriptions of their content.

University of Michigan Government Documents Center
www.lib.umich.edu/government-documents-center
Maintains a directory of links to major government websites worldwide.

GOVERNMENT PUBLICATIONS

Many governments have a central online portal where you can get news alerts and trace links to individual departments.

GRANTS AND FUNDING

Typical questions

- Where can I get information on bursaries for postgraduate students?
- Are there any lists of companies that offer sponsorship?

Points to consider

- Questions about funding can focus on grants for individuals or funding for organizational, institutional or departmental projects.
- Resources relating to funding for individual educational needs are often provided by local careers services. Other good starting-points are the professional organizations of the subject concerned.
- Specialist advice on research project grants can also usually be found on professional association websites as well as on those of the appropriate research councils.
- The resources listed in this section are general starting-points which will supplement the above. To be most successful in answering the query, try to get as much detail as possible about the type of information needed, because most types of funding have conditions attached.
- Finally, remember to check when the source was last updated!

Where to look

Individuals

GrantSpace

foundationcenter.org

Comprehensive website maintained by the Foundation Center to offer free support to organizations and individuals seeking funding. Although the main emphasis is on North America, it also has very useful advice for individuals covering all aspects of the application process. This includes a searchable directory of possible sources.

Grants Register: Complete Guide to Postgraduate Funding Worldwide. **Palgrave Macmillan. Annual**

Authoritative listing. Includes information on eligibility for and availability of grants for specific subject areas worldwide.

Guide to Grants for Individuals in Need. **Directory for Social Change. Annual**

Covers grants for poverty and disability as well as educational needs. Locate information on relevant charities and get advice on eligibility and how to make a successful application. Also available online at **www. grantsforindividuals.org.uk** (subscription required), with more regular updates and e-mail alerts when new opportunities arise.

Scholarship Search

www.scholarship-search.org.uk

Free website listing of institutions, companies and other organizations offering educational bursaries and funding to individuals. Search by type of funding and subject area.

Organizations

Company.giving.org.uk (subscription required)

www.companygiving.org.uk

Website maintained by the Directory for Social Change. Useful tool for fund raisers seeking to identify companies that may be sympathetic to their cause. Lists and profiles several hundred corporate organizations that regularly give. Includes profiles of past support, eligibility criteria and details of how to apply.

***Directory of Grant Making Trusts*. Directory of Social Change. Annual**

Well regarded comprehensive source intended for use by organizational fund raisers. Indexed by subject and geographical location. Entries include details on application procedures and previous beneficiaries. Also available from the same publishers is the online resource **Trustfunding.org.uk** (subscription required), **www.trustfunding.org.uk,** which complements the annual *Directory of Grant Making Trusts* with more regularly updated lists of information, e-mail news alerts and advice.

Government.funding.org.uk (subscription required)

www.governmentfunding.org.uk

Service of the Directory for Social Change. Access information on current and forthcoming UK local, regional and national government grants for organizations. Also has some coverage of European sources. Includes advice on how to apply successfully.

GrantSpace

foundationcenter.org

Site maintained by the Foundation Center, offering support to both organizations and individuals seeking funding. Although the main emphasis is on North America, it also has very useful advice (factsheets, sample letters, online films) covering proposal writing, searching for grants and making applications which would be useful for organizations elsewhere. It is also possible to search its library catalogue of non-profit literature to find references to recent books and reports covering all aspects of fund raising.

Grants and Resources
www.chapel-york.com/gandr2.php

Free e-mail service offered by Chapel & York. Get information/alerts on international grants for NGOs, charities and organizations. The company website also has other free guides to resources, plus guides and directories for purchase.

Guide to European Funding for Associations (2010) 16th edn, Directory for Social Change

Regularly updated guide which provides an overview of EU funds available for the non-profit sector. Also covers other European (non-EU sources).

HEADS OF STATE/HEADS OF GOVERNMENT

Typical questions

- Who is the Russian president?
- Where can I find the name of the British prime minister in 1974?

Points to consider

- Many governments now have websites with current and historic information on presidents and prime ministers. Some even have photographs, biographies, messages and speeches online. The University of Michigan Government Documents Center has a good collection of links to foreign government websites, which are a useful starting-point, **www.lib.umich.edu/government-documents-center.**
- Another starting-point for historic information is dictionaries of national biography. See the **Biographical Information** section for details.
- Always check when the information was last updated.

Where to look

Chiefs of State and Cabinet Members of Foreign Governments
www.cia.gov/library/publications/world-leaders-1/rss-updates/index.html
Free listing, regularly updated, by the CIA.

Statesman's Yearbook (subscription required)
www.statesmansyearbook.com
Online or in print, the annual publication lists current monarchs, presidents and heads of government. Online version covers 1860 onwards.

HIGHER EDUCATION

Typical questions

- I need to find statistics on student retention rates in English universities.
- Where can I search for recent articles on HE management?

Points to consider

- This section focuses specifically on Higher Education resources. General educational theory resources may also be found in the broader **Education** section.
- Increasing numbers of documents produced by government departments/educational think-tanks are being published on the web rather than in print. Therefore they may not be indexed on academic library catalogues. Remember to search the internet!

Where to look

Key organizations

UK

Government bodies

Remember that recent government reports are often online, while earlier ones can usually be located in paper in major libraries, including those listed in the **Education** section. Departmental names often change, so check details as carefully as possible.

Department for Business, Innovation and Skills (BIS)
www.bis.gov.uk/policies/by/themes/higher%20education
Currently responsible for higher and further education. Access policy, consultation, documents and full-text reports from the website.

Higher Education Funding Council for England (HEFCE)
www.hefce.ac.uk
Responsible for funding higher education and research activities. Note that Scottish higher education institutions are funded by the **Scottish Funding Council, www.sfc.ac.uk/about_the_council/council_funded_institutions/ council_funded_institutions.aspx**. Welsh higher education institutions are funded by the **Higher Education Funding Council for Wales, www.hefcw.ac.uk/about_he_in_wales/higher_education_institutions/he_ institutions.aspx**; and Northern Ireland by the **Department for Employment and Learning, Northern Ireland, www.delni.gov.uk**. Use the websites to trace names and contacts of all higher education (HE)

establishments, plus information on widening participation projects, the management of the HE workforce, statistics on budgets and research funding. The latter includes detailed documents relating to research assessment exercises and the Research Excellence Framework used to assess the quality of research in UK HE institutions.

IOE Digital Education Resource Archive
dera.ioe.ac.uk
Launched in 2011 by the Institute of Education (University of London). Aims to create a permanent web archive of documents published electronically by the UK government and related bodies in the area of education.

Office for Fair Access (OFFA)
www.offa.org.uk
Independent public body that helps safeguard and promote fair access to higher education. Its website provides free access to access agreements and monitoring reports on access by disadvantaged and minority groups. Topics covered include the impact of bursaries and tuition fees.

Quality Assurance Agency for Higher Education (QAA)
www.qaa.ac.uk
Seeks to ensure improvement of standards. Website provides free access to subject benchmark standards as well as individual reviews of colleges.

Professional and staff organizations

Use these to locate information on conditions and training for staff in UK higher education.

Higher Education Academy
www.heacademy.ac.uk
Aims to support excellence in teaching and learning. This includes support for subject-specialist activities. The home page includes free access to **Evidence Net**, a searchable database of useful resources (case studies, articles, reports) about teaching and learning in higher education, **www.heacademy. ac.uk/evidencenet**. It also has a section designed to support new lecturers (including graduate teachers). Explore the subject sections to find more specific resources such as case studies, syllabi and online projects relating to individual teaching areas.

Leadership Foundation for Higher Education
www.lfhe.ac.uk

Provides support and training in management and governance for individuals and corporate bodies. Get events listings and research publications. Topics covered include leadership development, succession planning and diversity.

Society of College, National and University Libraries (SCONUL)
www.sconul.ac.uk

Represents university libraries in the UK. Its website has news and policy documents covering such issues as library provision and funding, e-learning and the changing nature of scholarly communication.

Universities and Colleges Employers Association (UCEA)
www.ucea.ac.uk

Represents and advises UK higher education institutions on employment matters. Use the website to find news, information and facts about salaries, pay and terms of conditions in higher education.

University and College Union
www.ucu.org.uk

Largest trade union and professional association for academics, lecturers and academic-related staff working in further and higher education throughout the UK. Use to trace comment on government higher education policy as well as discussion of pay and conditions from a staff perspective.

Scholarly organizations

Society for Research into Higher Education
www.srhe.ac.uk

UK-based society with international membership. Website offers information on research networks, conferences and recent publications covering all aspects of higher education.

University groups and think-tanks

The following are influential organizations. Their websites are useful starting-points for tracing comment from the sector on government policy regarding such topics as research, curriculum content and student funding/tuition fees.

1994 Group
www.1994group.ac.uk

Established in 1994, the Group brings together 19 research-intensive universities.

Higher Education Policy Institute (HEPI)
www.hepi.ac.uk

UK's only independent think-tank devoted solely to higher education. Download its free reports from the website. Key topics include: educational funding, higher education supply and demand predictions, quality and standards of degrees and the impact of student tuition fees.

Million+
www.millionplus.ac.uk

Think-tank supported by a group of universities that, according to its website, 'provide courses and research programmes which promote aspirations and empower and equip students, employers and the "not for profit" sectors in the UK and in countries throughout the world'. Funds research into issues relating to student funding and the impact of universities on society and the economy. Examples can be read on its website.

Russell Group
www.russellgroup.ac.uk

Represents 20 leading UK universities often regarded as the elite research bodies. Includes Oxford, Cambridge and University College London.

Universities UK
www.universitiesuk.ac.uk

Founded in 1918, aims to be the definitive voice for all universities in the UK. Works with Higher Education Wales and Universities Scotland. Its website provides free access to many of its detailed policy and research reports. Key areas of concern are higher education sector funding, quality and standards, social mobility and access to higher education, international comparisons and research funding and governance.

University Alliance
www.university-alliance.ac.uk

Formed in 2006, comprising a mixture of pre- and post-1992 universities. Emphasis on business-focused courses and research.

International

AAU – Association of African Universities
www.aau.org

Non-governmental organization covering universities from Africa. Get news, information and reports from the region.

Association of Commonwealth Universities (ACU)
www.acu.ac.uk

Established in 1913, ACU is the oldest inter-university network in the world. Use its website to find news and reports on international student programmes, contact addresses of member organizations and news from different regions. Coverage includes colleges in developing nations.

European University Association
www.eua.be

Represents and supports higher education institutions in 46 countries, including non-EU members. Get news from member states, plus discussion and reports on issues relating to higher education management, policy, funding and international student mobility. Also includes news about the Bologna process, which is seeking to create a European higher education area.

International Association of Universities (IAU)
www.iau-aiu.net

Leading organization, founded in 1950. Its website is a useful starting-point for tracing information on universities worldwide. It publishes the annual *International Handbook of Universities*, which lists universities by country and indexes major regional and international higher education organizations. Some free access to basic listings taken from this can be found on the website. It also produces a database on higher education systems which profiles the nature and structure of higher education systems in over 183 countries worldwide. Again, the website offers basic access, although dates of last revision should be checked. A more detailed version is offered to subscribers online at **World Higher Education Database Online, www.whed-online.com.**

Journal article indexes

Use these in conjunction with the databases listed in the **Education** section.

HEDBIB (International Bibliographic Database on Higher Education)
hedbib.iau-aiu.net

Site maintained by International Association of Universities with contributions from UNESCO. Offers free access to abstracts of articles and reports covering higher education management, policy and planning. Registration required.

Higher Education Abstracts (subscription required)
www.wiley.com/bw/journal.asp?ref=0748-4364

Published quarterly by Claremont Graduate University. Indexes over 200 education titles, plus book chapters and government reports covering all aspects of higher education policy, theory and practice. Coverage strongest in terms of English-language materials from North America and Europe. Items from 1965 onwards.

Higher Education Empirical Research (HEER) database
heerd.open.ac.uk

Originally developed by the Centre for Higher Education Research and Information (CHERI) of the Open University. Transferred to the QAA (Quality Assurance Agency) in 2011. Provides free access to article abstracts and links to some full-text materials covering evidence-based research into education. Titles indexed include academic journals, statistics and government reports. Broad range of topics covered includes widening access, research assessments, the graduate labour market, curriculum content and the student experience. Most materials published since 1996. Free registration required.

Research into Higher Education Abstracts (subscription required)
www.srhe.ac.uk/publications.rhea.asp

Produced by the Society for Research into Higher Education. Comprehensive index of publications (articles, books, papers, government reports). Emphasis mainly on education systems of Britain, the Commonwealth and Europe. Selective coverage of elsewhere. Available in print or online (via databases such as Educational Research Online). Coverage from the 1960s to present.

News services

Most broadsheet newspapers provide coverage of educational policy. The following are specialist services for practitioners.

Chronicle of Higher Education
chronicle.com/section/Home/433

Weekday newspaper available in print or online. Some online materials for subscribers only. Focuses on American higher education, offering news, analysis and job listings.

Times Higher Education Supplement
www.timeshighereducation.co.uk

Renowned weekly newspaper. Website provides free access to world rankings of universities since 2004, plus recent articles, comment and job vacancies. Access to most archived materials requires subscription.

Statistical data

The organizations listed in the main **Education** section all provide access to some indicators relating to universities.

Higher Education Statistics Agency (HESA)
www.hesa.ac.uk

Official agency for the collection of higher education data in the UK. Offers free access to some datasets covering student numbers, qualifications obtained and student retention. Note that some detailed reports are offered to subscribers only.

Participation Rates in Higher Education
data.gov.uk/dataset/participation_rates_in_higher_education_academic_years

Published by the Department for Business, Innovation and Skills and the Department for Education.

HISTORY

Typical questions

- I need primary resource materials relating to the First World War.
- I want to find journal articles on emancipation.
- Where can I get a timeline of the British Empire?

Points to consider

- History is a vast topic. Not only does it include different time periods, it can focus on international, national or local histories; on different aspects, such as social, political or economic history; or on methods, such as oral history. Always check if the enquirer has a particular focus.
- This section cannot offer detailed guidance on all of these. Instead it concentrates on a number of key starting-points which students should explore in more detail. Related sections are: **Economic History**, **Census**, **Biographical Information** (for researching the lives of famous persons).
- Historians need to consult both primary and secondary sources in their research. Primary source materials provide first-hand accounts of historical events. These include artefacts, manuscripts, diaries, maps, photographs, government documents and contemporary newspaper reports. Secondary sources offer synthesis and interpretation of historical information. Examples include textbooks, journal articles and encyclopedias. Students are often confused by this distinction and need help in locating primary sources. Key starting-points for this are the resources in the **Archives**, **Government Publications**, **Maps** and **Images** sections. The **Freedom of Information** section offers advice on requests for the declassification of government papers. Note that primary resources are increasingly being made freely available on the internet by national archives and museums. However, students should always verify provenance before use.

Where to look

Key organizations

UK

Use these websites to trace news, events listings, project updates and reviews of new publications and electronic resources.

Arts and Humanities Research Council
   www.ahrc.ac.uk
   Key funding body. Get information on how to apply and browse information for outputs from recent projects.

British Association for Local History

www.balh.co.uk

Read copies of *Local History News*, access curriculum materials and explore links to recommended websites.

Federation of Family History Societies

www.ffhs.org.uk

Provides information on using archival resources for family history research. Includes a directory of local groups.

Higher Education Academy

www.heacademy.ac.uk

Supports lecturers in higher education, including coverage of History and Classics. Website is useful for tracing information about teaching and learning projects. Includes case studies of good practice. Also has information on research and funding opportunities.

Historical Association

www.history.org.uk

Seeks to promote history education at school, adult and higher education levels. Website provides free access to a wealth of resources. These include: lesson plans for teachers; a student resource bank of study notes and articles; and a section for the public with articles and research guides. Some materials are accessible by members only.

Royal Historical Society

www.royalhistoricalsociety.org

Long established organization. Website has contents pages from its *Transactions*, details of research funding and public lecture series.

Social History Society

www.socialhistory.org.uk

Promotes the study of social and cultural history.

Society for the Study of Labour History

www.sslh.org.uk

Covers co-operatives, industrial relations, history of the Labour Party. Website has useful research guides.

Women's History Network

www.womenshistorynetwork.org

United States

American Historical Association (AHA)
> www.historians.org
> Founded in 1884, covers all subject areas and periods of history for the public, researchers and students. Website is a key starting-point for tracing specialist research organizations in North America. It includes contents pages from its journals, doctoral dissertation listings and resource guides for students.

International

Use these to trace national members, plus news, new publications and conference listings.

EUROCLIO
> www.euroclio.eu
> European Association of Educators in Europe. Find information on History education in Europe. Get profiles of individual nations and access free online education resources.

International Commission for Historical Demography
> historicaldemography.net
> Specializes in population history. Website links to statistical datasets.

International Federation for Research in Women's History
> www.ifrwh.com

International Students of History Association
> www.isha-international.org

World History Association
> www.thewha.org

Libraries and archives

Use these to search catalogues for books and journals.

British Library
> www.bl.uk/reshelp/findhelpsubject/history/historyandsociety/
> historyandsocietyoverview/histandsocoverview.html
> Extensive holdings of national, local and world history from earliest times.

Institute of Historical Research
> www.history.ac.uk/library
> UK's largest open access reference library with extensive coverage of

history from the fifth century to the present day. Strong coverage in terms of history of Western Europe and its expansion overseas.

Senate House Library

www.ull.ac.uk/subjects/history/index.shtml

Research-level holdings of British, European and English/Welsh local history. Directory of links to history websites.

Chronologies

Use these for checking key dates

Britannica (subscription required)

www.britannica.com

Online version includes the *Britannica Book of the Year*, which has annual summaries of wars, world events and disasters.

Keesings World News Archive (subscription required)

www.keesings.com

Daily news coverage from 1931 onwards. Useful for checking dates and getting brief summaries of historical events.

Dictionaries and encyclopedias

Cambridge Histories Online (subscription required)

histories.cambridge.org

Renowned series of books available separately in print volumes or as a complete online cross-searchable database. Over 270 volumes published since the 1960s. Topics are broad ranging, including British and American History, Military History, Social and Economic History.

Oxford Reference Online (subscription required)

www.oxfordreference.com

Contains many history-related titles. They include dictionaries and companions (collections of scholarly articles). Topics covered include Military History, Ancient History, British and American History.

Electronic libraries

Use these to locate full-text primary source materials. Other starting-points for tracing these are national libraries and national archives.

UK

British History Online
www.british-history.ac.uk
Maintained by the Institute of Historical Research and the History of Parliament Trust, providing access to core primary and secondary materials. Includes sub-sections on Local History, Political History, Historical Geography, Ecclesiastical History and Urban History. Highlights include state papers and Victoria County Histories.

British Online Archives (subscription required)
www.britishonlinearchives.co.uk
Microform Academic Publishers publishes a number of series of digitized archives from major library collections covering Social, Economic and Political History. Examples include early colonial and missionary records and trade directories.

Connected Histories: British History 1500–1900
www.connectedhistories.org
Not-to-be-missed site which enables cross-searching of key databases covering all aspects of British History. Subscriptions required for access to some of the databases. Includes *Proceedings of the Old Bailey Online, 1674–1913*; *British Newspapers 1600–1900*; *Charles Booth Archive* (maps from Booth's survey into life and labour in London, 1886–1903); *London Lives 1690–1800* (over 240,000 manuscripts from eight London archives – key focuses on criminal justice and poverty); *House of Commons Parliamentary Papers 1715–1900*. Also provided are research guides.

Eighteenth Century Collections Online (EECO) (subscription required)
gale.cengage.co.uk/product-highlights/history/eighteenth-century-collections-online.aspx
E-books collection comprising over 136,000 titles published between 1701 and 1800. Mostly English language. Includes contemporary travel, science and economics.

Empire Online (subscription required)
www.empire.amdigital.co.uk
Designed for students. Includes essays, timelines and primary sources (maps, documents and manuscripts) relating to the social, political and economic history of the British Empire.

JSTOR 19th Century British Pamphlets Collection (subscription required)
about.jstor.org/content-collections/primary-sources/19th-century-british-pamphlets
Access over 26,000 social, political and economic pamphlets from the holdings of seven of the UK's major research libraries (including London School of Economics, University of Bristol, University College London). Many JSTOR subscriptions also offer access to extensive back files of historical journals.

Mass Observation online (subscription required)
www.massobs.org.uk/accessing_material_online.htm
Digitized version of parts of the major social history archive that recorded everyday life from 1930 to the 1950s. Website also has information on accessing original materials.

United States

American Memory Project
lcweb2.loc.gov/ammem
Maintained by the Library of Congress. Free access to thousands of printed, audio and visual resources arranged in themed collections. Highlights include African-American History, papers of presidents, Women's History and Military History. Also includes teachers' resources.

Avalon Project
avalon.law.yale.edu
Maintained by Yale University, offers free access to documents in Law, Diplomacy and History. They include treaties and Congressional reports. Emphasis upon American international relations.

Europe

EuroDocs: Online Sources for European History
eudocs.lib.byu.edu
Links to European primary source documents that are transcribed, reproduced in facsimile or translated, covering all periods of history. Maintained by Brigham Young University.

European Historical Bibliographies Project
www.histbib.eu
Hosted by the Berlin-Brandenburg Academy of Sciences and Humanities. Provides information on 15 bibliographic databases covering the history of individual European nations. Note that although links are provided to the websites, access to some requires a subscription.

European History Primary Sources
primary-sources.eui.eu

Great site created by European University Institute which offers hundreds of annotated links to online primary source collections covering all aspects of European History. Particularly good for locating the latest digitized collections from leading archives. Many in foreign languages.

Europeana
www.europeana.eu

Gateway to more than 15 million items from archives, library and museum collections in Europe. Includes digitized documents, maps, images and rare books.

International

Cold War International History Project
www.wilsoncenter.org/program/cold-war-international-history-project

Part of the Woodrow Wilson International Center. Provides free access to hundreds of documents relating to the history of the Cold War. They include US and Soviet declassified materials. Popular topics such as the Cuban Missile crisis and the fall of the Berlin Wall are covered. Site also has articles and working papers.

Internet History Sourcebooks
www.fordham.edu/halsall

Developed by Paul Halsall, Fordham University. Aims to provide free access to primary sources covering all aspects of history from ancient times. Includes sections for specific time periods, areas of the world and topics. Includes text, documents and annotated links. Note that the size of the site means some sections are updated irregularly.

Internet portals

These large sites have links to many high-quality specialist resources.

Best of History Websites
www.besthistorysites.net

Designed specifically for teachers. Offers links to curriculum-related materials and lesson plans covering all aspects and time periods of History.

History Guide
www.historyguide.de

Maintained by the Netzwerk Internetressourcen Geschichte (Network Subject Gateways History). Headed by German academic libraries. Over

13,000 links. Browse by region, time period, subject area.

Journal article indexes

America: History and Life (subscription required)
www.ebscohost.com/academic/america-history-and-life

Leading database indexing journal articles and books covering all aspects of Canadian and American History from ancient times to the present day. Coverage from 1969 onwards.

Bibliography of British and Irish History (BBIH) (subscription required)
www.history.ac.uk/projects/bbih/info

Maintained by Institute of Historical Research and the Royal Historical Society. Covers British History and the history of the British Empire from 55 BC to the modern day. Indexes books, journal articles and dissertations.

Historical Abstracts (subscription required)
www.ebscohost.com/academic/historical-abstracts

Covers World History (excluding North America) from 15th century onwards. Trace references from thousands of journals and books published since 1955.

News/current awareness resources

In addition to mailing lists maintained by the key organizations, try the following.

BBC History Magazine
www.historyextra.com

Intended for the general public. Useful for reading recent popular book reviews, getting TV and radio programmes listings and news about History on the net.

History Online
www.history.ac.uk/history-online

Maintained by the Institute of Historical Research. Provides a searchable database of history lecturers in the UK, listings of history projects and sources of funding available for researchers. Also includes the free e-journal **History Reviews, www.history.ac.uk/reviews**, which has reviews of books and digital resources.

Oral history

First-hand accounts by those involved in historic events. These resources offer insight into techniques and the latest research and enable access to examples of collections.

American Folklife Center Library of Congress
www.loc.gov/folklife/familyfolklife/oralhistory.html

Specialist research centre preserving American culture, whose collections include much of interest to oral historians. The website has a guide to oral history methods and relevant holdings.

British Library
www.bl.uk/reshelp/findhelprestype/sound/ohist/oralhistory.html

Has an extensive collection of recordings and supporting literature. Conducts its own recordings through the National Life Studies programme, many examples of which can be listened to via the Sound Archive website.

In The First Person
www.inthefirstperson.com

Index to letters, archives and oral history narratives in English written before 1900, which is made available by Alexander Street Press. Search by name, date, event to locate suitable collections. These include archives, free and subscription websites. A useful finding aid.

International Oral History Association
www.iohanet.org

Maintains a useful listing of national associations worldwide.

Oral History Association (USA)
www.oralhistory.org

Includes guidelines on principles and practice, plus news and events.

Oral History Society
www.ohs.org.uk

Key UK organization. Use its website to trace news, conferences, training and resources.

HUMAN RIGHTS

Typical questions

- Where can I get information on the human rights record of the Libyan government?
- Which countries still have the death penalty?
- I need information on international human rights cases.

Points to consider

- Human rights is a very large area. The term can be used broadly to include civil liberties and discrimination against certain groups. This section directs users to key academic information sources. They should be explored fully to retrieve information on individual nations. Other related sections include: **Women's Studies** and **Law**. Researchers are also advised to consult the **Journal Article Indexes** section.
- Note that increasing numbers of human rights organizations are publishing materials directly on the internet. This may mean that they are not indexed in library catalogues. Good sources for tracing these are in the internet gateways/digital libraries sub-section.

Where to look

Key organizations

Governments and international organizations

African Commission on Human and Peoples' Rights
www.achpr.org
Established in 1986 by the African Charter on Human and Peoples' Rights. Use its website to find reports relating to human rights across Africa.

Commission for Equality and Human Rights
www.equalityhumanrights.com
UK government body. Access government strategy documents, plus other research reports relating to the situation in Britain.

Council of Europe
www.coe.int/t/dghl/default_en.asp
Directorate General of Human Rights. Note this is a separate body from the European Union. Provides information on the application of the European Convention on Human Rights. Free online access to Human Rights Files monographs, handbooks and newsletters covering all aspects of human rights in Europe. The *Yearbook of the European Convention on Human Rights*

is currently published commercially by Brill but can be purchased from the website.

European Union
www.consilium.europa.eu

Council of the European Union publishes *EU Annual Report on Human Rights*. Free access from 1998/99 onwards. Publication provides an overview of conditions in EU nations (including major policy and legal instruments); also covers EU actions on international human rights.

Humanrights.Gov
www.humanrights.gov

Site maintained by the American government. In addition to materials relating to the USA, it also provides free access to annual human rights reports covering a large number of nations worldwide and international religious freedom annual reports. Some items available from 2004 onwards.

Inter-American Commission on Human Rights
www.cidh.oas.org

Body of the Organization of American States (OAS). Responsible for implementing and monitoring human rights in OAS members (North, South, Central Americas) working alongside La Corte Interamericana de Derechos Humanos. Website has documents, annual and country-specific reports from the late 1960s onwards.

Office of the High Commissioner for Human Rights
www.ohchr.org

Key website, with news, press releases and free access to a number of databases, including documents submitted to the Universal Periodic Review (four-yearly reviews of the human rights records of all UN member nations). The **Universal Human Rights Index, www.universalhumanrightsindex. org**, provides easy access to materials about individual countries published by UN bodies.

Organization for Security and Cooperation in Europe (OSCE)
www.osce.org

Regional security organization comprising members from Europe, North America and Asia. Includes as part of its remit monitoring of human rights issues relating to human trafficking, media freedom and minority rights in OSCE nations. Access all reports published since 1975.

United Nations

Produces extensive information relating to human rights. Basic guidance on research is given in the United Nations Documentation Research guide compiled by the **United Nations Dag Hammarskjöld Library,** **www.un.org/depts/dhl/resguide/index.html**. This highlights key bodies and assists users in navigating the often complex websites.

Legal organizations

African Human Rights Case Law Database
www.chr.up.ac.za/index.php/documents/african-human-rights-case-law-database.html
Access a database of several hundred cases decided by domestic courts, courts of sub-regional intergovernmental organizations, the African Commission on Human and Peoples' Rights and the African Court on Human and Peoples' Rights and United Nations treaty monitoring bodies.

Corte Interamericana de Derechos Humanos (Inter-American Court of Human Rights.)
www.corteidh.or.cr
Judicial body of the Organization of American States, aimed at the application and interpretation of the American Convention on Human Rights. Website includes basic facts, documents and decisions.

European Court of Human Rights
www.echr.coe.int/ECHR
International Court which rules on individual or state applications alleging violations of the European Convention on Human Rights. It is associated with the Council of Europe and should not be confused with the Court of Justice of the European Union. Its **HUDOC** database, **www.echr.coe.int/ ECHR/EN/hudoc,** enables users to access judgments, decisions and reports.

European Court of Justice
curia.europa.eu
Ensures application of European Union legislation in member states. Website provides information on its function, plus free access to case law.

International Court of Justice
www.icj-cij.org
Judicial organ of the United Nations, based in The Hague. Access news, reports, opinions and case-related materials from its origin in 1947.

Non-governmental organizations

These groups are renowned for their general work on human rights issues worldwide. They all have online libraries of press releases and full-text reports.

Amnesty International
www.amnesty.org

Publishes an annual human rights report, country reports and regular specialist reports on the death penalty and women's rights. Access materials from approximately 1991 onwards.

Freedom House
www.freedomhouse.org

Independent watchdog. Publishes the influential *Freedom in the World*, *Freedom of the Press* and *Freedom on the Net* surveys.

Human Rights Watch
www.hrw.org

Includes annual and country-specific human rights reports from approximately 1989 onwards.

Digital libraries and internet gateways

ASIL Guide to International Law
www.asil.org/erghome.cfm

Site compiled by the American Society of International Law. Has a specialist section on human rights law with detailed advice on tracing articles, treaties and case law.

Human Security Gateway
www.humansecuritygateway.com

Site maintained by Simon Fraser University, Canada. While focusing on broader issues relating to human security, it does have extensive coverage of human rights issues and abuses worldwide, especially those in conflict areas. It is particularly good for locating reports published by think-tanks.

HURIDOCS – Human Rights Information and Documentation Systems
www.huridocs.org

International NGO providing support to human rights organizations. Services include the specialist **HURISearch, www.hurisearch.org**, search engine, which enables users to quickly cross-search the websites of over 500 human rights websites (including academic research bodies, government and intergovernmental organizations).

University of Minnesota Human Rights Library
www1.umn.edu/humanrts

Specialist site for researchers providing free access to over 60,000 full-text documents plus extensive directories of links to websites. Key features include country profiles, information on international treaty ratification and subject-based bibliographies.

IMAGES AND PHOTOGRAPHS

Typical questions
- Where can I get hold of images of London that I can use in my coursework?
- I need a photograph to illustrate my lecture slides.

Points to consider
- This section highlights resources where still images (prints/photographs) suitable for academic use may be found. Moving images are covered in the separate **Film** section.
- Copyright can be a problem. Consult the separate section for advice.

Where to look

Support services

JISC Digital Media

> **www.jiscdigitalmedia.ac.uk**
> Provides advice, guidance and training to the UK's further and higher education community on still and moving images. Website has tips on tracing and using images legally.

Search engines

Most commercial search engines will retrieve some images. However, do remember to check copyright carefully!

Google Images

> **images.google.com**
> Has an advanced search form where you can restrict by image size and file format.

Digital libraries

For further examples of online libraries containing paintings and artworks see the **Art** section.

ARKive

> **www.arkive.org**
> Vast online library of images of the natural world (plants, animals, landscapes) from a project endorsed by leading conservation organizations.

British Cartoon Archive

> **www.cartoons.ac.uk**

Located at the University of Canterbury. Extensive holdings of cartoons, caricatures and comics from 1904 onwards. Catalogue provides access to thumbnail images. Copyright information is on the website.

Flickr

www.flickr.com/search

Famous photo-sharing site, increasingly being used by museums and archives to post historic images online. For effective academic use choose the advanced search form. This enables more specific phrase searching and allows searches to be restricted to Creative Commons use.

JISCMedia Hub (subscription required)

jiscmediahub.ac.uk

Enormous store of still and moving image collections specially selected for UK academic use. Includes thousands of images from the Getty Library covering famous persons, locations and social history topics.

Wellcome Images

images.wellcome.ac.uk

Over 40,000 historic images from the collections of the Wellcome Library. Strong coverage of medical topics and public health.

INFORMATION LITERACY

Typical questions

- Can you offer any advice on designing an information skills tutorial?
- Are there any agreed standards relating to information literacy?
- What skills do students need to conduct an effective literature search?

Points to consider

- The term 'information literacy' (IL) is widely used by librarians and information professionals. Their professional body CILIP defines it as 'Knowing when and why you need information, where to find it, and how to evaluate, use and communicate it in an ethical manner' (**www.cilip.org.uk/get-involved/advocacy/learning/ information-literacy/pages/definition.aspx**). Library staff are often interested in developing training programmes which encourage information literacy amongst staff/students.
- However, outside the profession other terms are often used when talking to academic staff/students. Common ones are information skills, information seeking or more generally library skills or literature searching skills.
- These resources offer starting-points for those wishing to learn more about IL and/or develop their own IL teaching materials.

Where to look

Definitions

These sites contain definitions and frameworks of competencies.

ACRL Literacy Competency Standards
  www.ala.org/ala/mgrps/divs/acrl/standards/
  informationliteracycompetency.cfm
  Devised by the Association of College and Research Libraries (ACRL). Predominately used in the USA.

SCONUL 7 Pillars
  www.sconul.ac.uk/groups/information_literacy/seven_pillars.html
  Widely used in UK universities.

Key organizations

Information Literacy Group
  www.informationliteracy.org.uk/cilip-csg-il
  Sub-group of the Community Services Group of the Chartered Institute of

Library and Information Professionals (CILIP). Provides a forum for discussion and dissemination on all aspects of information literacy. Its website has links to useful resources, including its e-mail discussion list. The group also organizes the prestigious annual LILAC conference, **lilacconference.com/WP**. It has its own website which provides free access to a selection of past conference papers. These encompass a wide range of issues, including teaching techniques, information literacy standards and practical examples of information skills tutorials and courses. All sectors of the profession are covered including, information literacy in school and university libraries.

National Forum on Information Literacy
infolit.org

Major US organization, created in 1989 as a response to the recommendations of an American Library Association committee. Website has news and events listings, links to key documents and a resource directory of programmes and projects.

Key websites

Explore these to find links to more useful resources.

Information Literacy Website
www.informationliteracy.org.uk

Maintained by information professionals from key UK organizations, including CILIP and SCONUL. Aims to support practitioners by offering free access to news, book reviews and case studies of best practice.

Journal of Information Literacy
ojs.lboro.ac.uk/ojs/index.php/JIL/index

Open access scholarly journal covering the philosophy, technology and practice of information literacy. Excellent starting-point for locating up-to-date materials.

LOEX: Clearing House for Library Instruction
www.emich.edu/public/loex/loex.html

International membership organization which supports training and information literacy in libraries. Website has an excellent archive of conference papers, plus a free directory of links to online tutorials, case studies and other recommended teaching and learning materials for library staff.

INTERNATIONAL ORGANIZATIONS

Typical questions
- Are there any international organizations covering coffee?
- What is WIPO responsible for?

Points to consider
- International organizations include both transnational non-governmental organizations (such as charities that operate across boundaries) and intergovernmental organizations (IGOS) (such as the UN, whose membership is composed of sovereign states). They can focus on specific regions of the world or on specific issues or commodities.
- Increasingly, websites are valuable for tracing information on international activities because they can offer free access to reports and statistics. In terms of developing nations, they may be the most reliable source of data.
- This section highlights major directories. The subject and area studies sections list more specific examples and there are separate sections for the **European Union** and **United Nations**.

Where to look

Europa Directory of International Organizations, **Routledge. Annual**
> Provides profiles of over 1900 regional and global international organizations.

Guide to the Archives of Intergovernmental Organizations
www.unesco.org/archives/sio/Eng
> Directory maintained by UNESCO which enables researchers to trace archive collections relating to international governmental and non-governmental organizations. Individual profiles have brief histories of the organizations and details of access and holdings.

Schechter, M. (2009) *Historical Dictionary of International Organizations,*
Scarecrow Press
> One of the influential *Historical Dictionaries of International Organizations* series published by Scarecrow Press since the 1990s. Over 20 titles have been issued, many covering regional or subject-based organizations. Each title has a chronology of key events, persons and actions and offers a bibliography of further readings.

Union of International Associations (UIA)
www.uia.be
Membership organization. Website has news and events listings. Publishes the *Yearbook of International Organizations*. Available in print or online. Subscription required. Extensive listing of several thousand international non-governmental and intergovernmental organizations. Includes profiles of recent activity, statistics and links to websites. Search by region or subject area.

INTERNATIONAL RELATIONS

Typical questions

- I need to do a literature search for materials on China's changing role in world affairs.
- How can I locate a definition of world systems theory?

Points to consider

- Many websites cover international affairs. However, students should check carefully because it is common for examples to be out of date and/or politically biased. The resources listed below should provide a basic grounding for academic research which they can then explore further.
- Students of international relations often study world conflicts. This section provides a starting-point for tracing authoritative datasets. However, note that this research can also overlap with foreign policy, so they may also find the resources in the **Political Science, Diplomatic, Consular and Foreign Service Lists** and **Treaties** sections useful.

Key organizations

Use these sites to trace conference listings, key academic journal titles and specialist research groups.

BISA: British International Studies Association
www.bisa.ac.uk
Leading professional organization. Website provides free access to many conference papers from 1996 onwards.

International Studies Association (ISA)
www.isanet.org
International network of scholars. Website also provides free access to a large archive of conference papers from its events. These cover all areas of international studies and include examples of the latest specialist research. There is an excellent directory of national International Relations organizations worldwide.

Libraries and archives

Chatham House Library (Royal Institute of International Affairs)
www.chathamhouse.org.uk
Influential research organization founded in 1920. Its library has collections covering all areas of international relations. Holdings focus on

the last 30 years. Strengths include security, defence, economics, politics and the environment.

LSE Library
www2.lse.ac.uk/library/home.aspx
Library of the London School of Economics and Political Science. Its catalogue is available online and can be searched to find relevant books and journals. The archives contain holdings from the British Studies Association and papers of eminent diplomats, **www2.lse.ac.uk/library/archive/holdings/international_history.aspx.**

Conflict data

FIRST: Facts on International Relations and Security Trends
first.sipri.org
Excellent free database maintained by leading research bodies (including Stockholm International Peace Research Institute, Heidelberg Institute for International Conflict Research). Get chronologies of conflicts and security-related events, country data, statistics on conflicts, military expenditure and reports on human rights and human security worldwide.

IISS Armed Conflict database (subscription required)
acd.iiss.org/armedconflict
Maintained by the International Institute for Strategic Studies (IISS). Includes reports, data and analysis of international and national conflicts and terrorism worldwide from 1997 onwards.

Dictionaries and encyclopedias

Griffiths, M. (2005) *Encyclopedia of International Relations and Global Politics*, **Routledge**
Covers all areas of International Relations theory and research. Each entry has a short bibliography to guide further reading.

Reus-Smit, C., Snidal, D. (eds) (2008) *Oxford Handbook of International Relations*, **Oxford University Press**
A collection of essays offering a wide ranging introduction to International Relations theories and research.

Journal article indexes

Use these to find references to journal articles and book chapters. You should also note that, increasingly, research bodies are publishing their reports online. Links to websites where these can be traced are listed in the internet portals sub-section.

Columbia International Affairs Online (CIAO) (subscription required)
www.ciaonet.org
Comprehensive resource covering all areas of international relations theory and research. Offers access to full-text journal articles, working papers and reports from leading academic research departments, aid agencies and think-tanks.

EINIRAS Database Network
einiras.coe.int/edn
European Information Network on International Relations and Area Studies (EINIRAS) is creating a virtual database for international relations researchers. Cross-search a growing number of leading bibliographies to find references to scholarly articles, books and reports. These currently include: the CERES database of the Council of Europe; the Finnish Institute of International Affairs; Sciences Po; the Royal Institute of International Affairs; and SIPRI (Stockholm International Peace Research Institute). Extensive coverage of European-language materials.

International Political Science Abstracts (subscription required)
www.ipsa.org/publications/abstracts
Published by the International Political Science Association with the support of the Fondation Nationale des Sciences Politiques and the American University of Paris. Coverage from 1951 onwards. Includes international affairs.

News services
Use these to supplement the national newspapers.

IRIN News
www.irinnews.org
Free humanitarian news and analysis service from the UN Office for the Coordination of Humanitarian Affairs.

Keesings World News Archive (subscription required)
www.keesings.com
Long established news service offering daily, concise updates of political, economic and social events in countries worldwide. Archive covers 1931 onwards.

Internet gateways and portals
Key resources for tracing full-text reports and links to recommended websites.

Human Security Gateway

www.humansecuritygateway.com

Not-to-be-missed resource. Database offers free access to over 27,000 full-text reports and news items covering human security worldwide. Excellent for tracing the latest academic research on a country. Project partners include Simon Fraser University, Canada.

ISN International Relations and Security Network

www.isn.ethz.ch/isn/Digital-Library

Service maintained by the Center for Security Studies (CSS), a leading Swiss academic research institute. Find news stories, online reports and links.

Margarita S. Studemeister Digital Collections in International Conflict Management

www.usip.org/publications-tools/digital-collections

Free access to a wealth of full-text resources maintained by the United States Institute for Peace (USIP). They include a peace agreements collection and the Truth Commissions digital library. The site also offers a directory of annotated links to recommended websites.

INTERNATIONAL STUDENTS

Typical questions

- I need help understanding if my overseas qualifications are equivalent to those in British universities.
- Where can I get advice on employment regulations for overseas students?

Points to consider

- This section covers resources for and about overseas students studying in the UK. Further related resources can be found in the **Qualifications** section. Materials relating to UK students wishing to study overseas can also be found there.
- International students may be unfamiliar with the UK education system. Other common questions relate to finance, immigration/visa regulations, English lessons and accommodation. In practice, many of these issues require specialist advice. Most universities have local offices for international/overseas students, where they can be referred. The resources below offer general introductions which may also be useful.

Where to look

Advisory services

Education UK

www.educationuk.org

Excellent website maintained by the British Council which explains the basics of the UK education system. This includes coverage of how to apply for courses, student finance and finding accommodation. There is also a section on UK life and culture.

National Union of Students (NUS)

www.nus.org.uk

Offers support and advice to all categories of students. Its website includes some information and news relating to international students.

Student Calculator

www.studentcalculator.org.uk

Website created by independent charity UNIAID, which aims to prepare international students for the financial side of living in the UK. Includes helpful tips on living costs and balancing budgets!

UK Border Agency

www.ukba.homeoffice.gov.uk/studyingintheuk

Branch of the Home Office, offers legal advice on requirements for entering the UK to study.

UK Council for International Student Affairs (UKCISA)
www.ukcisa.org.uk
National advisory body serving the interests of international students. Its website offers free access to a useful collection of factsheets covering basic questions asked by international students. Topics include regulations, finance and support services. It has also developed the free tutorial **Prepare for Success, www.prepareforsuccess.org.uk,** which takes potential overseas students through a series of interactive exercises designed to teach them about studying in the UK. Topics covered by this include what to expect from lecturers, and methods of teaching and assessment in the UK.

Statistical data

These resources provide information on the numbers of international students studying in the UK.

Higher Education Statistics Agency
www.hesa.ac.uk
Official agency for the collection of statistics relating to UK higher education. Some free access to headline data via the website. Other more detailed datasets offered to subscribers only.

Observatory on Borderless Education
www.obhe.ac.uk/home (subscription required for access to full text)
Membership organization, part of the International Graduate Insight Group. Offers news, reports and statistics on best practices and trends in international student mobility.

UKCISA
www.ukcisa.org.uk/about/statistics_he.php
Has a directory of links to potential sources of data.

JOURNAL ARTICLE INDEXES

Typical questions

- Where can I find recent articles on phenomenology?
- I need to do a literature search for my dissertation. Can you help?
- Has this author written any more articles?

Points to consider

- Most students will have used the internet for research. However they may be unaware of other sources where references to academic journal articles may be found. This section introduces some good general services which are available in many academic libraries. Examples of specific subject-based services are provided in all the subject sections.
- A common mistake is to search for journal articles in the main library catalogue. In most cases this will not retrieve any results because this type of material is not usually indexed.
- When confronted with this situation many students go for the easy option of searching on Google. The power of the internet means that this may retrieve many useful materials, including references to recent items which may not have been included yet in scholarly indexes! However, it is advisable to recommend that they use journal indexing services provided by the library as their starting-point because these will enable them to limit their searches to academic materials. Then, once this initial stage has been completed, supplement it with research on **Google Scholar, scholar.google.co.uk,** which searches the internet specifically for academic articles and books.
- Students often need help choosing which journal index to use. Many may be confused about the difference between journal indexing and abstracting services and e-journal databases. It may seem to them that databases which offer full-text e-journals must be better. However, it is advisable to recommend that indexes usually offer more comprehensive searches across larger numbers of journals. Many libraries have also implemented a facility that links them directly to their e-journal holdings so that full-text articles can be downloaded immediately.
- A final point to note is that students frequently need advice on how to access the full text of the articles they find. It is common for them to assume that all the items must be online. They may also have followed links that have taken them away from the subscription database. Advice should be given on how to double-check paper and e-journals holdings in the local library catalogue, search for the existence of journals in other local libraries (see the **Library Catalogues** section) and how to request interlibrary loans.

How to conduct effective searches

All journal indexing services have their own help screens, which offer more detailed advice. However, here are some general recommended strategies.

1 Analyse the research topic. Be clear about the type of information needed. Identify any concepts, dates, persons, geographical locations.

2 Select the search terms. It is necessary to choose these carefully. Ideally the number should not exceed six to eight keywords. Remember that journal indexes are machines. They will only search for the terms entered by the user. Their facility to interpret them is limited. Therefore some good tips are:
   — Check spelling; identify any terms which may have alternative spellings (e.g. labor and labour). Remember that many 'American spellings' may be different from British ones!
   — Identify any synonyms (e.g. women or female).
   — Identify any search terms that may have alternative word endings (e.g. Marx and Marxism). Many databases will allow you to use wildcard symbols to truncate and search for alternatives, e.g. enter advert* to retrieve materials containing the words adverts, advertising and advertisements in one search.
   — Identify phrases. Many databases will enable you to enter these in inverted commas (the symbol above the 2 on the keyboard). This can be helpful if they are common words. For instance, a search for "social policy" as a phrase is more specific than a search for social and policy, as the latter will retrieve items referring to foreign policy if the word social appears anywhere else in the text.
   — Avoid using prepositions, conjunctions or common verbs as search terms. These include: about, if, the, of, a, not, why, before, is, at. Databases refer to these as stop words and usually ignore them.
   — Search for authors by surname and initials, even if the full first name is known, as it is quite common for writers to publish under different variants of their name.
   — Consider the level of specificity. This is one of the most difficult things to get right. If the chosen search terms are too broad you will get too many hits. If they are too specific you will get too few. Be prepared to refine the search after reviewing the initial results.

3 Combine the search terms. Most searches require more than one keyword. Therefore you will need to combine terms. Check the help screens of the index for advice on this. Many databases use Boolean operators. These combine search terms using and, or and not (see table on next page).

4 Run the search and look at the results. Inspect the abstracts. These often give examples of subject indexing terms that can be used to refocus the

Boolean operators		
Combine terms using	Effect	Potential uses
AND	Requires all the search terms to appear somewhere in the document. Not necessarily in the same order. For instance a search for *Obama and tax* will retrieve all those documents which contain both terms. Any that contain just one of them will not be retrieved. This is represented in the diagram on the left by the darker colour.	Useful for narrowing a search by making it more specific.
OR	Requires any of the search terms to be found somewhere in the document. For instance, the search for *Obama or tax* will retrieve any documents which contain either of the terms or both of them. This is represented in the diagram on the left by the darker colour.	Useful for broadening a search, searching for synonyms and alternative word endings.
AND NOT	This excludes any documents containing the word following *and not* in your search term. For example if you entered *labour party and not Australia* you would retrieve all documents containing labour party, but those also containing the word Australia would be excluded. This would be useful if you wanted documents only on the British Labour Party. This is represented in the diagram on the left by the dark colour.	Useful for narrowing a search, especially where a word has several different meanings. However, it should be used with caution, as it is easy to exclude relevant results.

search terms. If you have too many results try to think of ways to narrow down your search. Some quick tips are:

— Look for an advanced search screen because it may enable you to limit by year of publication.
— Try limiting subject terms to specific geographical areas.
— Limit to a particular type of resource. Many databases include references to book reviews. You can narrow your search by excluding them.
— Look for a search history option. Many enable you to combine searches which you have done in the current session. This will make them narrower in focus.

5 If you have too few results, try to broaden your search to make it more general. Some quick tips are:

— Try to think of alternative spellings, e.g. color and colour.

— Truncate terms to see if any items are indexed under alternative word endings. In order to do this you must check the help screen of the database to see if it supports this type of searching. Many will enable you to enter a word root and then an asterisk to look for all alternatives, e.g. if searching for Marx try Marx★ to retrieve associated materials on Marxism and Marxists.

— Try to think of broader terms, e.g. replace Blair with Labour Party. The database may have a thesaurus, which will help you with this.

Where to look

The titles listed below are all recommended resources. It is advisable to search more than one database. This may retrieve some duplicate hits but is usually necessary because the range of titles indexed differs.

British Humanities Index (subscription required)
www.csa.com/factsheets/bhi-set-c.php
Interdisciplinary database which covers a wide range of subjects, including Literature, Economics, Religion, Gender Studies, History and Current Affairs. Indexes over 400 journal titles from 1962 onwards.

Google Scholar
scholar.google.co.uk
Specific service designed to facilitate academic journal article searching. Indexes millions of results, although a full listing of the journals covered is not readily available. Good for locating very recent articles.

For most effective use try the advanced search form, which allows searches to be limited by factors including date and author and enables exact search phrases to be used. It is also a good idea to look for the option to deselect patents (unless this is the topic of interest!) in order to make the search results manageable. Finally, remind students that the links to the full text may not work. They should always double-check availability using the local library catalogue and/or electronic library web pages.

International Bibliography of the Social Sciences (IBSS) (subscription required)
www.proquest.co.uk/en-UK/catalogs/databases/detail/ibss-set-c.shtml
Well regarded resource for tracing references to journal articles and book chapters covering social sciences subjects. Indexes over 2 million items

published since 1951. Key specialisms are: Anthropology, Sociology, Economics and Politics, although a wide range of interdisciplinary social science subject areas ranging from International Relations to Women's Studies and Healthcare are also covered. Extensive indexing of non-English-language resources.

Scopus (subscription required)
www.scopus.com
www.info.sciverse.com/scopus/about

Enormous cross-disciplinary database of abstracts and references to peer-reviewed literature covering all disciplines. Particularly noted for medical and scientific coverage. Indexes over 17,000 journal titles plus conference proceedings. Many references start at 1996, although selected titles go back to the 19th century. Includes the facility to conduct cited reference searches, analyse search results by number of times cited and set up personalised search alerts.

Web of Knowledge (subscription required)
wokinfo.com

Major service incorporating the *Social Sciences Citation Index*, *Arts and Humanities Citation Index*, *Science Citation Index* and a conference proceedings index. Libraries may also purchase subscriptions to other add-on databases. Dates of coverage differ according to the subscription package, but usually cover from the 1950s onwards. Key features include the ability to search for highly cited articles and the ability to set up and save search alerts.

LANGUAGES

Typical questions

- Has this book been translated into French?
- Which libraries in the UK hold Italian newspapers?

Points to consider

- Queries relating to languages tend to fall into a number of broad categories Students often require advice on language learning. See also the **Courses** and **Dictionaries** sections. Also relevant are the area studies sections, as most list resources in native languages.
- Students with existing language skills may wish to trace publications written in a foreign language. If these are not available locally, they will need help locating relevant resources.
- This section focuses on modern languages. Restrictions of space mean that it is not possible to list individual languages. Instead the section highlights general resources which should be explored fully to locate more specialist information.

Where to look

Key organizations

UK

Association for Language Learning (ALL)
 www.all-languages.org.uk
 Represents foreign-language teachers at all levels. Find news and events listings.

Association of University Language Centres
 www.aulc.org
 Covers university language departments in the UK and Ireland.

CILT: National Centre for Languages
 www.cilt.org.uk
 Seeks to promote language learning, and professionalism in language teaching. Website has careers advice for teachers, plus comment on languages policy at all levels. It includes news, training and events listings plus updates on recent research which it has conducted on language provision, learning and skills.

LANGUAGES

Higher Education Academy
www.heacademy.ac.uk
Aims to support higher education lecturers. This includes subject support for modern languages and linguistics. Website has news, events listings and online resources for teachers.

UKCASA (United Kingdom Council for Area Studies Associations)
www.ukcasa.ac.uk/index.html
Represents individual area studies associations. Many of these support language specialisms.

University Council of Modern Languages (UCML)
www.ucml.org.uk
Umbrella organization representing language teachers and area specialists. Website is useful for obtaining contact details of scholarly societies covering individual languages. It also discusses language teaching policy and funding at higher education level. Supports the **Routes into Languages** website, **www.routesintolanguages.ac.uk**, which seeks to increase take-up of language courses. This has details of events and promotional materials.

United States

Modern Language Association
www.mla.org
World-famous organization supporting the study and teaching of languages. Website has details about its style guide and the *MLA International Bibliography*.

National Resource Centers for Foreign Language, Area and International Studies
nrcweb.org
Created by the US government, specialist centres supporting teaching and research. Search the directory of members for information on courses and library collections.

International

CercleS: Confédération Européenne des Centres de Langues de l'Enseignement Supérieur
www.cercles.org/en/main.html
European Confederation of Language Centres in Higher Education. Find information on activities and policy in Europe, including European Union projects. Also has links to national language associations.

Council of Europe

www.coe.int/t/dg4/linguistic

Has a language section which seeks to promote linguistic diversity in Europe. Its website has news, policy documents (many relating to proficiency standards and assessment) and teaching resources which it has produced. It also has country profiles of language-learning trends and facilities.

UNESCO

www.unesco.org/en/languages-and-multilingualism

Promotes languages and multiculturalism. Find information on its activities and projects and access full-text reports. It includes the **Interactive Atlas of Languages in Danger, www.unesco.org/culture/ languages-atlas**, which offers free statistics and mappings of minority languages worldwide.

Indexes

Note that the resources in the **Journal Article Indexes** section and subject sections usually index foreign-language articles.

Index Translationum – World Bibliography of Translation

portal.unesco.org/culture/en/ev.php-
URL_ID=7810&URL_DO=DO_TOPIC&URL_SECTION=201.html
Maintained by UNESCO. This web version indexes translations of books published in 100 UNESCO member states since 1979. All subject areas are covered. It is possible to select a title and investigate what languages it has been translated into. The site also has some basic statistics on translated works, including top 50 authors, titles and languages. Check the site for details on transliteration standards, country coverage and last updates.

MLA Bibliography (subscription required)

www.mla.org/bibliography

Find references to journal articles and books covering all aspects of languages and literature. Language coverage is broad ranging. It includes all languages (excluding Latin and classical Greek), historical periods, plus language teaching and linguistics. Online version covers 1926 onwards.

Libraries

Use these resources to locate foreign-language journals and books.

British Library

www.bl.uk/reshelp/findhelplang/index.html

Excellent starting-point. The extensive collections include many materials supporting foreign languages which are managed by specialist curators. The website offers guides to the British Library's collections, plus directories of recommended websites.

Remember that you can also use **Copac, www.copac.ac.uk**, to search for foreign-language materials in other UK research libraries. These include books, journals and pamphlets. Always check access policies before sending students to other institutions.

Another starting-point is specialist library organizations. These support groups are headed by language specialists and often maintain their own directories of library holdings. Many also have mailing lists which discuss policy developments, new publications and training events.

Global Resources Network (GRN)
www.crl.edu/grn
Collaborative initiative of the Center for Research Libraries which seeks to improve access to international (including foreign language) materials in North American libraries. Website offers news of resources and digitization projects.

WESLINE: Western European Studies Library and Information Network
www.ulrls.lon.ac.uk/wesline
Umbrella organizations representing a number of individual UK groups, including: ACLAIIR (Advisory Council of Latin American and Iberian Information Resources); French Studies Library Group; German Studies Library Group; and Italian Studies Library Group.

Western European Studies Section (WESS)
wess.lib.byu.edu/index.php/Main_Page
Specialist group of the Association of College and Research Libraries. Represents American librarians. Website has information on member libraries, notes on activities and excellent directories of links to recommended web resources. Broad language coverage ranging from French, German and Dutch to Scandinavian languages.

Finally don't forget national library catalogues. Many have websites which also provide free access to digital versions of classic manuscripts. **The European Library Portal** has a directory, **www.theeuropeanlibrary. org/portal/libraries/map_en.html**.

Language learning

Includes resources for teachers and students!

Good starting-points for tracing courses are websites of the key organizations listed above.

Cultural institutions

Cultural institutions are also very useful. Many host courses and events and some have their own libraries. Examples include the following.

Goethe-Institut

www.goethe.de

Federal Republic of Germany cultural organization. Website has support and resources for learners and teachers of German.

Instituto Camões

www.instituto-camoes.pt

Information on the cultural life of Portugal and a virtual resource centre for teaching and learning Portuguese.

Instituto Cervantes (España)

www.cervantes.es

Resources, including courses, curriculum materials and links to recommended websites for learning Spanish.

Institut Français

www.institut-francais.org.uk

UK-based organization. Houses an extensive library collection which is open to the public. It also supports a digital platform, **Culturethèque**, **www.culturetheque.org.uk,** which offers remote access to webcasts and e-books. Some services are for subscribers only.

Istituto Italiano di Cultura

www.icilondon.esteri.it

Organization of the Italian government. Its London website has the online catalogue of its library, plus cultural and educational events listings.

TV/radio stations

Try national TV/radio stations. Many offer free sections for language learners. Good examples include the following.

BBC

www.bbc.co.uk/languages

Has a large languages site with online courses, interactive quizzes and games. Particularly strong coverage of French, German, Italian and Spanish. Includes a teachers' section.

LANGUAGES

Deutsche-Welle

www.dw-world.de/dw/0,,2547,00.html

Free access to German language courses, including video and audio content for a range of levels.

RAI TV

www.rai.it

Italian TV programmes.

RFI

www.rfi.fr

Has a section for students studying French, with regular news broadcasts (with transcripts) and associated language exercises.

RTVE

www.rtve.es

Spanish TV and radio programmes.

Online tools and resources

Lingu@net Europa

www.linguanet-europa.org

Free online learning tool covering 18 European languages. Includes online assessment tools, learning tips and links to thousands of accredited websites.

UCLA Languages project

www.lmp.ucla.edu

Database providing information and resources on 151 less commonly taught languages worldwide. Includes Asian languages, such as Chinese, which are gaining in popularity. Excludes Latin and Ancient Greek. Site includes language profiles with information on distribution and grammar. Also offers graded teaching materials at all levels.

Translation

Many students use **Babel Fish** for translating text, **babelfish.yahoo.com**. But for more specialist advice try the following professional organizations.

Institute of Translation and interpreting (UK)

www.iti.org.uk/indexMain.html

Search for a translator and consult the recommended websites.

International Federation of Translators

www.fit-ift.org

LATIN AMERICAN STUDIES

Typical questions

- Where can I find statistics on healthcare in South America?
- I want to search for articles about Chicano culture.

Points to consider

- Definitions of Latin America can differ. Enquirers may be referring to South America or the Caribbean. Check what is needed.
- This is an area studies section. It should also be used in conjunction with the appropriate subject studies sections.

Where to look

Key organizations

Scholarly societies

Use these to locate news, new publications, research and conference alerts.

Latin American Studies Association (LASA)
   lasa.international.pitt.edu
   World's largest organization. Find details of activities in North America and elsewhere.

Society for Latin American Studies UK
   www.slas.org.uk

International organizations

Use these websites to access reports, project information and data. Sometimes they are more up to date than national government websites!

Economic Commission for Latin America (ECLA)
   www.eclac.cl
   UN body with responsibility for the region. Spanish acronym is CEPAL.

Inter-American Development Bank
   www.iadb.org
   Information on development aid and projects.

Organization of American States (OAS)
   www.oas.org
   Promotes economic and social development in the region. Access treaties

and agreements on inter-American co-operation from the website. Strong coverage of human rights issues.

Pan-American Health Organization (PAHO)
new.paho.org
Regional office of the World Health Organization. Free access to regional core health indicator database, the regional mortality database and individual country reports.

Libraries

Use these to search for books and journals. The websites also have research guides.

British Library
www.bl.uk/reshelp/findhelpregion/americas/index.html
One of the most extensive collections in the UK. Mexico and Brazil are especially well represented.
To trace others try the following.

Advisory Council on Latin American and Iberian Information Resources: ACLAIIR
www.aclaiir.org.uk
Professional organization of information specialists. Maintains information on library book and newspaper holdings in the UK.

Journal article indexes

Chicano Database (subscription required)
www.oclc.org/support/documentation/firstsearch/databases/ dbdetails/details/ChicanoDatabase.htm
Interdisciplinary. Includes the Spanish-speaking *Mental Health Database*. Coverage from the 1960s onwards.

Handbook of Latin American Studies
lcweb2.loc.gov/hlas/hlashome.html
Compiled by Hispanic Division of the Library of Congress. Offers annotated references to books and journal articles covering the humanities and social sciences.

HAPI: Hispanic American Periodicals Index (subscription required)
hapi.gseis.ucla.edu
Articles about Central and South America and the Caribbean basin covering the social sciences and humanities from 1970 onwards.

Latin American Periodical Tables of Contents (LAPTOC)
lanic.utexas.edu/larpp/laptoc.html
Access tables of contents of more than 950 journals published in Latin America.

Latindex
www.latindex.unam.mx
Regional network disseminating information on scholarly journals from Latin America, the Caribbean, Spain and Portugal. Includes listings and links.

News services

Latin America Data Base (LADB) (subscription required)
ladb.unm.edu
Published by the University of New Mexico. English-language summaries of Latin American economic and political news. Coverage from 1986.

Latin American Newsletters (LatinNews) (subscription required)
www.latinnews.com
Established since 1967. Includes daily intelligence briefings.

Statistical data

Use this in conjunction with the **Statistical Data** section. The international organizations listed above are also useful.

Latin American Public Opinion Project (LAPOP)
www.vanderbilt.edu/lapop
Based at the Center for the Americas, Vanderbilt University. Offers access to polls with citizen views on political and social topics. Many can be downloaded free of charge.

Digital libraries and internet portals

Bibliotecas Virtuales de Ciencias Sociales de América Latina y el Caribe de la red
www.biblioteca.clacso.edu.ar
Virtual library maintained by a network of over 160 social science research institutions across 21 countries throughout Latin America and the Caribbean. Includes links to recent reports and online journals.

Choike.org: Portal on Southern Civil Societies
www.choike.org

Maintained by Instituto del Tercer Mundo, Uruguay. Aims to provide access to information and resources produced by social movements from the Southern hemisphere. Covers economic and social policy.

LANIC
lanic.utexas.edu

Comprehensive site from the University of Texas, Austin. Access a directory of links plus many full-text digitization projects, including: the Castro speech database; presidential messages; and Latin American Open Archives Portal, which indexes working papers.

Latin American and Caribbean Studies Research Portal
handbook.americas.sas.ac.uk

Maintained by Institute for the Study of the Americas. Searchable directory of Latin research resources in the UK. Includes lists of courses, academic staff and theses.

Political Database of the Americas
pdba.georgetown.edu

Project of Georgetown University and the Organization of American States. Find information and data on elections, political parties and electoral systems of Latin American nations.

LAW

Typical questions

- I need to find *McHale* v. *Watson* (1966) 115 CLR 199.
- How can I find out which cases have cited *Donoghue* v. *Stevenson* 1932?
- I want to trace recent journal articles on adoption law.

Points to consider

- Law enquiries can be complicated. Some universities have specialist law librarians. If one is not available another good starting-point are the websites of the law libraries listed here, as they contain detailed guides to legal research.
- Legal materials are increasingly being made available online; however, remember to check dates and jurisdiction before use.
- Related sections are **Criminology, Human Rights, Legislation, Treaties**. Information on EU law is also provided in the **European Union** section.

Where to look

Key organizations

Many students require information on how to enter a specific legal profession. The main organizations have websites which offer careers advice, plus news and events listings.

UK

Bar Council
   www.barcouncil.org.uk
   Approved regulator of the Bar of England and Wales. The starting-point for finding out about barristers and the Inns of Court.

ILEX
   www.ilex.org.uk
   Professional body representing legal executives.

Judiciary of England and Wales
   www.judiciary.gov.uk
   Provides information on the justice system, its evolution, the current court structure and the work of judges and magistrates.

Law Society of England and Wales
   www.lawsociety.org.uk

Represents solicitors. Website offers free access to the catalogue of its specialist legal library as well as advice on becoming a solicitor.

UK Centre for Legal Education (UKCLE)
www.ukcle.ac.uk
Works to improve the teaching and learning of law. Website contains news on courses, plus a useful collection of resources for lecturers.

International

International Bar Association (IBA)
www.ibanet.org
Established in 1947, the world's leading organization of international legal practitioners. Use its website to locate bar associations and law societies worldwide.

Law libraries

Use these websites to check the catalogues for relevant books and journals. They also have useful guides on how to research specialist legal topics.

Bodleian Law Library
www.bodleian.ox.ac.uk/law
Part of the University of Oxford.

Institute of Advanced Legal Studies Library (IALS)
ials.sas.ac.uk/library/library.htm
Part of the University of London. Extensive collection of UK and international law.

Law Library of Congress
www.loc.gov/law
World's largest specialist legal collection. Website has news and legal research guides covering international and comparative law.

Legal research guides

Clinch, P. (2001) *Using a Law Library: a student's guide to legal research skills*, **2nd edn, Blackstone Press**
Practical guide that introduces students to the main legal literature of England, Scotland, Wales and the European Union. Includes coverage of print and electronic resources.

Holborn, G. (2001) *Butterworth's Legal Research Guide*, **2nd edn, Oxford University Press**

Step-by-step guide to techniques and sources for legal research. Main focuses are on English and European Union law.

Legal citations and abbreviations

It is common for law reading lists to use abbreviations when referring to articles /cases.

- A typical case citation is:

  Donoghue v. Stevenson [1932] All ER Rep 1; [1932]

  It consists of:

  The names of the parties in a case (Donoghue v Stevenson)

  The year when the case was reported (1932)

  A volume number (1). This is included only when more than one volume was published in that year.

  The abbreviation for the name of a law report (All ER Rep). Note that it is common for famous cases to be cited in several places.

  Page number (or paragraph number) (1932)

- A typical citation for an article in a law journal is:

  [1990] J.B.L. 469.

  This similarly refers to the year of publication; abbreviation of the journal title; and page number.

If the reading list does not give the full title of the journal/law report abbreviation, check the following useful resources.

Cardiff Index to Legal Abbreviations
  www.legalabbrevs.cardiff.ac.uk
  Free index covering law reports and cases from over 290 jurisdictions worldwide. Search by abbreviation or by title.

OSCOLA: Oxford Standard for Citation of Legal Authorities
  www.law.ox.ac.uk/publications/oscola.php
  Standard widely used by law schools in the UK for citing legal materials. Free access to tutorials and guidance.

Raistrick, D. (2008) *Index to Legal Citations and Abbreviations*, **3rd edn, Martindale-Hubbell**
  Well regarded printed source; covers the legal literature of the UK, the Commonwealth, the USA and Europe.

Dictionaries and encyclopedias

Greenberg, D. (ed.) (2010) *Stroud's Judicial Dictionary of Words and Phrases*, **7th edn, Sweet & Maxwell**

Highly regarded dictionary first published in 1890. Offers authoritative definitions, discussion of the evolution of English legal terms and cross-references to related legislation and case law.

Halsbury's Laws of England

www.lexisnexis.co.uk

Available in print or online. Long established multi-volume work. A good starting-point for researching a specific legal topic because it offers summaries of subject areas, with notes referring to relevant cases and legislation.

Law, J. and Martin, E. (eds) (2009) *A Dictionary of Law*, **7th edn, Oxford University Press**

Focusing primarily on English law, this well regarded source contains over 4000 entries relating to the concepts, processes and organization of the legal system. Includes a guide to citing and referencing.

Directories (legal profession)

UK

Use these to locate contact names and addresses of practitioners.

Chambers and Partners Directory

www.chambersandpartners.com/UK

Free website; lists solicitors and barristers in over 70 specialist areas of UK practice. Detailed regional coverage.

Law Society's Directory

www.lawsociety.org.uk/choosingandusing/findasolicitor.law

Find solicitors in England and Wales. Users can look for a named firm or individual and search by region or specialism.

Legal Hub

www.legalhub.co.uk/legalhub/app/main

Provides free access to the *Bar Directory*, an annual listing of barristers published by the General Council of the Bar and Sweet & Maxwell.

International

Legal 500

www.legal500.com

Free website designed for use by clients. Provides listings and profiles of law firms in over 100 nations worldwide. Search by name, region and specialism.

Martindale
www.martindale.com

Website provides free access to an international directory which lists individuals and firms.

Waterlow International Legal Directory
www.waterlowlegal.com/directories/international-law-firms.php

Search by name or country. Free access.

Journal article indexes

Index to Foreign Legal Periodicals (subscription required)
www.law.berkeley.edu/library/iflp

Produced by the American Association of Law Libraries, it provides coverage of the law of all jurisdictions other than the United States, the UK, Canada and Australia, generally from 1981 onwards.

Index to Legal Periodicals (subscription required)
www.hwwilson.com/bus/legal.htm

Indexes over 1000 legal journals. Focuses mainly on articles from English-speaking countries (the US, UK, Canada etc). Coverage online is available in a number of different packages. Some entries date from 1908 onwards.

Legal Journals Index (subscription required)
www.westlaw.co.uk/journals/legal_journals_index.shtm

Forms part of *Westlaw*. Major source for UK law. Indexes over 400 titles from 1986 onwards.

Law reports

- Use these resources to locate examples of cases.
- Note that only a small proportion of law cases are published in law reports. In order to qualify, cases usually need to demonstrate a point of law. Guidance on obtaining transcripts of unreported cases is given on the main law library websites. Some are also available via court websites and selected electronic databases.
- Many students use electronic resources to locate cases. The major electronic databases are listed below. Use of such databases enables students to check quickly if a case has been upheld or overturned.

- Important cases are often published in several different law report series. Students are advised to cite the most authoritative source. In England this is the official law report series produced by the Incorporated Council of Law Reporting.

England

Historic cases before 1865

English Reports

www.justis.com/data-coverage/english-reports.aspx
Available in print or online. A compilation of over 100,000 of the most important cases reported between 1220 and 1873.

Post 1865

Law Report series – Incorporated Council of Law Reporting
www.iclr.co.uk
Established in 1865 and regarded as the 'authoritative version' because all materials are checked by judges. Over time, a number of sub-series have existed. All are now offered online via different legal databases. The website offers additional background information and updates. Note that it is common for most law reports to appear in other series before they are published in the official series. These can include the *Weekly Law Reports*, the *All England Law Reports* and selected newspaper reports. Using an electronic database makes it easy to locate all versions of the reports and check for subsequent judgments.

The following databases contain the official law reports series, plus large numbers of specialist commercial series, law encyclopedias and journals. The quantity of information can make them difficult to navigate. Guides are given on the major law library websites. A good tip is to ensure that students are searching within the correct jurisdiction! Check indexes and directories to find the right file.

British and Irish Legal Information Institute (BAILII)
www.bailii.org
Free access to a wealth of British legal resources. Content includes: transcripts of decisions from a range of courts (these include House of Lords and Supreme Court from 1838; High Court decisions). Also available is the text of legislation dating back several centuries.

Lawtel (subscription required)
www.lawtel.com

Content includes: summaries of reported and selected unreported cases from 1980 with links to some full text; summaries of UK statutes from 1984 with links to full text from 1987 and a range of articles.

Lexis Library (subscription required)
www.lexisnexis.co.uk
Produced by LexisNexis (formerly Butterworths). Content includes:

- Law reports and cases. The *Law Reports* series – from 1865; *All England Reports*; a number of specialist law reports series; *English Reports*; unreported transcripts.
- Legislation. Fully consolidated texts of Acts currently in force; Statutory Instruments currently in force.
- Journals. A number of full-text journals, including the *New Law Journal*, *Law Society Gazette*, *Oxford Journal of Legal Studies*.
- Books. Including *Halsbury's Laws of England*.

Westlaw (subscription required)
www.westlaw.co.uk
Produced by Thomson Reuters. Content includes:

- Law reports. The *Law Reports* series – 1865 onwards; *Weekly Law Reports*; a large number of subject specialist reports; *English Reports*; unreported transcripts.
- Legislation. Fully consolidated full text of Acts since 1267 (currently in force); Statutory Instruments since 1948 (currently in force).
- Journals. The *Legal Journals Index*, which has abstracts of every UK published legal article from 1986 plus other full-text titles.
- Books. Including The Common Law Series, *Chitty on Contract* and *Clerk and Lindsell on Tort*.

International/overseas

The major legal databases (Lexis, Westlaw) contain full-text case law from many jurisdictions. The resources listed below offer guidance on other resources.

ASIL Guide to Electronic Resources for International Law
www.asil.org/erghome.cfm
Maintained by the American Society for International Law. Excellent introductory guide to using the internet to trace legislation and case reports. Topics covered include European Union law, international criminal law, international human rights law and United Nations law.

FLAG Foreign Law Guide
ials.sas.ac.uk/flag.htm
Searchable catalogue of the printed holdings of many UK libraries. Useful for searching possible locations of foreign law reports.

World Legal Information Institute (WorldLII)
worldlii.org
Maintained by a number of leading national bodies, including the British and Irish Legal Information Institute (BAILII). An excellent starting-point for tracing links to websites where foreign and law reports can be found.

News services

Most newspapers cover legal news. Some broadsheets (such as *The Times*) even print law reports. Listed below are specialist law services for practitioners.

Current Awareness from the Middle Temple
innertemplelibrary.wordpress.com
Excellent blog maintained by Middle Temple library staff which highlights legal news, case law and changes in legislation relating to England and Wales.

JURIST
jurist.law.pitt.edu
Site maintained by the University of Pittsburgh. Offers free access to legal news and discussion of recent research articles. Main emphasis is on American law.

Law Society Gazette
www.lawgazette.co.uk
Weekly publication for solicitors produced by the English Law Society. Available online and in print. Includes legal news, City news, case discussion and jobs listings. Website offers free access to blogs and some articles. Archives for subscribers only.

Legal Week
www.legalweek.com
Online legal magazine featuring news, analysis and job listings. Main focus is on resources for commercial lawyers in the UK, some reference to other jurisdictions.

Internet gateways and portals

Eagle-i (Electronic Access to Global Legal Information)

ials.sas.ac.uk/eaglei/project/eiproject.htm

Directory of annotated links to high-quality websites which is being developed by the Institute of Advanced Legal Studies Library. Extensive coverage of resources (organizations, journals, websites, legislation, reports) relating to all aspects of UK, European, foreign, comparative and international law.

LawBore

lawbore.net

Guide maintained by City University which is designed for use by students of English Law. Includes a news section and directory of links by subject. It also has an excellent section on legal research skills called *Learnmore*, which offers free access to online tutorials covering subjects such as writing, researching and mooting.

LEGISLATION

Typical questions
- I need to consult the Welfare Reform Act 2007, c.5.
- Can I find EU legislation online?
- Is this Act still in force?

Points to consider
- Increasingly, it is possible to trace examples of full-text legislation online. However, students need to check the dates, jurisdiction and whether the text includes any subsequent amendments. Acts which incorporate later revisions in a single document are usually referred to as consolidated versions.
- The terminology used can be difficult to understand. Specialist legal libraries such as the Bodleian Law Library, **www.bodleian.ox.ac.uk/law**, and the Institute of Advanced Legal Studies, **ials.sas.ac.uk/library**, offer excellent guides to legal research, which are good starting-points.

Where to look
UK

There are two main types of legislation in the UK:

- Primary legislation – Acts of Parliament or Statutes. These are sub-divided into Public General Acts or Local and Personal Acts. A typical modern Public General Act consists of the following parts: title; year and chapter number (e.g. Welfare Reform Act 2007 c.5); purpose of the Act; date of Royal Assent; body of the Act; schedule providing information about repeals and amendments resulting from the Act.
- Secondary legislation – Statutory Instruments. These are often called Codes, Orders, Regulations, Rules and are usually preceded by the prefix SI and a number and date.

Detailed information about the law-making process can be found on the **UK Parliament** website, **www.parliament.uk/about/how/laws**.

Halsbury's Statutes
www1.lexisnexis.co.uk/hssi/hs-intro.html
Well regarded printed source. Its annotations are also offered online as part of the *Lexis Library*. Arranged by subject. Contains Acts currently in force and as amended. Acts no longer in force are omitted. Each Act is annotated with information on parliamentary debates, repeals, secondary legislation.

Legislation.Gov.UK

www.legislation.gov.uk

Official website maintained by The National Archives on behalf of HM Government Publishing. Aims to offer free access to legislation from 1267 to the present day. Includes Public General Acts, Local Acts and Statutory Instruments. It is intended to provide access to subsequent revisions to legislation. However, the website should be checked for information about exclusions because amendments are not currently available for all types.

Many libraries also have access to commercial subscription services which contain the full text of Acts (with revisions) plus links to related legislation and cases. Well known examples are the following.

Lexis Library

www.lexisnexis.co.uk/store/uk

WestLaw UK

www.westlaw.co.uk

Foreign law

Many commercial databases, such as Lexis and Westlaw, offer full-text European Union, international and foreign legislation. Additionally, a number of free websites are available.

EUR-Lex

eur-lex.europa.eu

Official EU website providing free access to European Union law. Most are consolidated versions. It is possible to browse a directory of European legislation in force.

FLAG Foreign Law Guide

ials.sas.ac.uk/flag.htm

Searchable catalogue of the printed holdings of many UK libraries. Useful for finding possible locations of foreign legislation.

World Legal Information Institute (WorldLII)

worldlii.org

Maintained by a number of leading national bodies, including the Australasian Legal Information Institute (AustLII) and British and Irish Legal Information Institute (BAILII). An excellent starting-point for tracing links to websites where full-text national legislation can be found.

LIBRARY CATALOGUES

Typical questions

- All the books on my reading list are on loan. Can I find them in another library?
- Where can I find a copy of the 20th edition of *Chitty on Contracts*?
- Which libraries in London take the *Journal of Common Market Studies*?

Points to consider

- Students should always be directed to search the catalogue of their own institution first. If items cannot be found it is always worth double-checking if books are on loan or if the search has been performed correctly!
- If items are not available locally, find out if your institution has any access agreements with other colleges and, if so, check their catalogues first, e.g. many UK universities are members of a scheme called **Sconul Access**, **www.access.sconul.ac.uk**.
- Visitors to other libraries may not be able to use certain categories of material such as e-journals or books in teaching collections. Always advise students to check before making a journey.
- When checking other library catalogues note that some universities have several sites and some items may be held in remote stores. If in doubt, check locations in advance.
- Most library catalogues do not index individual journal articles or government reports. These often need to be traced using other indexes. Information about these is usually given on the library website in subject or research guides.
- Library catalogues may retrieve several entries for what appears to be the same item. Remember to check all entries because there may be separate records for print and online versions!

Where to look

Union catalogues

These enable you to quickly cross-search the contents of more than one library catalogue. They are excellent for finding out which library in a specific area has a journal or book title. Remember to check which library catalogues are included and whether they have data on what books are on loan!

Regional union catalogues are good starting-points for locating local resources.

Inform25
www.inform25.ac.uk

A good example which has information on college and research libraries in the London and South-East M25 motorway area. It has options for searching for books and journals (via the University of London list of serials).

Other regional examples are listed on the **UK SUNCAT** website, **www.suncat.ac.uk/other.shtml**.

Links to all individual UK colleges are on the **UCAS** website, **www.ucas.com/students/choosingcourses/choosinguni/instguide**.

These websites usually have a link to the main library home page, where the catalogue is often found. Note that this is sometimes referred to as a learning resource centre or other similar title, so you may need to browse the website.

Also, don't forget public libraries in your area. They are often excluded from the main union catalogues but many have extra copies of basic textbooks and online newspaper databases.

An excellent public library list is maintained by Sheila and Robert Harden, **dspace.dial.pipex.com/town/square/ac940/weblibs.html**.

National and international union catalogues

COPAC

www.copac.ac.uk

Excellent national service which covers many UK university and research libraries, as well as the British Library. Especially suited for locating obscure book and journal titles.

European Library

search.theeuropeanlibrary.org/portal/en/index.html

Offers a federated search of all of the national libraries of European countries; many of these contain rare book and journal collections as well as extensive holdings of current and historical publications from their country. The site also provides access to some thematic online exhibitions.

SUNCAT – Serials Union Catalogue for the UK

www.suncat.ac.uk

Focuses on periodical holdings from major UK university and research libraries and the British Library. Coverage includes journals, magazines, annual reports and yearbooks. Some entries have recent tables of contents.

WorldCat

www.worldcat.org

Free version covers over 10,000 libraries worldwide. It includes books and journals. You can look for copies of books and journals near your location. Note that this covers only registered libraries.

LITERATURE

Typical questions

- What is an iambic pentameter?
- How can I trace recent literacy criticism of Charles Dickens?
- What poem does this line come from?

Points to consider

- This section focuses on the academic study of English and Comparative Literature. Those seeking recommendations of good books should consult the **Book Reviews** section. Information about individual authors can also be traced using the **Biographical Information** section. The **Languages** section has more links to literature in other languages.
- Due to limitations of space, this section cannot cover all forms of literature, genres and time periods! Explore the general indexes to find more specialized resources.

Where to look

Key organizations

Use the websites of these organizations to find news about publications, conferences and on-going research.

UK

Alliance of Literary Societies
www.allianceofliterarysocieties.org.uk
Useful for tracing research groups relating to individual authors/literary genres.

British Comparative Literature Association (BCLA)
www.bcla.org
Covers world literature in all languages, including translations. Website has good directory of links.

Council for College and University English
www.ccue.ac.uk
Professional organization for English lecturers in universities and colleges across the UK.

Higher Education Academy
www.heacademy.ac.uk

Aims to support UK higher education lecturers. Includes subject coverage of literature. Website highlights projects relating to teaching and learning.

Royal Society of Literature
www.rslit.org
Established in 1820. Renowned for its literary awards and lectures. Audio files of many are available from the website. They include discussions with authors.

International

European Society for the Study of English
www.essenglish.org
European federation of national higher education associations covering Literature and English Language. Find details of national members and Europe-wide activities.

Modern Humanities Research Association
www.mhra.org.uk
International organization promoting graduate study in the humanities. Special focus on modern languages and literature. Publications include: *Yearbook of English Studies, ABELL: The Annual Bibliography of English Language and Literature.*

Modern Language Association (MLA)
www.mla.org
Leading professional association for scholars of language and literature in the USA. Produces the specialist *MLA Style Guide* for writing research papers.

Libraries and archives

British Library
www.bl.uk
Extensive collections of books, journals and manuscripts covering English and post-colonial literatures. Search the catalogue and view examples of classic manuscripts online, **www.bl.uk/onlinegallery/onlineex/englit**.

Senate House Library
www.ull.ac.uk/subjects/comparativeliterature/index.shtml
Part of the University of London. Large English and Comparative Literature collections. Website has a good guide to key databases and websites for Comparative Literature.

LITERATURE

Dictionaries and encyclopedias

Baldick, C. (2008) *Oxford Dictionary of Literary Terms*, **Oxford University Press**

Useful for students needing to check difficult concepts. Companion website has associated web links, **www.oup.com/uk/booksites/content/9780199208272.**

Drabble, M. (2006) *Oxford Companion to English Literature*, **6th edn, Oxford University Press**

Regarded as a standard reference source for information on the history, persons and genres of English Literature from earliest times. Includes a listing of literary prize winners.

Journal article indexes

Note that the general **Journal Article Indexes** section includes some humanities material which provide coverage of Literature.

ABELL (Annual Bibliography of English Language and Literature) (subscription required)

collections.chadwyck.co.uk/home/home_abell.jsp

Compiled under the auspices of the Modern Humanities Research Association. Provides an annual listing of books, book reviews and book chapters covering all aspects of English-language prose, poetry and drama published worldwide.

MLA Bibliography (subscription required)

www.mla.org/bibliography

Published by the Modern Language Association. Search for references to books, articles and dissertations covering literature and language published since 1926.

World Shakespeare Bibliography Online (subscription required)

www.worldshakesbib.org

Over 127,000 references to articles, books and theatrical publications since 1960.

Digital libraries

See also the **E-books** section for other examples of online literature. Remind students to check edition details before use.

British Literary Manuscripts Online c. 1660–1900 (subscription required)
gale.cengage.co.uk/product-highlights/literature/british-literary-manuscripts-online-c16601900.aspx
Digital archive combining original works with manuscripts and diaries from authors. Covers major poets and writers from medieval to Victorian times. These include William Blake, the Brontë sisters and William Wordsworth.

Literature Online (subscription required)
lion.chadwyck.co.uk
Major resource providing access to over 350,000 full-text works of English and American fiction, poetry and drama from the seventh century to the present day. Also includes extensive literary criticism and reference works which explain literary concepts.

Voice of the Shuttle
vos.ucsb.edu
Annotated guide to thousands of humanities websites maintained by Alan Liu and staff at the University of California, Santa Barbara. Coverage of literature includes English and foreign-language writing and literary theory. Numerous links to e-book collections, literary journals and organizations.

Poetry

In addition to the general resources try these specialist ones!

Academy of American Poets
www.poets.org
Great website which provides free access to thousands of poems, plus audio/video readings by and interviews with famous American poets.

Gale, T. (2007) (ed.) *Columbia Granger's Index to Poetry in Anthologies*, 13th edn, Columbia University Press
www.columbiagrangers.org
Published for over a century. Recommended resource for tracing information about poets and poetry. Find where a poem was published, trace poetry by first or last lines. Also available online (subscription required).

Poetry Library
www.poetrylibrary.org.uk
Major UK library with extensive collections of modern poetry (post 1912). Website hosts an online digital poetry library, **www.poetrymagazines. org.uk**, containing full-text magazines.

LITERATURE SEARCHING

Typical questions

- How can I find materials for my dissertation?
- What has been published on the impact of climate change on the environment?

Points to consider

- Students need to conduct literature reviews to search for materials for their dissertations. Many need assistance on how to move beyond prescribed reading lists to active subject searching. In particular, they may be unaware of the differences between e-journals and journal article indexes and the fact that most library catalogues do not directly index journal articles.
- Researchers and academic staff need to conduct a literature review before undertaking a new project, in order to examine what has been written before. They often need to search more comprehensively.
- Stages in the literature review process include:
  — identifying the topic (setting the scope/parameters)
  — choosing the search tools, i.e. databases to search (see the subject and **Journal Article Indexes** sections). It may also be helpful when choosing the tools for students to consider the types of material they need because locating them often requires the use of different types of databases. Do they need primary or secondary resources, text or images? (See **Archives, Legislation, Government Publications, Statistical Data, Opinion Polls, Market Research, Maps, Treaties, Films, Images, Theses** and **Working Papers** sections where appropriate.)
  — constructing the search terms (see **Journal Article Indexes** section)
  — evaluating the search results (see **Journal Article Indexes** section)
  — recording/writing up (see **Citing and Referencing, Plagiarism, Writing and Style Guides** and **Reference Management Tools** sections). Note that tutorials designed to teach information-seeking skills can also be found by consulting the **Information Literacy** section.

Where to look

Key organizations

Use these sites to get general advice on training for researchers. Remember to check if your local university has any specialist student study/research support programmes.

Researcher Development Initiative

www.rdi.ac.uk

Supports social science researchers at all stages of their careers.

Vitae

www.vitae.ac.uk

National organization associated with Careers Research and Advisory Centre (CRAC) which offers support for postgraduate students and early career researchers. Website includes factsheets and resources covering general themes such as time management as well as research skills.

Online tutorials

Companion for Undergraduate Dissertations

www.socscidiss.bham.ac.uk

Developed by the Higher Education Academy's Centre for Sociology, Anthropology and Politics, it is designed for social science students; however, it contains some very good general advice which would be applicable to all. It guides students through each stage of the research process, from choosing a question to writing up, giving clear examples of good practice.

Further examples of information skills tutorials can be found in the **Information Literacy** section.

Systematic reviews

A particular method of literature review which is characterized by its insistence upon collecting all (as far as possible!) of the literature about a specific topic, using a rigorous systematic method. It is widely used in scientific subject areas. Due to its specialist nature it is advised that specialist advice is sought. Good starting-points are the following.

Centre for Reviews and Dissemination

www.york.ac.uk/inst/crd

Key organization. Its website provides free guides for researchers on using and conducting systematic reviews in healthcare. It maintains a number of important databases which can be used to trace examples (mainly in health and medicine). These include *DARE (Database of Abstracts of Reviews of Effects)* – a collection of systematic reviews which evaluate the effectiveness of healthcare interventions.

Evidence for Policy and Practice Information and Co-ordinating Centre (EPPI-Centre)

eppi.ioe.ac.uk

Based at the Institute of Education, University of London. Its website is a major resource for understanding systematic reviews. It defines what they are, the methods and tools used and gives case studies of good examples. It includes a catalogue of reviews which it has conducted.

National Institute for Health Research (NIHR)

www.nihr.ac.uk/research/Pages/Systematic_Reviews.aspx

Key organization promoting the use of systematic reviews in UK healthcare research.

UK Cochrane Centre

ukcc.cochrane.org

The Cochrane Library is a renowned source of systematic reviews in health and healthcare. The UK centre offers support to researchers on how to conduct Cochrane systematic reviews. Its website offers free access to online training modules, plus the facility to search the Cochrane Library to locate recent completed examples.

MANAGEMENT

Typical questions

- I want to trace some articles by Peter Drucker.
- What is PRINCE2?

Points to consider

- Management can be both a theoretical and a practical subject. Many internet sites are provided by commercial companies that expect payment. This section guides students to academic resources. It highlights commonly requested items such as management case studies.
- The resources should be used in conjunction with the **Business Studies** section. Refer in particular to the Libraries and Journal Article Indexes sub-sections, as these cover both business and management topics. Those studying Human Resource Management may also find the **Psychology** section (which encompasses Organizational Psychology) helpful.

Where to look

Key organizations

Scholarly

Academy of Management
   www.aomonline.org
   Leading international organization founded in 1936. Free access to current awareness resources, including conference listings and recent issues of newsletters. Full-text articles from Academy journals are for subscribers only.

British Academy of Management
   www.bam.ac.uk
   Supports the academic study of Management. Website has a student section, plus news, conference listings and research updates.

Higher Education Academy
   www.heacademy.ac.uk
   Part of the UK Higher Education Academy supports teaching and learning in Business Management, Accountancy and Finance. Website has useful updates on innovation in management education. It offers free access to the *International Journal of Management Education (IJME)*.

International Federation of Scholarly Associations of Management
www.ifsam.org
News and conference listings relating to the research and teaching of Management studies worldwide.

Professional bodies

American Management Association
www.amanet.org
Major organization offering support, job listings and training. Website has some free case studies and practical articles.

Chartered Institute of Personnel and Development
www.cipd.co.uk
Leading human resources organization. Website provides free access to news, blogs, surveys of human resources professionals and articles on practical management issues. Other online courses and journals offered to subscribers only.

Chartered Management Institute
www.managers.org.uk
Provides training and support for practising managers. Website includes news, events and career guidance. It is also possible to download case studies and research reports, including surveys of managers and assessments of the economy. All topics ranging from human resource management to negotiation and employee relations are covered.

European Management Association
www.europeanmanagement.org
Unites national professional and academic organizations across Europe. Use the website to get news and trace members.

Society for Human Resource Management (SHRM)
www.shrm.org
International association. Website has news, events and careers advice. Case studies available to members.

World Federation of People Management Associations (WFPMA)
www.wfpma.com
Focuses specifically on human resource management. Trace news about global trends and information on national members.

Dictionaries and encyclopedias

Cooper, C. L. (2004) *The Blackwell Encyclopedia of Management*, **2nd edn, Blackwell Publishing**

Available in print or online. Comprehensive 12-volume set covering all aspects of Management, including entrepreneurship, international management and human resource management. Online version has expanded content.

Law, J. (2009) *A Dictionary of Business and Management*, **5th edn, Oxford University Press**

Over 7000 entries covering theories and concepts of all aspects of Business and Management. Companion website has links to recommended internet resources, **www.oup.com/uk/booksites/content/9780199234899**.

Management case studies

Most professional bodies listed in the organizations sub-section offer some free access. However, this is often limited. Internet searches frequently produce commercial resources which require payment. Check local subscriptions first.

British Library Business and Management Portal
www.mbsportal.bl.uk

Search the British Library catalogue, plus associated indexes and websites, to locate books, journals and articles covering all aspects of Business and Management. Increasing numbers (including some case study-based materials) can be downloaded free of charge by registered users. Registration is currently free of charge. Other items can only be accessed by subscribers to the individual e-journal titles. Remind students to check local subscriptions because access may be possible via their institution.

ECCH (European Case Clearing House) (subscription required)
www.ecch.com

Based at Cranfield University. Over 39,000 management case studies for undergraduates and Masters students, plus associated teaching notes. A limited range can be accessed free of charge, other items can be purchased online.

Harvard Business School Case Studies (subscription required)
hbsp.harvard.edu/product/cases

Over 13,000 examples available for both undergraduate and postgraduate use covering a broad range of Business and Management topics. Free access to blogs containing discussion of case study use by academics.

Project management

Association for Project Management

www.apm.org.uk

UK professional association. Website provides free access to news, careers guidance, events listings and some free case studies of good practice.

Best Management Practice

www.best-management-practice.com

Site supported by UK government departments to provide guidance on good practice relating to project, risk and portfolio management. Offers a knowledge centre of articles and papers, many of which can be accessed free of charge.

PRINCE

www.prince-officialsite.com

PRojects IN Controlled Environments (PRINCE) is a common method of project management which has been developed by the British government. The official website offers authoritative information on content, qualifications and courses, plus some free case studies.

Internet gateways and portals

Human Resource Management

www.nbs.ntu.ac.uk/research/depts/hrm/links.php

Extensive directory of links maintained by Nottingham Business School. Includes organizations, news sites, courses and employment.

MAPS

Typical questions

- I need to get maps of current local authority boundaries in London.
- What did Zimbabwe used to be called?

Points to consider

- Increasing numbers of maps (both historical and current) are being digitized. However users should be careful to check dates, scale and coverage before use. Remember that many examples may still exist only in paper, so searches should be made of the large map libraries recommended in this section.
- Copyright can also be a problem. See the **Copyright** section for advice.
- Recommended resources for GIS mapping can be found in the **Geography** section.

Where to look

Map libraries

British Library

www.bl.uk/reshelp/findhelprestype/maps

Extensive national collection of current and historic maps of all regions of the world. Website has many extremely useful guides, including map scales, digital mapping, mapping terminology and a directory of links to free map websites. The **Mapping History** section, www.bl.uk/learning/artimages/maphist/mappinghistory.html, provides free access to an exhibition (with associated classroom activities) that spotlights key resources and introduces students to map research skills.

For a full listing of UK map libraries consult the national directory offered on the **British Cartographic Society** website www.cartography.org.uk/default.asp?contentID=705.

Library of Congress Geography and Map Reading Room

www.loc.gov/rr/geogmap/gmpage.html

Explore the world-famous collections of the Library of Congress. Increasing online exhibitions provide free access to important examples. The *Places in the News* section highlights resources relating to current news stories.

Gazetteers

Often referred to as geographic dictionaries. Use them to find out information about places and place names.

Columbia Gazetteer of the World (subscription required)

www.columbiagazetteer.org

Encyclopedia-style entries on places and regions. These cover demography, geological features, land, area and political and administrative boundaries worldwide.

Gazetteer of British Place Names

www.gazetteer.co.uk

Free access to this extensive list created by the Association of British Counties. Find information on the county, administrative district and map location of specific places. Includes information about historical name changes. Further details can be located on the **Historic Counties Trust** website, **www.historiccountiestrust.co.uk.**

GEOnet Names Server (GNS)

geonames.nga.mil

National Geospatial-Intelligence Agency's (NGA) and US Board on Geographic Names' (US BGN) database. Gives approved names of places, map co-ordinates and, in many cases, links to Google maps of the area.

Online maps

UK maps

Digimap (subscription required)

edina.ac.uk/digimap

Service hosted by Edina for the UK higher education community. Provides access to current and historical collections. These include Ordnance Survey products, postcode and administrative boundaries. The historical collections include Landmark historic data (county series maps 1843–1939; town plans 1848–1939 and National Grid maps published before 1945).

Ordnance Survey

www.ordnancesurvey.co.uk

Britain's national mapping agency. Website provides information on its role and products. It includes a section on support for higher education and some free access to maps (including current administrative districts and some annotated with notes on landmarks and routes by the community) on its **OpenData** website, **www.ordnancesurvey.co.uk/oswebsite/products/os-opendata.html.** Note that many UK academic libraries subscribe to

Ordnance Survey products via databases such as those offered by Edina, so check local access. Also available is the separate **Election Maps** website, **www.election-maps.co.uk/index.jsp**, which has maps of constituency and local authority boundaries.

Royal Mail Online Postcode Finder
postcode.royalmail.com

National service for locating the postcode of specific addresses. Currently offered free for personal use only, with restrictions on the number of searches per day.

The National Archives
www.nationalarchives.gov.uk/maps

Extensive collections of historical materials relating to the UK and overseas. Collection strongest from the 17th to 20th centuries. Website has a detailed guide to holdings.

United States maps

National Atlas
www.nationalatlas.gov

Registered site of the US Department of the Interior. Provides free access to an excellent collection of maps of the USA. These include: congressional districts, time zones, Native American reservations, presidential election results. Includes a section of raw data for serious researchers!

United States Geological Survey
www.usgs.gov/pubprod

Website provides information on products, plus free access to online maps and images of the USA and other world regions. Links are provided to many major map websites and mapping resources.

US Census Bureau Maps
www.census.gov/geo/www/maps

Official site of the US government. Includes recent printable maps of congressional districts and other administrative boundaries, plus historical mappings of population distribution taken from American censuses.

World maps

Google Earth
www.google.com/earth/index.html

Free service offered by Google. Includes street-view imagery and some 3D and historical maps. Read the help screens and tutorials to understand the content and use it effectively.

MAPS

National Geographic

maps.nationalgeographic.com/maps

Website offers free access to a selection of different types of maps and mapping activities. Note that in some cases more recent versions of maps are available for purchase only.

Perry-Castañeda Library Map Collection

www.lib.utexas.edu/maps

Based at the University of Texas. World-famous collection which provides free access to thousands of online maps of different regions of the world (both current and historical), including maps produced by the US Central Intelligence Agency.

United Nations Cartographic Section

www.un.org/Depts/Cartographic/english/htmain.htm

Free access to maps of the world supplied by the UN. Includes some thematic maps of UN peace-keeping missions and world events. Check when individual maps were updated.

UNOSAT

www.unitar.org/unosat

Get free access to some recent satellite maps supplied by United Nations agencies. Main emphasis on mapping recent conflict/disaster zones.

Historical maps

Good starting-points for tracing the existence of historical maps in print or online are national archives and/or national libraries, including those listed in the sections above. UK academic libraries may also have access to subscription services via the Edina Digimap service described above. Other recommended sources are the following.

David Rumsey Maps

www.davidrumsey.com

Free access to over over 26,000 maps. Coverage strongest in terms of 18th- and 19th-century North and South American maps, although other areas of the world are also well represented.

Europeana

www.europeana.eu

Indexes major collections from libraries in Europe, including the national libraries, so offers the facility for a broader search. The advanced search option allows searches to be limited by resource type.

MARKET RESEARCH

Typical questions

- What is the market share of frozen foods in the UK?
- I need statistics on market trends in pharmaceuticals for the last five years.

Points to consider

- Students often need market research studies to obtain data on trends and projections for specific industries. They are also useful insights into consumer lifestyles. However, tracing them can sometimes be difficult. Incomplete references are often given by media coverage. It is good practice to remind students to refer to the original survey and to evaluate the sample size and methodology used.
- Access can be another problem. Internet searches often retrieve items for sale at exorbitant prices! Visitors to academic libraries may be unable to use online reports, due to strict licensing conditions. If items are unavailable locally, refer students to the libraries listed in the **Business Studies** section, which all have excellent specialist public collections. The databases listed in that section also provide financial data on markets. Students interested in social attitudes should also refer to the **Opinion Polls** section. Those seeking advice on how to conduct market research studies should consult the **Social Research Methods** section.

Where to look

Key organizations

ESOMAR

> www.esomar.org
> International industry body. Use the websites to consult codes of practice and search its online directory of market research organizations worldwide.

Market Research Society

> www.mrs.org.uk
> UK-based professional association. Website has an introductory guide to understanding the nature and techniques of market research. It also has a news section with information on recent trends.

Databases

Euromonitor (subscription required)

> www.euromonitor.com

Offers a range of databases which specialize in combining intelligence reports (about markets, companies and countries) with macroeconomic data analysis that provides contextual background.

Key Note
www.keynote.co.uk

Market intelligence, assessments and reports covering all areas of UK industry. Some free executive summaries available from the website.

Mintel (subscription required)
www.mintel.com

Well known supplier of market intelligence. Offers a range of products covering consumer and market intelligence on a global scale.

MARKETING

Typical questions

- I want to search for articles on direct marketing
- Are there any websites that provide access to advertising campaign materials?

Points to consider

- Marketing is a rapidly evolving field because it develops to take account of new technologies. Space limitations mean that this section cannot cover all resources. Explore the major organizations' websites to find specialist sub-groups.
- Use the resources in conjunction with the **Business Studies** section. Those listed in the Libraries and Journal Article sub-sections cover both subjects. Students may also find the **Market Research** section useful.

Where to look

Key organizations

Use these websites to trace news, events, careers and training advice.

American Marketing Association (AMA)
www.marketingpower.com
Worth checking this site for its extensive resource directory containing online dictionary, articles, webcasts and market research directory.

Chartered Institute of Marketing (CIM)
www.cim.co.uk
UK professional organization. Website is a rich source of information. Get online articles, case studies and links to key organizations. Use the learning zone site to read CIM syllabi, past papers and study guides. All topics are covered, from planning to market research.

European Marketing Academy (EMAC)
www.emac-online.org
Focuses on marketing education and research. Get news about teaching and learning initiatives.

European Marketing Confederation
www.emc.be
Pan European federation. Get information on Europe-wide trends.

MARKETING

Marketing Society
www.marketing-society.org.uk
British professional association. Access online videos of past lectures. Many with famous businessmen/women!

Libraries

Chartered Institute of Marketing Information and Library Service
www.cim.co.uk/resources/libraryservices/libraryservices.aspx
Specialist library open to non-members. Website offers free access to detailed research guides with reading lists covering specific topics such as branding, marketing plans and market segmentation.

Dictionaries

AMA Dictionary

www.marketingpower.com/_layouts/Dictionary.aspx
American Marketing Association free online dictionary. Up to date with the latest terms.

Harris, P. (2009) *Penguin Dictionary of Marketing*, **Penguin**
Designed for student use. Covers international marketing terms.

News services

Use these to locate news, market trends and job listings from marketing professionals.

Ad Week
www.adweek.com
Covers weekly trends in advertising and branding. American focus.

Marketer
www.themarketer.co.uk
Official magazine of the Chartered Institute of Marketing. Many articles are for subscribers only.

Marketing Week
www.marketingweek.co.uk
UK based. Includes blogs, special reports and a resource library of factsheets on improving marketing skills.

Digital libraries

Ad*Access

> **scriptorium.lib.duke.edu/adaccess**
>
> Free access to information and fascinating images from 7000 advertisements printed in North American media between 1911 and 1955. Main subject areas are TV, transport, beauty and hygiene, and World War II.

Creative Club (subscription required)

> **www.creativeclub.co.uk**
>
> Large archive of UK ads from 1997 onwards. Includes spending data. Search by company or sector.

Statistical data

Use with the databases in the **Business Studies** section!

Expenditure Report from the Advertising Association and Warc (subscription required)

> **expenditurereport.warc.com**
>
> UK ad expenditure data from 1982 onwards with forward projections. Covers cinema, radio and TV advertising. Some free summaries on the website.

MATHEMATICS

Typical questions

- Are there any websites where I can download recent Maths working papers?
- Where can I find articles on discrete algorithms?

Points to consider

- Many examples of scholarly Maths publications are published in preprint or working papers series. Students conducting literature searches are recommended to use the resources in the **Journal Article Indexes** and **Working Papers** sections. Many of the latter are now free online!

Where to look

Key organizations

Use these to locate forthcoming conferences, links to key journals and new publications, plus lists of specialist sub-groups (which often conduct cutting-edge research).

American Mathematical Society (AMS)

> www.ams.org
>
> Founded in 1888, and covering all branches of Mathematics, the AMS website has resources for students, indexes of journal articles and conference listings.

International Mathematical Union (IMU)

> www.mathunion.org
>
> International organization which seeks to promote co-operation in Mathematics scholarship. Its website is a good starting-point for tracing names, addresses and websites of key national Maths organizations worldwide.

London Mathematical Society (LMS)

> www.lms.ac.uk
>
> Established in 1865, its website has advice on Mathematics education, career opportunities, plus free access to the LMS newsletter and information about its library and archives.

Society for Industrial and Applied Mathematics (SIAM)

> www.siam.org
>
> Leading organization in the field of applied Maths. Website provides free access to many recent conference papers.

Dictionaries

Clapham, C. and Nicholson, J. (2009) *Concise Oxford Dictionary of Mathematics*, 4th edn, Oxford University Press
Useful for students, covers commonly encountered concepts and terms.

Hazewinkel, M. (ed.) (2002) *Encyclopedia of Mathematics*, Springer
eom.springer.de
Authoritative reference source with over 7000 articles. Available in print or online. Use it to check the precise names of concepts and theorems, find out about the applications of a specific concept and get bibliographies of references.

Journal article indexes

MathSciNet (subscription required)
www.ams.org/mathscinet
Essential tool produced by the American Mathematical Association. Covers Maths reviews from 1940 onwards.

Zentralblatt MATH
www.zentralblatt-math.org/zbmath
Free site edited by the European Mathematical Society, Fachinformationszentrum Karlsruhe and Heidelberger Akademie der Wissenschaften. References (and some full-text links) to articles published since 1848.

Working papers

arXiv
arxiv.org
Maintained by Cornell University. This great site provides free access to over 500,000 e-prints in Mathematics, Quantitative Finance, Statistics and other scientific disciplines.

Internet gateways and portals

Digital Mathematics Library
www.mathematik.uni-bielefeld.de/~rehmann/DML/dml_new.html
Maintained by Ulf Rehmann, Fakultät für Mathematik, Universität Bielefeld, Germany. Links to thousands of full-text journals and books. Specializes in listing historical works.

European Mathematical Information Service (EMIS)
www.emis.de
Supported by the European Mathematical Society. Offers free access to

MATHEMATICS

ELibM – Electronic Library of Mathematics, an enormous repository of full-text Maths e-books, journals and papers. Other features include free access to major indexes of Maths literature and news from mathematical organizations.

TechXtra
www.techxtra.ac.uk

Specialist search engine for Engineering, Mathematics and Computing created by Heriot Watt University. Quickly find academic working papers, news, technical reports and announcements. Many have links to full text.

MEDIA STUDIES

Typical questions

- Where can I find information on the theories of Marshall McLuhan?
- I want to search for articles about women in Bollywood films.

Points to consider

- Media studies can be a very broad area, encompassing the media industry (**Business Studies**); media regulation (**Law**), popular culture (**Sociology** of the media), studies of new media (**Computer Science**) and/or film studies. Try to identify the focus of interest and refer to the appropriate area of this book where needed.
- Other common queries from media students include tracing **Newspapers**, **Images** and **Films**. These are also covered in separate sections.

Where to look

Key organizations

Academic research

International Communication Association (ICA)

   www.icahdq.org

   Leading international scholarly association covering all aspects of human and computer-mediated communication. Website is an excellent starting-point for tracing research news, conference listings, specialist research groups and links to national communication associations worldwide.

MeCCSA

   www.meccsa.org.uk

   Subject association for the field of Media, Communication and Cultural Studies in UK higher education. Website provides details about conferences, recent research and publications.

Royal Television Society

   www.rts.org.uk

   Leading forum for debate on all aspects of TV in the UK. Website has details of awards and lectures.

Society for Cinema and Media Studies

   www.cmstudies.org

   Leading society for academic study of film, TV, radio and digital media. Has listing of conferences, publication and on-going research.

Trade organizations

UK

Community Media Association

www.commedia.org.uk

Covers local radio and TV. Website includes news, membership lists and links to key research publications.

National Union of Journalists (NUJ)

www.nuj.org.uk

Website has information on training and news about developments in the profession.

Press Association

www.pressassociation.com

National news agency. Website includes trade news, useful contacts for journalism training, links to news providers and breaking headlines.

International

European Broadcasting Union

www.ebu.ch

Association of national broadcasters in Europe. Its website offers news, events listings and free publications. Links are provided to national member websites.

International Federation of Journalists

www.ifj.org

World's largest organization of journalists. Find membership lists, information about journalism and human rights, and news.

World Broadcasting Unions

www.worldbroadcastingunions.org

Body which co-ordinates the work of regional broadcasting unions. Members include the European Broadcasting Union (EBU), the International Association of Broadcasting (IAB/AIR), the North American Broadcasters Association (NABA). Website is a good starting-point for keeping up to date with developments in technology, regulation and policy.

Media regulators

These websites cover issues relating to media law and licensing.

European Union Audiovisual Portal

ec.europa.eu/avpolicy/info_centre/index_en.htm

Provides free access to information about EU policy, legal documents, law reports and research studies on media policies in EU nations.

ITU (International Telecommunications Union)
www.itu.int/ITU-D/treg/index.html
United Nations agency for information and communication technology issues. Its website has a large section on radio, TV and telecommunications regulation and standardization issues.

Ofcom
www.ofcom.org.uk
Independent regulator and competition authority for the UK communications industries, with responsibilities across TV, radio, telecommunications and wireless communication services. Its website includes a large section of research reports.

Libraries

BFI National Library
www.bfi.org.uk/filmtvinfo/library
World's largest specialist collection of moving image books and journals. Covers both film and TV. Also contains UK national film archive. Fee based. Website has guidance on research.

British Library Business and IP Centre
www.bl.uk/bipc
Extremely useful for media industry resources. Website has an industry research guide.

Media Studies at UC Berkeley
www.lib.berkeley.edu/doemoff/mediastudies
Site includes bibliographies and research guides created by library staff.

Dictionaries and encyclopedias

Chandler, D. and Munday, R. (2011) *A Dictionary of Media and Communication*, **Oxford University Press**
Definitions of over 2000 commonly used terms. Covers terminology, concepts and theories from a wide range of subject areas, including media culture, journalism, new media, radio studies and telecommunications. References are made to key websites.

International Encyclopedia of Communication Online (subscription required)

www.communicationencyclopedia.com

Published in association with the International Communication Association. Available in print or online. Over 1300 essays covering theories, concepts and scholarship covering all areas of Media and Communication Studies.

Journal article indexes

Communication Abstracts (subscription required)

www.ebscohost.com/academic/communication-abstracts

Covers all aspects of Media and Communication Studies, including advertising, broadcasting, journalism and the role of technology in communication. Coverage from 1977 onwards.

IZI-Datenbank.de

www.izi-datenbank.de

Excellent free resource maintained by the International Central Institute for Youth and Educational Television (IZI), Germany. Provides free access to over 20,000 references to articles, books and reports relating to all aspects of children's TV and children's use of the internet. Particularly strong coverage of German-language materials, although English-language materials are also widely indexed.

NCOM: Nordic Media Research

www.nordicom.gu.se

Site maintained by NORDICOM, which disseminates media research from Nordic nations (chiefly Denmark, Finland, Iceland, Norway and Sweden). Find references to articles from approximately 1975 onwards.

News services

These are trade newspapers for the media industry.

Columbia Journalism Review

www.cjr.org

Website associated with the leading academic title is updated frequently with news, blog postings, discussion and analysis on the changing nature of the profession.

Media Week

www.mediaweek.co.uk

Breaking news, jobs and analysis for media professionals. Covers cinema, radio, TV, digital and local media. Some features of the site offered to subscribers only.

Press Gazette
www.pressgazette.co.uk

Jobs and journalism industry news for journalists. UK focus. Some magazine content and archives are offered to subscribers only.

Statistical data

The sites listed below offer some free statistics which are of relevance to media researchers. Note, however, that full access often requires a subscription. Users may also find the resources listed in the **Business Studies** section useful.

ABC (Audit Bureau of Circulations)
www.abc.org.uk

Measures circulation figures for UK newspapers and magazines.

BARB (Broadcasters' Audience Research Board)
www.barb.co.uk

Organization responsible for providing the official measurement of UK TV audiences.

ITU
www.itu.int/ITU-D/ict

Publishes *World Telecommunication/ICT Indicators Database* (containing access and tariff data) and other statistics on internet use and mobile phone access.

OECD
www.oecd.org/sti/telecom/outlook

Publishes a range of titles, including *Communications Outlook*. This contains annual data on the performance of the communications sector in OECD countries.

Trade directories

Benn's Media Guide
www.wlrstore.com/benns/index.aspx

Online or in print. Long established annual trade directory. Covers publishing, newspapers, TV and radio stations and online media. Gives profiles, circulation figures and contacts. Several editions are published. *UK Media Guide*, *Benn's Media Guide Europe* and *Benn's Media Guide World*.

MEDIA STUDIES

UK Media Yearbook, Zenithoptimedia
Annual compendium covers national and regional newspapers, TV, digital media, magazines and cinema. Each section has an overview of market trends, key owners and basic statistics.

Willings Press Guide
www.willingspress.com
Online or in print. Long established guide. Brief profiles and contacts listings of local and national press publishers. Brief profiles of individual titles. Coverage worldwide.

Internet gateways and portals

Explore these sites to find links to academic-quality media websites.

International Clearinghouse on Children, Youth and Media
www.nordicom.gu.se/clearinghouse.php
Hosted by NORDICOM. Links to new publications, organizations and databases.

MCS
www.aber.ac.uk/media
Award-winning guide to internet-based media resources, hosted by the University of Wales, Aberystwyth. Covers a range of topics, including IT and telecoms, textual analysis, media industry and more.

Film studies

American Film Institute
www.afi.com
Leading institute promoting film education. Website has training events, news and a searchable catalogue of American films. Some features offered to subscribers only.

British Film Institute
www.bfi.org.uk
Key organization promoting film and TV heritage and culture. Website has events calendars, a database of film listings/reviews and a searchable *Moving Image Research Registry*, which contains details of recent and on-going work.

International Federation of Film Archives (FIAF)
www.fiafnet.org
Association of the world's leading film archives. Details of conferences,

training and national projects. Produces the *International Index to Film Periodicals* (subscription required), covering articles published since 1972.

Television programmes

- Many students require access to recordings of TV programmes. Most UK universities have a licence to make off-air recordings. For advice on copyright, see the separate **Copyright** section.
- Older materials can be difficult to trace and access if not held locally. Useful starting-points include the following.

Box of Broadcasts (subscription required)
bobnational.net
Off-air recording and media archive service. Users can record programmes, watch programmes from the archive, create clips and search for programmes.

British Universities Film and Video Council (BUFVC)
bufvc.ac.uk
Supports UK higher education use of moving images. Offers a specialist advice service and back-up TV recording service.

Television and Radio Index for Learning and Teaching (TRILT)
(subscription required)
bufvc.ac.uk/tvandradio/trilt
Useful for tracing the existence and transmission dates of TV programmes. Covers over 300 TV and radio channels from 1995 onwards. It is also possible to set up alerts for forthcoming programmes.

MEDICINE AND NURSING

Typical questions
- Where can I find recent articles on HIV prevention programmes?
- I need information on clinical trials of anti-malarial drugs.
- Does the NHS have any guidelines on treatment for obesity?

Points to consider
- It is essential that all medical researchers obtain access to high-quality current information. This frequently needs to be evidence based. This section highlights useful subscription and free databases. It has specialist sub-sections on nursing and health policy information. However, users should be reminded of the need to check when resources were last updated!

Where to look

Key organizations

Professional bodies

Use these to locate news, professional development resources and careers advice for students. They are also useful starting-points for tracing comment (sometimes critical!) on government health policy.

UK

British Medical Association
>**www.bma.org.uk**
>Represents British doctors. Use the website to search the **BMA Library catalogue, www.bma.org.uk/library_services/index.jsp** and find information on the latest activities.

General Medical Council (GMC)
>**www.gmc-uk.org**
>Regulatory body. Consult the online register of approved doctors, plus advice on standards and ethics.

Higher Education Academy
>**www.heacademy.ac.uk**
>Supports teaching and learning in UK higher education. Subject coverage includes Medicine, Dentistry and Veterinary Medicine. Website lists events and highlights curriculum innovation.

Royal College of Physicians
www.rcplondon.ac.uk

Royal College of Surgeons of England
www.rcseng.ac.uk
Website highlights news, courses and online resources relating to surgical practice. It includes access to the catalogue of its specialist library.

Royal Society of Medicine
www.rsm.ac.uk
Independent membership organization which is a leading supplier of continuing professional development training for the medical profession. Use its website to get access to news, events listings and webcasts of recent lectures. It also includes details about its renowned postgraduate biomedical library. Other features include resources (news, articles and training) relating to global public health and useful directories of links to recommended health websites.

International

American Medical Association
www.ama-assn.org
Includes some free access to blogs, careers information and news/articles from *JAMA* – its leading weekly general medical journal.

Association for Medical Education in Europe
www.amee.org
Find information on medical education in over 90 countries. Website has a directory of links to medical students' associations worldwide.

European Union of General Practitioners (UEMO)
www.uemo.eu
Represents GPs in European nations. Website has links to national bodies.

World Medical Council
www.wma.net
Represents physicians worldwide. Website is useful for tracing contacts for national medical associations. It also contains documents relating to medical ethics.

Government bodies

These websites have news and policy documents. See also the statistical data sub-section below for key international bodies covering healthcare.

Note that the names and responsibilities of government bodies and agencies can change – the **Government Publications** section has further advice.

Department of Health
www.dh.gov.uk

Main UK government body. Its website is complex in structure, providing information on its main specialisms and associated sub-agencies. Online publications include circulars, reports and statistics. There is a separate **NHS** website, **www.nhs.uk/Pages/Homepage.aspx**, which provides information to the public on using and locating the services of the National Health Service.

NHS Information Centre
www.ic.nhs.uk

This is a more specialist website designed for practitioners and researchers, and has a large statistics section.

Research organizations

Medical Research Council
www.mrc.ac.uk

Central starting-point for finding information and news about on-going research in the UK. It also offers guidance on obtaining funding.

National Institute for Health and Clinical Excellence (NICE)
www.nice.org.uk

Makes recommendations and provides guidelines to the NHS on medicines and medical treatments. A key starting-point for locating evidence-based research.

National Institutes of Health
www.nih.gov

Find information on medical research projects, grants, funding and on-going clinical trials from the USA's leading organizations.

Libraries

Use these websites to locate books and journals. They also offer helpful research guides!

British Library
www.bl.uk/reshelp/findhelpsubject/scitectenv/medicinehealth/ healthcareinformation/healthcareinfo.html

Comprehensive medical collection, including complementary and allied healthcare and the pharmaceutical industry.

Wellcome Library

library.wellcome.ac.uk/collections.html

London-based specialist library which is open to the public. Renowned collection of medical history materials, plus contemporary printed and electronic resources. The website provides free access to:

- **Wellcome Images** collection, **images.wellcome.ac.uk**. Thousands of images and photographs (many historical) covering all aspects of clinical and biomedical sciences – ranging from diseases to tattoos!
- **Wellcome Film** collection, **library.wellcome.ac.uk/wellcomefilm.htm**. Over 450 examples of historical health-related films, including early examples of UK public health information films on subjects such as immunization and smoking.

Health Libraries Group

www.cilip.org.uk/get-involved/special-interest-groups/health/pages/alpha.aspx

Special-interest group of the Chartered Institute of Library and Information Professionals. Provides support and training on issues relating to medical and health librarianship. Website includes links to other professional organizations. Helps to maintain **HLISD** (Health Libraries and Information Services Directory), **www.hlisd.org**, which provides over 800 links to key libraries in the UK and Ireland.

National Library of Medicine

www.nlm.nih.gov

World's largest medical library. Its extensive website is worth exploring in detail. It offers free access to its catalogues, databases for locating recent medical literature and images from the History of Medicine collection. It includes links to the US network of Medical Libraries.

Dictionaries and encyclopedias

British National Formulary

bnf.org

Published twice annually by the British Medical Association and the Royal Pharmaceutical Society. Available in print or online (subscription required). Leading medical and pharmaceutical reference book for healthcare professionals containing information on the pharmacology of drugs, along with prescription advice. It also offers details about all medicines available on the National Health Service.

Embase (subscription required)
www.embase.com

Leading biomedical and pharmacological database. Indexes thousands of articles and evidence-based reviews. Dates of coverage differ according to subscription, but back-files often offered from 1947 onwards. Coverage includes medicine and pharmaceutical properties of drugs. Main emphasis on European sources.

History of Science, Technology and Medicine (HistSciTechMed) (subscription required)
www.oclc.org/support/documentation/firstsearch/databases/dbdetails/ details/HistSciTechMed.htm

Indexes over 9000 journal titles, plus conference proceedings and books, covering all aspects of medical history. Coverage from 1975 onwards.

Marcovitch, H. (ed.) (2009) *Blacks Medical Dictionary*, 42nd edn, A & C Black

World-famous dictionary first published in 1906, which covers medical terms, concepts and abbreviations. Includes appendices of medical measurements, tests, and lists of professional organizations.

Medpedia
www.medpedia.com

On-going collaborative project being created in association with Harvard Medical School, Stanford School of Medicine and other leading health organizations. It is compiling a searchable medical encyclopedia of terms, concepts and treatments. All contributions are peer reviewed.

Journal article indexes/Digital libraries

MEDLINE
www.nlm.nih.gov/databases/databases_medline.html

Premier database produced by the National Library of Medicine. Provides extensive coverage of all forms of Medicine, Healthcare, Dentistry, Veterinary Sciences and Biomedicine from 1946 onwards. Available via a number of subscription databases. Also offered in a free online version called **PubMed, www.ncbi.nlm.nih.gov/pubmed**. This includes references to in-press articles and links to online versions (where available). Guidance on differences in coverage between the free and subscription services, as well as advice on effective searching can be found at **www.nlm.nih.gov/ pubs/factsheets/dif_med_pub.html**. The databases are renowned for the quality of their controlled vocabulary and Medical Subject Headings

(MeSH®). It is worth consulting the online thesaurus to obtain guidance on construction, broadening and narrowing of search terms. The **NLM** also supports a gateway search facility, **gateway.nlm.nih.gov**. This enables users to quickly cross-search PubMed with a number of other medical databases. These include the *NLM Library catalogue*; *ClinicalTrials.gov* (information from the US government about clinical trials); *Hazardous Substances Data Bank*; *TOXLINE* (toxicology citations).

POPLINE
www.popline.org
Free access to the world's largest citation database covering all aspects of population, fertility, family planning and health-related issues. Maintained by the Johns Hopkins Bloomberg School of Public Health and funded by the United States Agency for International Development (USAID). Indexes books, journal articles and reports. Coverage from 1973 onwards.

PubMed Central (PMC)
www.ncbi.nlm.nih.gov/pmc
Free open access archive of hundreds of full-text life sciences and medical journals which is maintained by the US National Library of Medicine.

UK PubMed Central
ukpmc.ac.uk
British equivalent of PubMed Central. It includes PubMed articles, plus references to UK biomedical theses, research grant outputs and NHS clinical guidelines.

Alternative health

AMED: Allied and Complementary Medicine (subscription required)
www.ovid.com/site/catalog/DataBase/12.jsp
Created by the Health Care Information Service of the British Library. Indexes journals covering occupational therapy, physiotherapy and all forms of complementary and alternative medicine. Coverage from 1985 onwards. Main emphasis on English-language materials.

National Center for Complementary and Alternative Medicine
nccam.nih.gov
Maintained by the US National Institutes of Health. Offers free access to evidence-based research, Cochrane systematic reviews, clinical trials from *PubMed*, patient sheets and clinical guidance for practitioners.

Evidence-based practice

Cochrane Library

www.thecochranelibrary.com

Free access to several leading databases:

- *Cochrane Database of Systematic Reviews*. Key resource for practitioners of evidence-based medicine because it contains comprehensive literature reviews of clinical trials, treatments and health systems interventions.
- *Database of Abstracts of Reviews of Effects (DARE)*. Assesses the conduct and quality of systematic reviews.
- *Cochrane Central Register of Controlled Trials (CENTRAL)*.
- *Health Technology Assessment (HTA) Database* and the *NHS Economic Evaluation Database*. Produced by the Centre for Reviews and Dissemination (CRD) at the University of York. Contains assessments of the health outcomes and cost-effectiveness of particular technologies and techniques used in healthcare.

NHS Evidence

www.library.nhs.uk/default.aspx

Maintained by the National Institute for Health and Clinical Excellence (NICE). Formerly known as the National Library for Health. Excellent one-stop shop for cross-searching and accessing clinical and non-clinical information about UK health and social care. It contains many full-text items such as systematic reviews (including the Cochrane Library), NHS and NICE guidelines and articles. Also available are medical images and a directory of links to accredited health information sites for patients. Note that some items are restricted to NHS staff.

TRIP (Turning Research Into Practice) Database

www.tripdatabase.com

Free service enabling rapid cross-searching of around 150 resources containing high-quality evidence-based health information. They include the Cochrane Library, *PubMed Clinical Queries* and journals such as *Evidence-Based Medicine*.

News services

Keeping up to date is crucial for medical students. Recommend the resources in the **Current Awareness Tools** section for setting up tables of contents alerts and check the websites of the main professional organizations.

British Medical Journal

www.bmj.com

Leading journal of the British Medical Association. Some research articles and news freely available.

Grey Literature Report

www.nyam.org/library/online-resources/grey-literature-report

Bimonthly publication of the New York Academy of Medicine Library. Alerts researchers to new grey literature publications (reports from think-tanks, working papers and conferences) in health services research and selected public health topics. Some North American bias. Available free from website.

Lancet

www.thelancet.com

World's leading general medical journal. Website provides free access to some online articles, jobs listings and blogs. Some services offered to subscribers only.

Statistical data

UK

Department of Health

www.dh.gov.uk/en/Publicationsandstatistics/Statistics/index.htm

Website contains reports and data on UK health policy. It includes performance data on National Health Service waiting lists.

NHS Information Centre

www.ic.nhs.uk

Also has information and statistics relating to services. Includes performance and National Health Service workforce data.

Office for National Statistics

www.statistics.gov.uk

Key starting-point. A major series is *Health Statistics Quarterly*. This covers births, conceptions, abortions and mortality. Some online data available from 1970s onwards. For earlier resources see the libraries sub-section.

United States

National Center for Health Statistics

www.cdc.gov/nchs

Official data from government resources covering all topics.

International

OECD Health

www.oecd.org/health

Statistics on health and healthcare in OECD countries. Topics covered include health expenditure, the state of health in individual nations and available health resources. Some data offered to subscribers only.

Pan-American Health Organization (PAHO)

www.paho.org

Regional body of the World Health Organization. Website has data for Latin, Central and South America covering a variety of indicators.

UNAIDS

www.unaids.org/en

Specialist body of the United Nations. Publishes an annual report and regular epidemiology updates.

WHO Europe

www.euro.who.int/en/what-we-do/data-and-evidence/databases

Provides free access to statistics on health in Europe. It includes the *European Hospital Morbidity Database* and mortality data.

World Health Organization (WHO)

www.who.int/gho

Maintains a Global Health Observatory offering free access to reports and data covering health and healthcare worldwide. It includes the annual *World Health Report*, reports on child and maternal health and health risks. Also accessible is the *WHO Bibliographic Database (WHOLIS)*, which is the library catalogue of the WHO library.

Health policy

Use these resources to supplement those listed above. Pay particular attention to the key government organizations and professional bodies. Note that the resources listed in the **Journal Article Indexes** and the **Social Welfare and Social Work** sections are also relevant.

UK

Health Management Information Consortium (HMIC) Database (subscription required)

library.nhs.uk/help/resource/hmic

Combines data from the King's Fund Information and Library Service and the Department of Health's Library and Information Services database (references to official publications, grey literature mainly from 1983 onwards). Focuses on UK healthcare delivery, policy and administration.

The King's Fund
www.kingsfund.org.uk
Leading charity which focuses on understanding and reforming the UK health system. Its website contains news, comment and free research reports covering a wide range of topics, from NHS funding, to end-of-life care, health service governance, health inequalities and workforce management. It also provides information on its specialist library, **www.kingsfund.org.uk/library/index.html**, which is open to the public. The library website offers free access to the library database, which has thousands of references to books, journal articles, grey literature and government reports. Main emphasis on the UK and items published since 1979.

International

European Observatory on Health Systems and Policies
www.euro.who.int/en/home/projects/observatory
Collaboration between WHO-Europe and leading academic institutions, including UNCAM (French National Union of Health Insurance Funds) and the London School of Economics. Website has profiles, statistics and analyses of health services in European nations. It also offers free access to news and working papers.

World Health Organization
www.who.int
Website has reports and data on health systems and workforces worldwide. In addition, it maintains a useful directory of links to the websites of national health ministries and statistical offices, **apps.who.int/whosis/database/national_sites/index.cfm**.

Nursing

Use these to supplement the general resources listed above!

British Nursing Index (subscription required)
www.bniplus.co.uk
Compiled by libraries of Bournemouth University, Poole Hospital NHS Foundation Trust, Royal College of Nursing, Salisbury NHS Foundation Trust. Indexes 240 British nursing and midwifery journals. Coverage from 1985 onwards.

CINAHL (subscription required)
www.ebscohost.com/cinahl

Well established nursing and allied health professions database. Indexes articles, case studies, reports and clinical trial results covering all aspects of healthcare from 1937 to the present.

Global Network of WHO Collaborating Centres (WHOCCs) for Nursing and Midwifery Development
www.parlatore.com.br/whocc

International Council of Nurses
www.icn.ch

Global network seeking to promote standards and co-operation. Website has a useful directory of national members.

Royal College of Midwives (UK)
www.rcm.org.uk

Professional organization and trade union. Website includes news and careers information. It includes free access to its research database of current and completed midwifery projects.

Royal College of Nursing
www.rcn.org.uk

Largest professional association and trade union representing nurses and nursing students in the UK. Website has news, conference listings and extensive careers and professional development resources relating to general nursing and special interest nursing groups. The **RCN Library**, **www.rcn.org.uk/development/library**, has a specialist collection of books, journals and theses relating to nursing research and practice. Its catalogue can be searched online and the web pages also offer links to recommended internet resources. Online access to databases is for members only.

MUSIC

Typical questions

- I want to research the life of Beethoven.
- I need to locate articles on the role of music in Soviet Russia.
- Can you recommend some good classical music websites.

Points to consider

- Most students have used music downloading websites such as iTunes, but they may be unfamiliar with academic resources. This section offers a series of good starting-points which can be explored to find more specialist resources on specific instruments, time periods and genres. Information about musicians can also be found using the **Biographical Information** section.

Where to look

Key organizations

Use the websites of these scholarly societies to trace news, careers advice, events listings and specialist research groups.

American Musicological Society

www.ams-net.org

Influential organization with international membership. Website provides free access to *Doctoral Dissertations in Musicology (DDM)*, an international database of references to theses in Music, Music Theory and Ethnomusicology. It also has an extensive directory of links to specialist music websites.

International Musicological Society (IMS)

www.ims-online.ch

Member of the Conseil International de la Philosophie et des Sciences Humaines (CIPSH). Website has an excellent directory of links to national music societies worldwide.

Royal Musical Association

www.rma.ac.uk

Founded in 1834. Supports many conferences and study days.

Libraries and archives

Use these websites to locate books and journals. They also provide handy research guides and links to key websites.

British Library Music collections
www.bl.uk/reshelp/bldept/music/index.html
World-famous collection of printed music, manuscripts and sound recordings. Website has a concert programme database.

Royal College of Music Library
www.rcm.ac.uk/RCMLibrary
Extensive collections of manuscripts, orchestral sets, books and journals dating from the 16th century to the present.
To trace other library collections try the following.

Cecilia
www.cecilia-uk.org
Searchable database of music collections held in UK libraries, museums and archives.

International Association of Music Libraries, Archives and Documentation Centres
www.iaml.info
Get information and links to the websites of major music libraries worldwide. Also provides free access to *Recent Publications in Music* – an annual bibliography listing major new books and reference works. The UK branch has its own website, **www.iaml.info/iaml-uk-irl/index.html**.

RISM: Music Manuscripts after 1600 in British and Irish Libraries
www.rism.org.uk

Dictionaries and encyclopedias

Oxford Music Online (subscription required)
www.oxfordmusiconline.com
Cross-search the content of a number of leading reference sources, including: *Oxford Companion to Music*, *Grove Music* and *Encyclopedia of Popular Music* to find articles, definitions and biographies.

Sadie, S. and Tyrrel, J. (2003) *New Grove Dictionary of Music and Musicians*, 2nd edn, Oxford University Press
Twenty-nine-volume set available in print or online (to subscribers). Regarded as a classic source on music theory, instruments, musicians and musical genres.

Journal article indexes

International Index to Music Periodicals (IIMP) (subscription required)
iimp.chadwyck.com/home.do
Indexes over 470 international scholarly and popular music journals. Covers all genres. Most items published since 1996.

RILM Abstracts of Music Literature (subscription required)
www.rilm.org
Répertoire International de Littérature Musicale. Comprehensive bibliography of books, chapters, articles and reports covering all aspects of Music. Coverage from 1967 onwards.

Music recordings

British Library Archival Sound Recordings (subscription required)
sounds.bl.uk
Widely available to UK higher education. Includes extensive collections of classical music, world music and jazz.

Naxos Music Library (subscription required)
www.naxosmusiclibrary.com
Comprehensive collection over 750,000 tracks covering classical music, jazz, pop and world music.

NEWSPAPERS

Typical questions
- Can I get copies of *The Times* newspaper from the 1950s online?
- I want to research contemporary news coverage of the 1930s economic crash.

Points to consider
- Newspapers are valuable both for coverage of the most recent events and for offering insight into social, political and economic history.
- Most libraries subscribe to large newspaper databases containing hundreds of titles. These are usually accessed via the library catalogue/e-library rather than via the newspapers' home pages or a Google search.
- Note that newspaper titles are not usually indexed by journal article databases. Therefore separate searches of these resources may be necessary.
- This section highlights general resources. Specialist services are mentioned in the subject sections.

Where to look

Libraries

British Library Newspaper Collections
> **www.bl.uk/reshelp/inrrooms/blnewspapers/newsrr.html**
> World-famous collection of current and historical British and overseas newspapers. Website provides access to the catalogue and research guides. A key starting-point for researchers seeking to trace items not available locally. Also useful is the **Copac** union catalogue, **www.copac.ac.uk**, which cross-searches titles held in major UK and Irish research libraries.

Commercial databases
- These are commonly available titles. Check for local access/alternatives.
- Note that some services have a time delay, so for the latest headlines the newspaper's home page may be more up to date.
- Some databases do not contain images or page layouts. If these are unavailable locally refer to the British Library, which has major microfilm collections.
- All these services offer the ability to set up e-mail alerts.

Factiva
> **www.factiva.com**

Currently owned by Dow Jones. Thousands of newspapers and newswires worldwide. Renowned business coverage.

Nexis
www.lexisnexis.com
Currently a division of Reed Elsevier. Access to thousands of national and regional newspapers worldwide, many from 1980 onwards.

Newspaper websites

Note that the **Media Studies** section lists trade directories, which have circulation figures.

Alternative Press Index
www.altpress.org/index.php
Site provides an impressive directory of links to radical and activist newspapers worldwide.

EU feeds: news feeds from European newspapers
www.eufeeds.eu
Site created by the European Journalism Centre. Get news feeds of the latest headlines from over 300 European national and local newspapers.

Online newspapers.com
www.onlinenewspapers.com
Directory of thousands of online newspapers worldwide. Arranged by geographical area. Not all are free.

Historical newspapers

UK

Good examples include the following.

British Newspapers 1600–1900 (subscription required)
www.gale.cengage.com/index.htm
Widely available in UK higher education. Cross-search the 17th- and 18th-century Burney Collection (full-text newspapers and news pamphlets gathered by the Reverend Charles Burney) and 19th-century British Library Newspapers (46 regional titles).

Times Digital Archive (subscription required)
archive.timesonline.co.uk/tol/archive
Currently covers 1785 to 1985.

NEWSPAPERS

International

Chronicling America: Historic American Newspapers
www.loc.gov/chroniclingamerica
Excellent free website maintained by the Library of Congress. Search hundreds of full-text newspapers from 1860 to 1922. Site also has information about American newspapers from 1690 onwards.

Papers Past
paperspast.natlib.govt.nz/cgi-bin/paperspast
Maintained by the National Library of New Zealand. Access hundreds of national and regional titles from 1839 to 1945.

Proquest Historical Newspapers (subscription required)
www.proquest.co.uk/en-UK/catalogs/databases/detail/
pq-hist-news.shtml
Full-text coverage of leading titles, including *Guardian* (1821–2003), *The Observer* (1791–2003), the *New York Times* (1851–2006), the *Irish Times* (1859–2006).

To trace other projects try searching national library websites.

Europeana
www.europeana.eu/portal
Good at picking up digitized content from Europe.

ICON – International Coalition on Newspapers
icon.crl.edu
Another good starting-point. Consortium of member libraries (mainly USA based) that are seeking to preserve and improve access to newspapers worldwide. The website includes a database of bibliographic information about newspapers published worldwide. It also maintains an excellent directory of links to historical newspaper digitization projects.

NON-GOVERNMENTAL ORGANIZATIONS (NGOS)

Typical questions

- Where can I get a list of NGOs who operate in DRC Congo?
- What NGOs are active in healthcare in Europe?

Points to consider

- Non-governmental organizations operate independently of governments. However, their definition is loose and can include charities, campaign groups, grassroots organizations, civil society or third sector organizations operating at both local and transnational levels.
- Students may wish to contact them to get information about scholarships (see the **Grants and Funding** section), internships (see **Volunteering**) or to trace details of their on-going work. Their websites can be rich sources of information, containing online reports and news about current and historic fieldwork that may be difficult to obtain elsewhere.
- This section contains references to general directories. More specific subject-based resources are listed separately in the appropriate sections. There is also a more detailed **Charities** section. Note that enquirers may not be certain of the status of an organization, so it is advisable to try both sections.

Where to look

Duke University NGO Research Guide
library.duke.edu/research/subject/guides/ngo_guide
Excellent starting-point. Although intended for local students, its guidance is widely applicable. Includes definitions, a civil society bibliography, a database of over 600 NGOs and a directory of links to other key websites. Also provided is a specialist search engine which searches the websites of major NGOs.

UK

National Council for Voluntary Organisations (NCVO)
www.ncvo-vol.org.uk
Supports and acts on behalf of community and voluntary organizations in the UK. Use the website to trace news and training events and browse its database of organizations.

NGOs in Britain Project

www.ngo.bham.ac.uk

Leverhulme-funded project (due to end late 2011) examining the history of NGOs and their activity in Britain post 1945. Website provides free access to research guides and the *DANGO Database of Archives of NGOs* active in Britain during this period.

Third Sector Research Centre

www.tsrc.ac.uk

Focal point for tracing recent research-based evidence about civil society (charities, pressure groups and NGOs) operating in the UK today. Read news, research reports and papers. Topics covered include governance, operation, economic and social impact and community involvement.

International

UN NGO Branch

www.csonet.org

United Nations Department of Economic and Social Affairs (UNDESA) maintains information on over 3000 organizations in consultative status with the UN. View by region, type and activity.

World Association of Non-Governmental Organizations (WANGO)

www.wango.org

Membership organization which represents NGOs worldwide. Website provides free access to news and the *NGO Handbook*, which has legal definitions of NGO status, statistics on numbers and useful website links. Also available is the *Worldwide NGO Directory*, a searchable database of national and international NGOs. Browse by nation and subject area.

Yearbook of International Organizations (subscription required)

www.uia.be/yearbook

Published annually by the Union of International Associations. Maintains a comprehensive listing of NGOs which operate internationally. It highlights those affiliated to intergovernmental organizations and gives statistics on staff, budgets and main areas of activity.

OPEN ACCESS PUBLISHING AND REPOSITORIES

Typical questions

- Can I upload a copy of an article published last year to my personal website?
- Does this publisher allow draft versions of articles to be made freely available online?

Points to consider

- Open access usually refers to making material available to everyone via the internet free of charge.
- Increasingly, academic institutions are establishing websites called institutional repositories, where they are making available outputs from their research (papers, reports, journal articles, theses and learning materials). Where copyright allows, they are placing full-text versions online. However, in terms of commercially published materials the version they make available is subject to copyright restrictions and is often an author version (pre-proof or draft) rather than the final, published version. Therefore students should check carefully the content and how to cite it.
- This section offers guidance on where to find information about maintaining and populating a repository, the growth of the open access movement and examples of key directories of open access repositories. More specific subject-based examples are found in the subject sections.

Where to look

Open access support

Eprints.org

> **www.eprints.org**
> Site developed by the School of Electronics and Computer Science, University of Southampton to support EPrints open source software. It provides free access to a wealth of resources, including technical support documents, FAQs on self-archiving for authors and an extensive directory of useful links. Also available is the EPrints *ROARMAP* service, **roarmap.eprints.org**, a searchable register of mandates and policies on open access publishing from institutions and research funders.

JISC Repositories and Support Programme

> **www.jisc.ac.uk/programme_rep_pres.aspx**
> JISC supports the innovative use of new technology in the UK higher and

further education sectors using funding received from the UK government. It has been heavily involved in promoting the management and development of institutional repositories. Its website is a key starting-point for tracing both historic and current programmes. Topics covered include technical infrastructure, digital preservation and legal concerns. A major initiative is the **Repositories support project (RSP), www.rsp.ac.uk** (funded 2006–12). This has a separate website with sections covering starting up a repository, advocacy and technical support. There are links to many examples of open access repository projects.

SHERPA
www.sherpa.ac.uk
Consortium led by the University of Nottingham that is investigating issues in the future of scholarly communication, focusing in particular on open access repositories. Key resources offered include:

- **RoMEO, www.sherpa.ac.uk/romeo.php**. Searchable listing of journals and publishers, providing information on their policies regarding self-archiving and open access.
- **JULIET, www.sherpa.ac.uk/juliet/index.php**. Summary of policies given by various research funders as part of their grant awards.
- Glossary of acronyms and abbreviations commonly used by the open access movement, **www.sherpa.ac.uk/glossary.html**.

SPARC
www.arl.org/sparc/openaccess/index.shtml
International consortium of research libraries, which seeks to influence models of future scholarly communication to increase access and reduce financial pressure. Its website has online forums, newsletters and documents covering all aspects of open access.

Directories

Directory of Open Access Journals
www.doaj.org
Maintained by Lund University Libraries. Get links to thousands of titles.

Open Access Directory (OAD)
oad.simmons.edu/oadwiki/Main_Page
Wiki about open access (OA) hosted by the Graduate School of Library and Information Science at Simmons College and supervised by an independent editorial board. It relies on the OA community to help maintain and keep the links up to date. A key feature is the **Open Access**

Bibliography, oad.simmons.edu/oadwiki/Bibliography_of_open_access, which is based on Charles W. Bailey, Jr. (2005) *Open Access Bibliography: liberating scholarly literature with e-prints and open access journals*, Washington, DC: Association of Research Libraries. It seeks to list and link to articles and reports covering all aspects of OA. Topics include mandates, copyright, institutional repositories and interviews.

OpenDOAR
www.opendoar.org
Comprehensive list of institutional and subject-based repositories worldwide. It is possible to cross-search the content to locate individual articles.

Bibliographies

OpCit Project
opcit.eprints.org/oacitation-biblio.html
Based at the Department of Electronics and Computer Science, University of Southampton. Provides free access to a bibliography of articles and reports that focus on the impact of open access publishing on citations. Aims to show that making articles open access increases the number of citations.

News services

Open Access Newsletter
www.earlham.edu/~peters/fos/newsletter/archive.htm
Free access to this excellent service produced by Peter Suber and supported by the Scholarly Publishing and Academic Resources Coalition (SPARC) which covers all aspects of the movement in extensive detail, highlighting events, news and publications. Sign up to receive the current issue via e-mail or view the archives online.

OPINION POLLS

Typical questions

- How can I trace changing public attitudes towards the government?
- What do British people think about the EU?

Points to consider

- Large-scale surveys can be useful starting-points for tracing changing public attitudes over time. However, many surveys which appear in the media have incomplete details and are sponsored by lobbying or commercial interests. Always check the original, and evaluate the methodology used. Here are some recommended examples!

Where to look

UK

British Social Attitudes Survey

www.britsocat.com

Largest survey of British economic, social and political attitudes. Carried out annually since 1989 by **National Centre for Social Research**, **www.natcen.ac.uk**. Published in print or online. Latest issues, data and questions, plus a bibliography of associated readings, can be accessed via the website.

Survey Question Bank

surveynet.ac.uk/sqb

Site co-ordinated by the UK Data Archive. Contains a catalogue of questions asked by major British social surveys since the 1990s. Use to trace relevant surveys by topic. Note that the site does not provide results. The **ESDS catalogue, www.esds.ac.uk,** is a good starting-point for locating these. Check local data subscriptions.

United States

Gallup

www.gallup.com/Home.aspx

World-famous company. Some recent polls can be downloaded from the home page. **Gallup Brain, brain.gallup.com/home.aspx,** has a searchable question archive from 1935 onwards. Access to full results requires a subscription.

Roper Center for Public Opinion Research (subscription required)
www.ropercenter.uconn.edu
Over 500,000 US polls from 1935 onwards with associated reports and datasets. Covers political, economic and social topics.

International

Afrobarometer
www.afrobarometer.org
African-led surveys on attitudes towards democracy and governance. Access data from more than a dozen nations from 1999 onwards.

Arab Barometer
www.arabbarometer.org
Established in 2005 by the Institute for Social Research, University of Michigan. Free access to surveys of citizens' political attitudes in a number of Arab states, including Palestine, Jordan and Morocco.

Asian Barometer
www.asianbarometer.org
Comparative studies of changing political attitudes in 13 Asian nations, including China and Japan. Results from 2001 onwards.

Centre for Comparative European Survey Data
www.ccesd.ac.uk/Body.aspx
Cross-search questions used in major European social attitudes surveys. Free registration required.

Eurobarometer
ec.europa.eu/public_opinion/index_en.htm
Access official public opinion analysis from the European Commission. Covers a range of economic, political and social topics, including attitudes towards the European Union and European integration, allowing for cross-national comparisons over time.

International Social Survey programme (ISSP)
www.issp.org
Cross-national programme. Find information about surveys conducted in over 40 nations worldwide, including the USA and UK. Access arrangements for individual surveys are provided.

Latinobarometer (subscription required)
www.latinobarometro.org
Annual polls of citizens in 18 Latin American nations covering economic,

social and political attitudes. Access to full data requires a subscription. A similar site, **Latin American Public Opinion Project (LAPOP)** at Vanderbilt University, **www.americasbarometer.org** or **www.vanderbilt. edu/lapop,** offers some free Americas Barometer results and data.

Polling the Nations (subscription required)
www.orspub.com

Contains over 500,000 surveys conducted after 1985. Includes major USA, national and regional polls as well as results from Europe (Eurobarometer) and other world regions.

WorldPublicOpinion.org
www.worldpublicopinion.org

Managed by the Program on International Policy Attitudes, University of Maryland. Opinion poll research on international issues (such as attitudes towards specific nations, religions, international security) from 25 nations worldwide.

World Values Survey
www.worldvaluessurvey.org

International project to map changing world attitudes. Get results and reports from 1981 onwards. Includes national and international mappings of cultural attitudes and happiness levels!

PARLIAMENTS/PARLIAMENTARY PROCEEDINGS

Typical questions

- Can I get a list of MPs who voted against the recent Student Finance Bill?
- I want to trace all the parliamentary debates and bills relating to the Dangerous Dogs Act 1991.

Points to consider

- The internet has made it possible to find a wealth of information on parliaments worldwide. Typical information found on parliamentary websites includes:
  — lists of current MPs
  — information on parliamentary committees. These often include useful scrutiny of Acts of Parliament and the performance of the government in certain policy areas
  — information on the legislative process. This can include lists and the texts of bills being debated
  — the official reports of proceedings. Often these are called *Hansard*. They include records of voting in the House
  — useful factsheets which explain the parliamentary procedure of the nation concerned.

They may also have statistics and summaries of recent bills. However, do remember to check when the website was last updated!

Where to look

UK

Dods Parliamentary Companion
www.dodsshop.co.uk
Available in print or online. Well respected annual listing of MPs and parliamentary committees. Includes biographical information on individuals and statistics on the composition of Parliament.

House of Commons Library Research papers
www.parliament.uk/business/publications/research/research-papers
Can be really useful for summarising clearly how parliament works and the content of recent parliamentary bills.

Hansard 1803–2005

hansard.millbanksystems.com

Website of the Hansard Digitization Project, led by the Directorate of Information Services of the House of Commons and the Library of the House of Lords. Searchable by date, keyword or MP.

Theyworkforyou.com

www.theyworkforyou.com

Project of UK Citizens Online Democracy (registered charity) which aims to help citizens keep tabs on UK parliamentary activity. Look up an MP and see their expenses claims, recent attendance in Parliament and how they voted.

UK Parliament website

www.parliament.uk

Official website. Includes Parliament TV (live broadcasts), plus the full text of *Hansard* from session 1988–89 onwards. Use the advanced search form to quickly locate specific references.

International

International Parliamentary Union (IPU)

www.ipu.org/english/home.htm

International organization of parliaments. Key starting-point for tracing the names, addresses and websites of national and regional parliaments worldwide. A section contains statistics on the representation of women in national parliaments. Also offers free access to the *PARLINE* database, **www.ipu.org/parline-e/parlinesearch.asp**, which has information on the structure and working of several hundred parliaments.

PHILOSOPHY

Typical questions

- Where can I find recent articles by feminist philosophers?
- I need a summary of the writings of Kant.
- Are any of Hegel's essays online?

Points to consider

- Note that increasing numbers of classic (out of copyright) philosophy texts can now be found online. However, students need to check the details of the edition and/or translation carefully before use. They should be reminded to check any local subscription services which may have more authoritative versions!

Where to look

Key organizations

American Philosophical Association

www.apa.udel.edu/apa/index.html

Main professional organization for philosophers in the United States, founded in 1900. Its website has newsletters, job listings and information on forthcoming conferences.

British Philosophical Association

www.bpa.ac.uk

Key organization representing philosophers in the UK. Its website has information for students on courses, careers and research funding. It also has a directory of key websites.

Royal Institute of Philosophy

www.royalinstitutephilosophy.org

Charity renowned for its publications and lectures. Information (and the full text) of some of these can be viewed online.

Libraries and archives

Use these to locate lists of books, guides to research sources.

Bodleian Philosophy Faculty Library

www.bodleian.ox.ac.uk/philosophy/collections

Part of Oxford University. Covers ancient and contemporary Western Philosophy. Extensive manuscript holdings, including those of John Locke (1632–1704).

Senate House Library

www.ull.ac.uk/subjects/philosophy/index.shtml

Leading national resource, acts as the Library of the Royal Institute of Philosophy. Strong collections in Western and Continental Philosophy. Admission fee for non-members.

Dictionaries and encyclopedias

Routledge Encyclopedia of Philosophy Online (subscription required)

www.rep.routledge.com

Over 2000 articles by experts. Covers all branches of ancient and contemporary Philosophy and includes non-Western thought. Good introductions to the work of leading philosophers, with references to guide further reading.

Stanford Encyclopedia of Philosophy

plato.stanford.edu

Unique free digital library being created as an on-going process by a team of experts. Will cover thinkers and concepts from all branches of Philosophy.

Journal article indexes

Philosopher's Index (subscription required)

philinfo.org

Pre-eminent abstracting service. Provides coverage of all major Philosophy journals in English, French, German, Spanish and Italian and some books. From 1940 onwards.

Electronic libraries

Find full-text Philosophy books and papers online.

Marxists Internet Archive

www.marxists.org

World's largest online library of Marxist Philosophy. Full-text writings from over 400 historic and contemporary thinkers.

PhilPapers

philpapers.org

Supported by the Institute of Philosophy, University of London and other partners. Online directory of contents pages of over 300 Philosophy journals, plus links to full-text papers from authors' home pages and institutional repositories.

Super-Enlightenment
collections.stanford.edu/supere
Maintained by Stanford University, provides free access to 36 texts, written in French between 1716 and 1835, that are important for the history of Philosophy.

Internet gateways and portals
Philosophy at Large
www.liv.ac.uk/pal
Maintained by University of Liverpool. Locate links to associations, e-mail discussion lists and websites for specific sub-fields.

PLAGIARISM

Typical questions

- Where can I get some advice on avoiding plagiarism?
- What anti-plagiarism programmes are available?

Points to consider

- Students are often worried that they might accidentally commit plagiarism. Many therefore also need advice on citing and referencing correctly. Refer to that section for useful sources.
- Lecturers may need help in using plagiarism detection software. Note that many universities have a preferred product. Check locally first.

Where to look

Plagiarism.advice.org

> www.plagiarismadvice.org
>
> Supported by **JISC** (**www.jisc.ac.uk**), a resource centre for the UK higher and further education communities. Includes useful help guides, news and advice.

Plagiarism Teaching Online (PLATO) (subscription required)

> www.preventplagiarism.co.uk/index.asp
>
> Tutorial developed by the University of Derby which develops student awareness of plagiarism. Focuses on avoidance through learning how to cite correctly.
>
> Note that many general information literacy courses include sections on citing, which can also help. A good directory of these is offered on the **Information Literacy** website, **www.informationliteracy.org.uk**.

Turnitin

> turnitin.com/static/index.php (subscription required)
>
> Leading plagiarism detection product. Website includes news and user advice.

POLITICAL SCIENCE

Typical questions

- Where can I find journal articles about politics?
- Are there any forthcoming conferences on Latin American politics?

Points to consider

- This section will provide you with a brief overview of where to begin subject searching. Many politics students also study conflict, so the **International Relations** section is also worth exploring.

Where to look

Key organizations

Use these to locate forthcoming conferences, lists of specialist sub-groups (which often conduct cutting-edge research) and links to key journals and new publications.

American Political Studies Association
    www.apsanet.org
    Main professional body for the USA. Extensive coverage of all areas of Politics, including a large collection of materials on teaching and learning.

International Political Science Association (IPSA)
    www.ipsa.org
    Key international body. Consult the website for links to the latest conference news, national political associations worldwide and *IPSA Portal*, its list of recommended websites.

Political Studies Association (UK)
    www.psa.ac.uk
    Main professional body for the UK. The website has an online portal of recommended Politics websites and an extensive collection of online conference papers from 1996 onwards.

Libraries and archives

Bodleian Library
    www.bodleian.ox.ac.uk/bodley/library/specialcollections/ western_rarebooks/political
    Holds one of the largest concentrations of modern British political manuscripts and archives. It also has extensive collections of journals and books.

POLITICAL SCIENCE

LSE Library

www2.lse.ac.uk/library/home.aspx

Established in 1896, the working library of the London School of Economics and Political Science and is one of the largest libraries in the world devoted to the economic and social sciences. Its website has subject guides to the collections and a separate archives section.

Dictionaries

Bealey, F. (1999) *Blackwell Dictionary of Political Science: a user's guide to its terms,* **Wiley-Blackwell**

Defines 1000 words and phrases in Political Science. Particularly suitable for those new to the field.

McLean, I. and McMillan, A. (2003) *The Concise Oxford Dictionary of Politics,* **Oxford University Press**

Contains more than 1700 entries covering political thinkers, institutions and theories.

Journal article indexes

International Bibliography of the Social Sciences (IBSS) (subscription required)

www.proquest.co.uk/en-UK/catalogs/databases/detail/ibss-set-c.shtml

Interdisciplinary database. One of the main areas covered is Politics. Coverage from 1952 onwards.

International Political Science Abstracts (subscription required)

www.ipsa.org/publications/abstracts

Published by the International Political Science Association. Coverage from 1951 onwards. Extensive indexing of foreign-language materials.

News services

Most online national newspapers and TV stations have a Politics section. The following are examples of services that specialize in Politics.

C-SPAN

www.c-span.org

Independent non-profit company created by the American cable TV industry. Focuses specifically on American Politics, providing free access to news, analysis and educational resources. Live coverage of congressional hearings and debates and an online video library of archived recordings.

Epolitix.com

www.epolitix.com

Free access to latest UK politics and parliamentary stories, also includes political interviews and extensive links to major UK blogs, Twitter news feeds.

Internet gateways and portals

Keele Guides to Government and Politics

www.keele.ac.uk/depts/por

Maintained by the School of Politics, International Relations and Philosophy, Keele University. Includes directories for individual nations, areas of the world and thematic topics.

Richard Kimber's Political Science Resources

www.politicsresources.net

Over 17,000 links to major government and politics websites worldwide. Extensive coverage of British elections and political parties. This includes transcripts and links to UK general election manifestos from 1945 onwards.

PSYCHOLOGY

Typical questions
- Where can I find articles about Evolutionary Psychology?
- Are there any psychological tests online?
- Where can I get advice on careers in Psychology?

Points to consider
- Psychology can encompass many sub-fields. Those studying clinical practice may benefit from consulting the sources listed in the **Medicine and Nursing** section. Organizational Psychology students often focus on human resources or personnel management issues. They may therefore find the **Management** section useful.

Where to look

Key organizations
Use these to find specialist sub-groups, mailing lists, lists of key journals and forthcoming conferences.

American Psychological Association (APA)
www.apa.org/careers/index.aspx
Largest association of psychologists worldwide. Features of website include extensive resources for early-career psychologists, a section on research methods and ethics codes and *PsycPORT: Psychology newswire*, which is excellent for keeping up to date with the latest psychological research in the news.

British Psychological Society (BPS)
www.bps.org.uk
Major body representing researchers and practising psychologists in the UK. Website includes information about tests and lists of test providers. It is also possible to sign up to the free fortnightly BPS research digest, which reports on the latest research.

International Union of Psychological Science (IUPsyS)
www.iupsys.net
International organization which seeks to promote Psychology as a science and a profession. Website offers links to many national psychology organizations worldwide.

Libraries and archives

Institute of Psychoanalysis

www.psychoanalysis.org.uk/library.htm

Library of the British Psychoanalytical Society, which houses the finest collection of psychoanalytic material in the world.

Senate House Library

www.ull.ac.uk/subjects/psychology/index.shtml

Part of the University of London. The collection houses the library of the British Psychological Society. Website has guides to tracing psychological tests.

Dictionaries and encylopedias

Colman, A. (ed.) (2008) *A Dictionary of Psychology*, **3rd edn, Oxford University Press**

Over 11,000 definitions covering all branches of Psychology.

Davis, S. and Buskist, W. (2008), *21st Century Psychology: a reference handbook*, **SAGE Publications**

Highlights over 100 key topics for students, offering summaries of past research, possible future directions and suggestions for further reading.

Journal article indexes

Students may also find it helpful to supplement these with the resources listed in the working papers sub-section.

PEP-Web

www.pep-web.org

Free archive of classic psychoanalytical texts and articles. Includes the standard edition of the *Complete Psychological Works of Sigmund Freud* as well as the 18-volume German Freud standard edition, *Gesammelte Werke*, and references to journal articles.

PsycInfo (subscription required)

www.apa.org/pubs/databases/psycinfo/index.aspx

Key resource produced by the American Psychological Association, indexes articles, technical reports and papers from the 19th century onwards. Note that many universities also have access to **PsycArticles**, **www.apa.org/pubs/databases/psycarticles/index.aspx**. While it offers the full texts of over 70 journals published by the APA, the overall number of titles indexed is narrower in scope than PsycInfo.

Working papers

CogPrints

cogprints.org

Free access to thousands of working papers covering Psychology, Neurosciences and Linguistics.

PsycDok

psydok.sulb.uni-saarland.de

Open access repository for Psychology maintained by Saarland University and State Library (Germany). It is a good resource for locating abstracts and many full-text papers published by European researchers.

Internet gateways and portals

Psychology Virtual Library

www.vl-site.org/psychology/index.html

Forms part of the WWW Virtual Library. Annotated directory of links to organizations and online libraries.

Social Psychology Network

www.socialpsychology.org

Excellent site maintained by Scott Plous, Wesleyan University. Includes psychology news headlines (including a searchable database going back to 2004), links to online textbooks, journals and teaching resources.

QUALIFICATIONS

Typical questions

- What is an HND?
- Is there a website where I can compare international qualifications with UK ones?

Points to consider

- These resources offer general guidance on academic qualifications. Students seeking advice on whether they meet the entrance criteria for specific courses should always be referred to the institution concerned. Look for the admissions section on the website.
- Another possible source of information is professional associations. They will be able to provide advice on accredited courses and/or qualifications for entering their field.
- Don't forget that the UK is comprised of a number of regions with different education systems. Information on Scotland and Northern Ireland will often be listed separately.
- Finally, remember to check when the website/directory was last updated!

Where to look

UK

British Qualifications, Kogan Page. Annual

Long established guide to academic and vocational qualifications in the UK. Includes information on all further and higher education colleges and professional institutions granting awards. Also includes background information on the structure of the education system.

Education UK

www.educationuk.org

Site created by the British Council. Provides a general introduction to the British education system which explains simply its structure and the types of qualifications awarded. Useful as an introduction for overseas students.

National Recognition Information Centre for the United Kingdom (NARIC)

www.naric.org.uk

National agency responsible for offering individuals and businesses advice on comparing overseas skills and qualifications with their British equivalents. Website contains basic information. Most services are fee based.

QUALIFICATIONS

Quality Assurance Agency for Higher Education (QAA)
www.qaa.ac.uk
Government body responsible for overseeing standards in UK higher education. Website includes framework statements and benchmarking reports which set out the standards required for the award of higher degrees.

International

Erasmus
ec.europa.eu/education/lifelong-learning-programme/doc80_en.htm
Major programme of the European Union which aims to encourage international mobility in higher education. Its website provides information on the programme. The **British Council** website offers more support for UK students, **www.britishcouncil.org/erasmus.htm**.

International Bureau on Education
www.ibe.unesco.org/en.html
UNESCO institute. Website gives free access to its international directory of education systems, *World Education Data*. This offers a profile of the education system and accreditation process in many nations worldwide. Notes cover schooling and higher education. There are references to the names of the main agencies and their websites.

UK Council for International Student Affairs (UKCISA)
www.ukcisa.org.uk
The UK's national advisory body serving the interests of international students. Its website offers some useful advice for British students on how to study overseas. Topics covered include visas, recognition of qualifications, sources of funding and a directory of support organizations in specific countries.

UNESCO
www.unesco.org/new/en/education
Maintains a portal on higher education systems which provides information on the organization of the systems and on standards bodies. Links are provided to key information websites.

World Higher Education Database (subscription required)
www.whed-online.com
Compiled by the International Association of Universities (IAU). Offers information on courses from thousands of colleges in over 180 nations worldwide. Also includes descriptions of the education system of each

nation and types of qualifications awarded. The **IAU** website, **www.iau-aiu. net/content/servicespublications,** provides free access to a less detailed directory of information on higher education systems worldwide. This gives details of the awards and lists the national bodies responsible for overseeing standards. Many entries helpfully provide internet addresses.

QUANGOS

Typical questions
- Where can I get a list of all the current government quangos?
- How much money was spent on funding quangos by the Department of Health last year?

Points to consider
- The term 'quango' is an abbreviation for a quasi-autonomous, non-governmental organization. In the UK, an official term which is often used is non-departmental public body or NDPB.
- It can be an emotive term. Searches on the internet for quango often generate hits containing polemic both for and against levels of government expenditure on such bodies. Students seeking economic analysis of quangos may therefore benefit from consulting the resources listed in the **Economics** section.

Where to look

Public Bodies

www.civilservice.gov.uk/about/resources/ndpbs.aspx

Since 1990, the Cabinet Office has produced an annual directory of NDPBs. This contains a definition of the different types of quango, listing of total number, number by department and statistics on staffing and expenditure. Free access to issues from 1998 onwards.

More in-depth information on the activities and governance of NDPBs can usually be found on their individual websites. These can be traced via the main **UK DirectGov** directory, **www.direct.gov.uk/en/Dl1/Directories/A-ZOfCentralGovernment/index.htm**.

UK Parliament website

www.parliament.uk

Parliamentary discussion on the numbers and roles of quangos can be traced by searching the main website. This will retrieve any debates, committee reports and factsheets produced by the House of Commons Library.

QUOTATIONS

Typical questions

- Did Tony Blair really say 'education, education, education'?
- Where can I find some quotations from Barack Obama?

Points to consider

- It has become increasingly easy to trace quotations online. However, note that some websites have been set up by unqualified individuals and may not be accurate!
- Good starting-points are established reference works such as those listed in this section. See also the **Speeches** section.
- Other possibilities include prime ministers'/presidents' and parliamentary websites (for political quotations) and personal home pages maintained by film stars, university lecturers and other personalities.
- Try to get as much information as possible about name, occupation, dates and any institutional affiliations because this will help in searching.

Where to look

Bartlett, J. and Kaplan, J. (2002) *Bartlett's Familiar Quotations: a collection of passages, phrases, and proverbs traced to their sources in ancient and modern literature*, **Little, Brown and Company**
Arranged chronologically with detailed author and keyword indexes. Strong content for literature, Shakespeare and the Bible.

Jay, A. (ed.) (2010) *Lend Me Your Ears: Oxford dictionary of political quotations*, **4th edn, Oxford University Press**
Specialist resource for tracing quotes from politicians and political leaders, covering all time periods.

Knowles, E. (ed.) (2009) *Oxford Dictionary of Quotations*, **7th edn, Oxford University Press**
Contains over 20,000 quotations covering all topic areas from earliest times to the 21st century. Includes categories for catch phrases, newspaper headlines and advertising slogans. Companion website has a good directory of free websites, **www.oup.com/uk/booksites/content/9780199237173**.

There is also some free access to quotations contained in the online directory at the **Oxford Dictionaries** website, **oxforddictionaries. com/page/quotations**. However, be aware that this is not so comprehensive.

QUOTATIONS

Platt, S. (1989) *Respectfully Quoted: a dictionary of quotations requested from the congressional research service*, **Library of Congress**
www.bartleby.com/73
Free online access to over 2000 of the most popularly requested American political quotations. Note date of publication – the most recent items will not be listed!

REFERENCE MANAGEMENT TOOLS

Typical questions

- Are there any online tools for managing the citations for my dissertation?
- Are there any programmes which will format my references into APA style?

Points to consider

- Reference management tools provide a place where students/researchers can effectively organize, store and format bibliographic references to books, journals, papers and websites etc. They can save researchers time and effort because in many cases lists of references can be directly exported from commercial journal indexes and databases. The best services also automatically format citations into specific styles (such as APA and MLA) which can be output as a bibliography at the end of a dissertation or article.
- In addition to established commercial products, an increasing number of free reference management tools are being made available on the web. Note that some have storage limits and offer fewer facilities for automatic formatting in bibliographic styles, so check capabilities carefully.
- This section introduces a selection of well known commercial and free examples. When deciding which to use, students should first check if local library/IT services provide support for any specific services. Major library services also produce comparison guides. A good example is **Yale University, guides.library.yale.edu/tutorials**. However, do bear in mind that some of the advice given may be geared towards local IT networks, so check versions, compatibility and date last updated before relying on it!
- Finally, remember that students who enquire about reference management tools may also benefit from the general advice about **Citing and Referencing** given in this book.

Where to look

Connotea
> www.connotea.org
> Free web-based service created by Nature Publishing and used heavily by scientists. Users can save, tag and share citations. References can be imported from any website.

EndNote (subscription required)
> www.endnote.com
> Well known commercial product. The website offers factsheets, tutorials and a users' forum.

REFERENCE MANAGEMENT TOOLS

EndNote Web

www.endnote.com/enwebinfo.asp

Free web-based version of EndNote. Has more limited functionality, but a good capability for sharing references with others. Online tutorials are available.

Menderley

www.mendeley.com

Free service aimed at researchers which is both a reference management tool and a social network because, in addition to storing, downloading and formatting citations, it enables users to view and exchange information on popular papers. Data can be imported into Mendeley from a variety of other reference management tools, such as EndNote and Zotero.

RefWorks (subscription required)

www.refworks.com

Web-based competitor to EndNote. Website also includes tutorials and free trials.

Zotero

www.zotero.org

Free service originally developed by George Mason University. Installation requires Firefox. Some restrictions on the free storage space, although extensions can be purchased.

RELIGIOUS STUDIES AND THEOLOGY

Typical questions
- Where can I search for literature on the ordination of women?
- What is the difference between Sunni and Sufi Muslims?

Points to consider
- Religion can be a contentious subject. Many websites are maintained by biased or unqualified persons. Always encourage students to evaluate them carefully.
- The resources listed below are recommended for academic use. They are sub-divided into general and then more specific faith-based resources. Explore them to find more in-depth material. Remember that material may be produced by believers, which can affect its content. Students of theology may also find the **Philosophy** section useful. Those researching Islam and Asian religions may also want to refer to the **Asian Studies** section.

Where to look
General and comparative religion
Key organizations

American Academy of Religion (AAR)
www.aarweb.org
Large scholarly society supporting teachers. Website includes an online collection of syllabi and other classroom resources.

Association of University Lecturers in Religion and Education
www.aulre.org.uk
Supports UK-based academic staff. Get news and updates on UK educational policy, curriculum content and course delivery.

British Association for the Study of Religions (BASR)
www.basr.ac.uk
Formerly the British Association for the History of Religions. Promotes the academic study of all religions.

European Association for the Study of Religions
easr.org
Supports research in Europe. Website has a useful directory of national member organizations.

Higher Education Academy
www.heacademy.ac.uk

Supports teachers in UK higher education institutions. Subject coverage includes Religion, Philosophy and Theology. Website has some useful online learning resources and lists of training events.

International Association for the History of Religions (IAHR)
www.iahr.dk/iahr.html

Key international body. Links to all major regional and national associations covering religion.

Libraries and archives

Association of British Theological and Philosophical Libraries (ABTAPL)
www.newman.ac.uk/abtapl/index.html

Network supporting specialist UK libraries. Website is of great value in locating libraries with large Religious Studies collections. It includes a union list of their journal holdings.

Association of Religion Data Archives
www.thearda.com

Based at Pennsylvania State University, this wonderful online resource aims to provide free access to statistical information about religion. While this originally focused on the USA, increasingly international datasets are being added. Topics covered include church membership, surveys of lifestyle and public attitudes towards religion. Most information is post 1990. The site also contains religious profiles of nations worldwide.

BETH European Theological Libraries
theo.kuleuven.be/beth

Organization of national theological library associations. Its website provides links to specialist library websites and catalogues.

Heythrop College Library
www.heythrop.ac.uk/about-us/library-and-learning-resources.html

One of the finest collections of theological and philosophical books in the UK. Part of the University of London. The library admits postgraduate researchers and academics. Search the online catalogue to find references to books and journals.

Dictionaries and encyclopedias

Eliade, M. (ed.) (2004) *Encyclopedia of Religion*, **2nd edn, MacMillan Reference**

Monumental work containing over 2500 entries on persons, practices and topics relating to world religions from earliest times.

Von Stuckrad, K. (2007) *The Brill Dictionary of Religion*, **Brill**
Available in print or online. Over 500 entries focus on the history and modern practice of religions and religious beliefs worldwide.

Journal article indexes

ATLA Religion Database (subscription required)
www.atla.com/products/catalog/Pages/rdb-db.aspx
Produced by the American Theological Library Association. Indexes articles from over 600 journals covering Theology and all aspects of Religion from 1949 onwards.

Internet gateways and portals

Use these to locate examples of recommended websites.

Virtual Religion Index
virtualreligion.net/vri/index.html
Created by Mahlon H. Smith. Award-winning collection of links covering all world religions plus Theology. Highlights journals, conference listings and online texts.

Wabash Center Internet Guide to Religion
www.wabashcenter.wabash.edu/resources/guide_headings.aspx
Excellent collection of links designed for use by students and academics. Contains useful annotations on content. Includes large numbers of links to online syllabi.

Buddhism

Singh, N. (ed.) (1996–99) *International Encyclopaedia of Buddhism*, **Anmol Publications**
Comprehensive 75-volume work arranged by country. Covers rituals, beliefs, history and culture.

Tibetan Buddhist Resource Center (TBRC)
www.tbrc.org
Access examples of literature, plus links to Buddhist websites.

World Buddhist directory
www.buddhanet.info/wbd

Directory of local and national associations worldwide. Useful for locating addresses and events listings.

Christianity

Anglican Communion

www.anglicancommunion.org

Worldwide network of Anglican/Episcopal churches. Website contains news, events and texts.

Church of England

www.churchofengland.org

Includes news from the Archbishop of Canterbury and meetings of the governing body, the General Synod.

Holy See

www.vatican.va

Official website of the Vatican. Includes liturgies of the Catholic faith, Vatican Council documents and papal encyclicals from the 19th century onwards.

The New Catholic Encyclopedia (2002), 2nd edn, Gale

Published jointly by the Catholic University of America and the Gale Group, this 15-volume work contains authoritative entries on the history, practices and famous persons of the Catholic church from earliest times. It includes biographies of saints, information about individual popes and explanation of Catholic liturgy.

Journal article indexes

Catholic Periodical and Literature Index

www.cathla.org.catholic-periodical-and-literature-index.

Coverage 1981 to the present. Indexes articles published in Roman Catholic periodicals, papal documents, church promulgations and books about the Catholic faith that are authored by Catholics and/or produced by Catholic publishers. Produced by the American Theological Library Association and Catholic Library Association.

New Testament Abstracts (subscription required)

www.ebscohost.com/academic/new-testament-abstracts-online

Produced by the American Theological Library Association in partnership with Boston College. Indexes periodicals and monographs relating to the Gospels and New Testament published from 1985 onwards.

Old Testament Abstracts (OTA) (subscription required)
www.atla.com/products/catalog/Pages/ota.aspx
Produced by the American Theological Library Association with the Catholic Biblical Association. Indexes periodicals (plus some monographs) relating to the Hebrew Bible. Coverage 1978 to present.

Hinduism

Hindu Forum of Britain (HFB)
www.hinduforum.org
Largest representative body for British Hindus with over 420 member organizations. Find, news, events and contact addresses.

Kapoor, S. (2002) *Encyclopaedic Dictionary of Hinduism*, Cosmo Publications
Covers the beliefs, mythology, religion, history and literature of Hinduism.

School of Oriental and African Studies Library (SOAS)
www.soas.ac.uk/library
Part of the University of London and one of the world's most important academic libraries for the study of Africa, Asia and the Middle East. Use the online catalogue to trace examples of key books and journals. Includes extensive collections in vernacular languages.

Islam

Encyclopaedia of Islam, new edition (subscription required)
www.brillonline.nl/public
Available in print or online. Invaluable reference tool covers the religion, people and lands from earliest times.

Index Islamicus (subscription required)
www.brill.nl/indexislamicus
Leading bibliography on Islam and the Muslim world from 1906 onwards. Indexes over 3000 journal titles, plus monographs and book chapters.

Islamic Studies Reading Room
www.columbia.edu/cu/lweb/indiv/mideast/cuvlm/Islam.html
Extensive directory of links to web resources compiled by Columbia University. Covers religion, history and culture.

Muslim Council of Britain
www.mcb.org.uk

National Muslim umbrella body representing Islamic religious groups. Website includes news, events and resources on Muslims in Britain today.

School of Oriental and African Studies Library (SOAS)
www.soas.ac.uk/library

Judaism

Academic Jewish Studies Internet Directory
www.jewish-studies.com
Maintained by the Institute for Jewish Studies, Düsseldorf University. Over 500 links to high-quality resources covering Jewish religion, history and culture.

Encyclopaedia Judaica (2007), 2nd edn, Macmillan
www.encyclopaediajudaica.com
Comprehensive resource. Available in print or online (subscription required). Over 21,000 articles about all aspects of Jewish life, history, religion and culture.

Library of the Jewish Theological Seminary
www.jtsa.edu/Library
Based in New York. Contains one of the world's largest library collections of Hebraic and Judaic materials. Search the online catalogue to find references to books and journals covering the Jewish faith. Website also includes research guides.

RAMBI: Index of Articles on Jewish Studies
jnul.huji.ac.il/rambi
Free index produced by the Jewish National and University Library. Covers all aspects of Jewish life. Includes materials published in Yiddish. Material dates from the 1960s onwards.

United Synagogue
www.theus.org.uk
Information on the Orthodox Jewish faith. Website includes contact addresses, plus events and a Hebrew calendar.

World Union for Progressive Judaism
www.wupj.org
Umbrella organization of reform, liberal, progressive and reconstructionist movements worldwide. Find links to national bodies and news about events.

RESEARCH COUNCILS

Typical questions

- Where can I get a list of the main bodies that fund scientific research in the USA?
- Where can I get alerts about the latest Psychology research projects?

Points to consider

- Research councils usually co-ordinate funding and organization of research projects at a national level.
- Doctoral students may find their websites useful for advice on how to get funding, for news about recent projects and for information on training schemes for researchers.
- Academic staff can use them to locate sources of funding and keep up to date with the latest research (both completed and in progress).
- Note that individuals seeking advice on funding may also find the **Grants and Funding** section relevant.

Where to look

UK

There are currently seven publicly funded research councils. They all have individual websites with training sections, news about government funding policies and databases of completed and on-going research projects. In many cases this also includes links to full-text articles and reports which they have produced.

Arts and Humanities Research Council (AHRC)
www.ahrc.ac.uk

Biotechnology and Biological Sciences Research Council (BBSRC)
www.bbsrc.ac.uk

Economic and Social Research Council (ESRC)
www.esrc.ac.uk

Engineering and Physical Sciences Research Council (EPSRC)
www.epsrc.ac.uk

Medical Research Council (MRC)
www.mrc.ac.uk

Natural Environment Research Council (NERC)
www.nerc.ac.uk

Science and Technology Facilities Council (STFC)

www.stfc.ac.uk

All seven form part of the **Research Councils UK partnership**, www.rcuk.ac.uk. This website provides a focus point for news and information. It is particularly good for locating cross-disciplinary topics.

International

EUROHORCs

www.eurohorcs.org

Informal association of heads of national research councils and public non-university research organizations of the European Union member states. Website is a useful starting-point for locating lists of national councils, plus news on current trends.

National Research Council (NRC)

sites.nationalacademies.org/NRC/index.htm

Working arm of the national academies in the USA. These currently comprise: National Academy of Sciences (NAS), National Academy of Engineering (NAE), Institute of Medicine (IOM). Website includes news and training opportunities. The NRC also conducts regular research-based assessments of doctoral programmes in the USA.

UNESCO

www.unesco.org/new/en/education

UNESCO has a responsibility covering higher education. Its website has news about cross-border research programmes. These can be useful for identifying key players and trends worldwide. It maintains a portal on higher education systems, which provides information on national systems.

SCIENCE

Typical questions

- Where can I find an introduction to quantum mechanics?
- What is the boiling point of helium?

Points to consider

- Science is such a broad concept that it is worth asking the enquirer to be more specific about their area of interest. Definitions can differ! This section focuses on resources for tracing high-quality scientific literature. It has specialist sub-divisions for Physics, Biology and Chemistry. See separate sections for **Mathematics, Psychology, Medicine and Nursing, Engineering** and **Environment.**

Where to look

Key organizations

UK

British Council
www.britishcouncil.org/science-uk.htm
Promotes Britain overseas. Website has a good introductory guide to the organization of British science and technology which identifies key organizations and bodies. It also maintains information on research funding and international collaboration.

British Science Association
www.britishscienceassociation.org
Seeks to improve public understanding of science. Organizes regular science festivals, details of which can be found on its website, along with classroom activities for teachers and advice on how to get funding for scientific study.

Foundation for Science and Technology
www.foundation.org.uk
Promotes debate between Parliament, government departments, business and academia on policy issues relating to science. Copies of many debates are published on the website.

Higher Education Academy
www.heacademy.ac.uk
Supports lecturers in UK higher education. Subject coverage includes

Chemistry, Physics, Astronomy and Forensic Science. Website includes information and news about teaching and learning initiatives.

The Royal Institution of Great Britain
www.rigb.org

Conducts research and promotes science to the public through its lecture series. Some of its famous lectures can be viewed online.

Science Council
www.sciencecouncil.co.uk

Umbrella organization which represents the views of over 30 scholarly and professional bodies from all areas of science. Website provides access to events listings, careers information and policy statements. Many of the latter cover attitudes towards government policy and funding.

UK Research Councils
Those relevant to science are:

Biotechnology and Biological Sciences Research Council (BBSRC)
www.bbsrc.ac.uk

Engineering and Physical Sciences Research Council (EPSRC)
www.epsrc.ac.uk

Natural Environment Research Council (NERC)
www.nerc.ac.uk

Science and Technology Facilities Council (STFC)
www.stfc.ac.uk

They all have individual websites with training sections, news about government funding and databases of completed and on-going research projects. In many cases this also includes links to full-text articles and reports.

Wellcome Trust
www.wellcome.ac.uk

Major funder of scientific research. Website can be used to locate funding opportunities, plus news and reports from on-going projects. It also has a large educational resources section where teachers can find online curriculum materials covering all aspects of science and researchers can view case studies on public communication and ethics.

United States

American Association for the Advancement of Science

www.aaas.org

International organization which seeks to promote scientific research. Publishes the journal *Science*, which offers free access to some research news, articles and blogs.

National Science Foundation

www.nsf.gov

Independent federal agency created by US Congress in 1950 to promote scientific progress. Website has scientific discovery news and statistics on funding in the USA.

Science.Gov

www.science.gov

Portal to scientific news, policy, statistics and research from American government agencies. Also includes thesauri and image databases.

International

COST

www.cost.eu

Intergovernmental framework for European Cooperation in Science and Technology.

European Science Foundation

www.esf.org

Non-governmental organization dedicated to pan-European scientific networking and collaboration. Find news on research projects.

International Center for Scientific Research

www.cirs-tm.org

International organization, created to foster and promote all aspects of science and scientific research. Maintains a directory of scientific organizations worldwide.

Libraries

British Library

www.bl.uk/science

Houses one of the world's largest scientific research collections, including books, journals and electronic databases. Search the online catalogues and read the online research guides.

Radcliffe Science Library, University of Oxford
www.bodleian.ox.ac.uk/rsl

Legal deposit library entitled to receive copies of all published British scientific literature. These cover all aspects of science, with strong holdings in the history of science.

Encyclopedias

eLS: citable reviews in the life sciences (subscription required)
www.els.net

Over 4000 articles covering all aspects of the life sciences, from Biochemistry to Genetics and Virology.

Journal article indexes

Note that scientific publication often occurs first in working papers/pre-print series. Recommend that students check these as well!

Sciverse (subscription required)
www.info.sciverse.com

Maintained by Elsevier. Enables rapid cross-searching of a number of leading databases, including **ScienceDirect**, www.sciencedirect.com, which can be used to locate scientific articles, reference sources and e-books.

Web of Science (subscription required)
wok.mimas.ac.uk

Offers access to the *Science Citation Index*. Contains references to journal articles, book reviews and papers from 1956 onwards. Results can be sorted to highlight highly cited papers.

News services

AlphaGalileo
www.alphagalileo.org

Free independent, multilingual research news service covering science, applied science, business and the arts. Highlights the latest projects and findings from across Europe.

EurekAlert!
www.eurekalert.org

Maintained by the American Association for the Advancement of Science. Provides free access to the latest news and press releases from leading science research institutes and government departments. Some North American bias, although European news is also covered.

Nature

www.nature.com

Weekly science journal which publishes the latest research. Website also has blogs and jobs listings. Some materials limited to subscribers.

New Scientist

www.newscientist.com

Website of the famous magazine provides access to articles, videos, blogs, news and comment covering science and society. Some articles offered to subscribers only.

SciCentral

www.scicentral.com

Aggregates the latest news stories from a variety of science sites covering Biosciences, Chemistry, Physics.

Scientific American

www.scientificamerican.com

Founded in 1845. Oldest general scientific magazine designed for the public. Reports on the latest research. Some articles limited to subscribers only.

Talking Science

www.britishcouncil.org/talkingscience.htm

Site maintained by the British Council which has good snippets of general science news and events listings for the general public.

Working papers/Internet portals

arXiv.org

arxiv.org

Maintained by Cornell University. Search for open access working papers in a range of scientific subject areas including Physics, Mathematics, Computer Science, Quantitative Biology.

National Digital Library for Science

nsdl.org

Funded by the National Science Foundation. Free gateway to teaching and learning resources for Science, Technology, Engineering and Mathematics. Covers school and higher education levels. Links to high-quality organizations, journals and databases.

ScientificCommons

en.scientificcommons.org

Project of the University of St Gallen, which is creating a central place to search for scientific literature. It includes references (and many full text) papers and reports, many in European languages.

Scitopia

www.scitopia.org

Cross-search the research outputs of over 20 leading American scientific organizations to find references and many full-text links to papers, reports and articles covering all aspects of science and technology. Contributors include American Institute of Physics, Institute of Physics Publishing and Society for Industrial and Applied Mathematics.

WorldWideScience.org

worldwidescience.org

Developed and maintained by the Office of Scientific and Technical Information (OSTI). Enables rapid cross-searching of a growing number of national and international scientific databases and major websites.

Biology

BiologyBrowser

www.biologybrowser.org

Produced by Thomson Reuters. Provides links to many useful resources for students and researchers. They include news stories, an index of organism names and *Nomenclatural Glossary for Zoology*.

Biosis (subscription required)

thomsonreuters.com/products_services/science/science_products/a-z/biosis_previews

Search for references to journal articles, conference proceedings and papers. Back-file data from 1926 onwards is available via some subscription packages.

Biotechnology and Biological Sciences Research Council

www.bbsrc.ac.uk

Leading UK funding agency. Find details of cutting-edge research, conference listings and advice on how to apply for funding.

Higher Education Academy

www.heacademy.ac.uk

Supports lecturers in higher education. Subject coverage includes Biochemistry and Microbiology. Website has news on education policy and curriculum innovations. It includes free access to the *Bioscience Education* journal and the *ImageBank*, which contains thousands of copyright-cleared photographs for use in teaching.

National Biological Information Infrastructure (NBII)
www.nbii.gov
Managed by the US Geological Survey's Biological Informatics Office. Provides free access to data, information and images relating to the flora, fauna and environment of the USA. It includes reference tools for checking the scientific names of species.

Society of Biology
www.societyofbiology.org
Professional organization whose members include scientists, academics and students. Website includes job listings and links to educational resources.

Zoological Record (subscription required)
thomsonreuters.com/products_services/science/science_products/a-z/zoological_record
The world's oldest database of animal biology and taxonomy. Find references to literature from 1864 onwards.

Chemistry

American Chemical Society
portal.acs.org
Professional organization whose website is a rich source of information on news, events and on-going research. It also has a large educational section with resources for schoolteachers and lecturers.

Chemistry Central
www.chemistrycentral.com
Publishes open access peer-reviewed journals in Chemistry.

ESIS (European chemical Substances Information System)
esis.jrc.ec.europa.eu
EU database provides information on chemicals, covering subjects such as classification and labelling, risk assessments.

Merck Index (subscription required)
www.merckbooks.com/mindex
Available in print or online. Well established reference source covering chemicals, drugs and biologicals. Entries include chemical, common and generic names, molecular formulae, scientific and patent literature references.

ReAxys (subscription required)

www.reaxys.com

Chemical reaction and substance information. Merges the content of the *Patent Chemistry* database and *Beilstein* databases (journal literature on the structures, reactions and properties of organic carbon compounds). Records date from 18th century onwards.

Royal Society of Chemistry (RSC)

www.rsc.org

Largest professional organization in Europe. Website has news, events, publication reviews and job listings. It also provides information on the specialist RSC library, **www.rsc.org/Library/Services/index.asp**, and has a large education section with resources for teachers. They include online lesson materials and an extensive directory of links to free Chemistry websites.

The RSC also supports **ChemSpider, www.chemspider.com**, a free searchable database of chemical structures and properties.

TOXNET

toxnet.nlm.nih.gov

Free service of the United States government. Search many databases on toxicology, hazardous chemicals, environmental health and toxic releases. These include dictionaries and journal article indexes.

Physics

American Institute of Physics

www.aip.org

Federation of leading US Physics societies. Find news, research and conference listings and a resource directory of recommended websites.

European Physical Society

www.eps.org

Leading international forum. Use the website to locate research, publications, projects and conferences. It includes links to European Physics departments.

Inspec (subscription required)

www.theiet.org/publishing/inspec

Journal index published by the Institution of Engineering and Technology (IET), covering Physics, Electrical Engineering and Electronics.

Institute of Physics (IOP)

www.iop.org

World-famous organization representing physicists and promoting the teaching and learning of Physics. Website provides information on news, conferences and research. Features include:

- **IOP Journals, iopscience.iop.org/journals.** Has tables of contents and some free pre-print articles from leading IOP journals
- **PhysicsWorld, physicsworld.com.** A free news service
- **Physics.org, www.physics.org.** An extensive directory of links to recommended Physics websites.

Physical Sciences Resource Center

www.compadre.org/PSRC

Free service maintained by the American Association of Physics Teachers. Provides hundreds of links to online teaching and learning resources. These include simulations.

SciFinder (subscription required)

www.cas.org/products/scifindr/index.html

Cross-search the *Chemical Abstracts Service* with the *Medline* database of the National Library of Medicine. Coverage includes articles from 1907 onwards, plus chemical source information and chemical reaction databases.

SLAVONIC AND EAST EUROPEAN STUDIES

Typical questions

- How can I search for journal articles about post-communist transition in Hungary?
- Which libraries have good collections of Polish newspapers?

Points to consider

- This section concentrates on area studies. Many students will need to combine its use with resources listed in the relevant subject sections of this book. Common queries relate to post-1989 economic and political transitions (see **Economics** and **Political Science**) and Cold War studies (see **History**).

Where to look

Key organizations

Association for Slavic, East European, and Eurasian Studies (ASEEES)
www.aseees.org
Leading American scholarly society. Website has details of its journal *Slavic Review*, plus other research, conference and publication news.

British Association for Slavonic and East European Studies (BASEES)
www.basees.org.uk
Major scholarly society supporting many specialist study groups. Use the website to find out about its annual conference and on-going research activities.

International Council for Central and East European Studies (ICCEES)
www.iccees.org
Global network of research associations and scholars. Website provides free access to copies of its newsletter containing conference listings, book reviews and other research news. The site also has a directory of links to national societies worldwide.

Libraries and archives

Search the catalogues to find references to journals, books and newspapers. The websites have guides on how to search for Cyrillic items.

British Library Slavonic and East European Collections
www.bl.uk/reshelp/bldept/eurocoll/easteuropean/easteuropean.html
Largest collection in the UK. Website has guidance on holdings and a
useful directory of relevant resources elsewhere on the web.

**Council for Slavonic and East European Library and Information Services
(COSEELIS)**
www.lib.gla.ac.uk/COSEELIS/index.html
Organization representing libraries with major collections. Use the website
to find out about potential sources in the UK. Involved in the creation of
**COCOREES (Collaborative Collection Management Project for
Russian and East European Studies), www.cocorees.ac.uk,** a searchable
catalogue of East European and Slavonic book and journal holdings in
major UK libraries.

Slavic and East European Microform Project (SEEMP)
www.crl.edu/area-studies/seemp
Special project of the Center for Research Libraries which focuses on
preserving rare collections such as newspapers and pamphlets. Website has
lists and a catalogue for tracing libraries with holdings. Most are based in
North America.

UCL School of Slavonic and East European Studies Library (SSEES)
www.ssees.ucl.ac.uk/library
Leading teaching and research collection. Part of the University of
London. Website has an excellent internet directory.

Journal article indexes

**ABSEES: American Bibliography of Slavic and East European Studies
(subscription required)**
www.library.illinois.edu/absees
Leading index of journal articles, book chapters, dissertations, online resources and selected government publications on East-Central Europe and the
former Soviet Union published in the United States and Canada since 1990.

News services

Radio Free Europe/Radio Liberty (RFE/RL)
www.rferl.org
Service funded by the US Congress through the Broadcasting Board of
Governors (BBG). Covers regions where it regards news services as 'unfree'.
Includes the Balkans and Eurasia. Access stories, blogs and multimedia.

319

Transitions Online

www.tol.org

Covers political, social, cultural and economic issues in the former communist countries of Europe and Central Asia. Renowned for its use of local reporters. Headlines free, many articles and special reports require a subscription.

Statistical data

Use these in conjunction with the resources listed in the main **Statistical Data** section.

Centre for the Study of Public Policy, University of Aberdeen (CSPP) (subscription required)

www.abdn.ac.uk/cspp

Has conducted regular social surveys of the inhabitants of former Soviet regions since 1991. Examples include the *New Europe Barometer* and the *New Russia Barometer*. They are extremely useful for studying post-communist transitions in attitudes and behaviours.

European Bank for Reconstruction and Development (EBRD)

www.ebrd.com

Major development bank financing projects in Central and Eastern Europe and Eurasia. Get reports, publications and statistics on development and economics for individual countries. Includes the annual *Transitions Report.*

Nations in Transit

www.freedomhouse.org/template.cfm?page=17

Annual survey of democratic development in 29 countries from Central Europe to Eurasia, conducted by Freedom House. Access all issues from 2003 onwards.

Internet portals and digital libraries

Use these to locate high-quality academic resources. Especially good for finding Cyrillic-language resources.

CEEOL – Central and East European Online Library (subscription required)

www.ceeol.com

Database of articles from over 580 journals covering all subject areas. Many published in the region.

REENIC: Russian and East European Network Information Center
reenic.utexas.edu

Maintained by the University of Texas. Extensive regional and subject directories of academic resources with helpful comment on content.

REESWEB: Russian and East European Studies Server
www.ucis.pitt.edu/reesweb

Maintained by the University of Pittsburgh. Interdisciplinary. Search by keyword or browse to find websites (organizations, journals indexes etc.) Annotations on content provided.

ViFaOst: Virtuelle Fachbibliothek Osteuropa
www.vifaost.de

Great service funded by the German government, forming part of the Vascoda Network and involving leading German research institutions. Cross-search specialist journal article databases, library catalogues, data sources, online digital libraries and find relevant internet sites relating to all aspects of the history, politics, economics and culture of the nations of Eastern Europe. Some databases may be restricted to subscribers only. Also supports the **Slavistiks Portal, www.slavistik-portal.de,** which offers similar access to high-quality interdisciplinary resources. Specialist coverage includes Polish-language materials.

SOCIAL RESEARCH METHODS

Typical questions
- Where can I find information on qualitative research methods?
- What is mixed-methods research?

Points to consider
- This section focuses on social research methodology. It offers advice on how to conduct research. Students who need to access examples of completed social research should also consult the **Opinion Polls**, **Market Research** and **Statistical Data** sections. The latter highlights key data archives which have catalogues of surveys. To search for journal articles, consult the general **Journal Article Indexes** and **Sociology** sections.
- A major distinction is between qualitative and quantitative research. Very basically, qualitative research is usually concerned with understanding/interpreting human behaviour. Its methods often include fieldwork, focus groups, unstructured interviews and observation. Quantitative research focuses on the collection of empirical data and testing of hypotheses. This often involves the handling and evaluation of statistical data. Examples include longitudinal surveys, controlled trials and cohort studies. Some subjects, primarily the sciences, concentrate on this method. Others, including social sciences, often use a combination or mixed-methods approach, combining both qualitative and quantitative methods.
- A key area of concern is research ethics. The organizations listed below can offer advice on this, and those listed in the individual subject sections of the book are another starting-point.

Where to look
Key organizations
ESRC National Centre for Research Methods
> www.ncrm.ac.uk
> Central focus for research training in the UK. Use the website to access news, training and events listings. Linked with this is the **Researcher Development Initiative (RDI)**, www.rdi.ac.uk, which supports training for Social Science researchers at all stages of their careers. Its website has news plus some resources from projects which teach specific research skills.

Government Social Research Unit
> www.civilservice.gov.uk/my-civil-service/networks/professional/gsr/index.aspx

Provides the British government with social research. Its website has news and policy documents.

NatCen: National Centre for Social Research
www.natcen.ac.uk
Organization which conducts leading social research and offers training in qualitative and quantitative methods for researchers.

Social Research Association
www.the-sra.org.uk
Acts as a forum for researchers and practitioners in the UK. Use its website to locate news, jobs listings, training events covering the conduct, development and application of social research. Encompasses both qualitative and quantitative methods. Website includes a section on ethical guidelines.

Dictionaries and encyclopedias

Kempf-Leonard, K. (ed.) (2004) *Encyclopedia of Social Measurement,* **Elsevier**
Three-volume set available in print or online. Over 300 articles covering theory, techniques and applications of methods associated with qualitative and quantitative research.

SAGE Social Methods Online (subscription required)
srmo.sagepub.com
Access the full text of over 600 dictionaries, encyclopedias and handbooks published by SAGE covering all aspects of the research process.

News/Current awareness

Methodspace
www.methodspace.com
Online user discussion forum covering the full range of social research methods. Supported by Sage Publishing. Includes a useful directory of links to online resources.

Online tutorials

Research Ethics Guidebook
www.ethicsguidebook.ac.uk
Developed by a team at the Institute of Education. Guides researchers through the main issues and offers advice on writing research proposals, getting ethics committee approval and dealing with issues arising during fieldwork.

Social Research Methods

www.socialresearchmethods.net

Developed by William Trochim, Cornell University. This great site offers guidance to students in applied social science research. Features include online tutorials and a knowledgebase textbook on methods.

Qualitative research

Association for Qualitative Research

www.aqr.org.uk/about/index.shtml

UK-based professional association. Website has news, courses, job listings for practitioners.

ESDS Qualidata

www.esds.ac.uk/qualidata

Specialist research support centre based at the UK Data Archive. Offers assistance to creators and users of qualitative data. Website has a catalogue of datasets, including some designed for teaching and learning which can be used online. These include Dennis Marsden's study *Mothers Alone: Poverty and the Fatherless Family, 1955–1966*. Training is also offered in using qualitative data.

Forum: Qualitative Social Research

www.qualitative-research.net

Open access scholarly journal supported by the Institute for Qualitative Research, Freie Universität Berlin. Access articles, books reviews and news published since 1999.

International Institute for Qualitative Methodology

www.ualberta.ca/~iiqm

Hosts regular conferences on qualitative health research and methods. Website offers free access to its International Journal of Qualitative Methods.

Qualitative Report

www.nova.edu/ssss/QR

Online journal published since 1990 by Nova Southeastern University. Has online articles, conference listings, book reviews and links to key websites.

Social Research Update

sru.soc.surrey.ac.uk

Quarterly electronic and print publication from the University of Surrey. Covers theoretical, ethical and methodological issues in qualitative research. All issues from 1993 onwards can be read online.

Quantitative research

See also the **Statistical Data** section.

American Statistical Association Survey Research Methods Section

amstat.org/sections/srms

Website highlights news, conferences, specialist publications.

Centre for Longitudinal Studies

www.cls.ioe.ac.uk

Based at the Institute of Education, University of London. Houses several internationally renowned birth cohort studies, including the *1958 National Child Development Study*. It offers support in using the studies and training in research methods and techniques.

Institute for Social and Economic Research (ISER)

www.iser.essex.ac.uk

Specializes in the production and analysis of longitudinal data. Its website provides free access to working papers, research summaries and details of its forthcoming training for researchers.

Survey Resources Network (SRN)

surveynet.ac.uk

Funded by the Economic and Social Research Council (ESRC). Co-ordinates training and resources. Website offers free access to the *Survey Question Bank*, which has a searchable catalogue of questions used in UK cross-national surveys. It also has factsheets relating to social survey methodology.

SOCIAL WELFARE AND SOCIAL WORK

Typical questions

- I need to find recent statistics on child adoption.
- Where can I locate government guidance on standards of care?
- Where can I find journal articles on the impact of the Baby P case on child social services?

Points to consider

- Social welfare is a very broad-ranging topic which can be difficult to define. This section aims to highlight good general resources – covering social policy, social work and social care. It also has two specialist sub-divisions: studies of children and older persons. Particular care has been taken to highlight those resources which contain or link to evidence-based studies because these are often required by students.
- Note that researchers of children's issues may also benefit from consulting the **Education** section. Those interested in health issues relating to specific age groups should also consult the **Medicine and Nursing** section. In addition, many students will need to consult legislation (**Law**) and/or official publications (such as guidelines, circulars and research reports). These are covered separately in the **Government Publications** section.

Where to look

Key organizations

Professional bodies

British Association of Social Workers (BASW) – College of Social Work
www.basw.co.uk
Largest professional organization for social workers in the UK. Its website offers information on social work training and careers, a directory of social workers, plus lists of forthcoming events and comment on recent government policy.

International Association of Schools of Social Work (IASSW)
www.iassw-aiets.org
International body which supports social work education organizations worldwide. Useful directory of links to national bodies.

International Federation of Social Workers
www.ifsw.org

Global network of national social work organizations. Use the website to trace news, events and links to key bodies worldwide.

National Association of Social Workers
www.naswdc.org
Largest professional body in the USA. Find out about careers and get news, events and research listings.

Social Care Institute for Excellence (SCIE)
www.scie.org.uk
Organization seeking to improve quality by promoting good practice amongst the UK's social care workforce. Broad remit includes social work, plus services for adults and children. Site provides free access to the **Research Register for Social Care, www.researchregister.org.uk/ default.asp**, a database of current and recent social care research in England, Wales and Northern Ireland. Other features of the site include news stories, events listings, case studies of good practice and free access to its bibliographic indexing service, *Social Care Online*.

Scholarly bodies

UK

Higher Education Academy
www.heacademy.ac.uk
Seeks to support teaching and learning in UK higher education. Includes subject coverage of social policy and social work. Its website has details of events and useful teaching and learning resources for lecturers.

Social Policy Association
www.social-policy.org.uk
Professional association supporting researchers and students of social policy in the UK. Use its website to trace examples of recent research from specialist groups, events lists and news.

International

European Centre for Social Welfare Policy and Research
www.euro.centre.org
United Nations-affiliated intergovernmental organization concerned with all aspects of social welfare policy and research. In addition to news and conference listings, its website links to national organizations in Europe.

International Council on Social Welfare (ICSW)
www.icsw.org

Non-governmental organization which represents national and local organizations in more than 70 countries throughout the world. Website is useful for keeping up to date with global trends. It can also be used to locate relevant national organizations worldwide.

International Social Security Association (ISSA)
www.issa.int

International organization supporting good practice in social security. Its website provides free access to a detailed database of country profiles, an observatory monitoring news stories and links to social security legislation worldwide. Topics covered include social benefits, pensions, unemployment and child care.

Network for European Social Policy Analysis
www.espanet.org

Association of academics interested in social policy in Europe. Its website offers good starting-points for keeping up to date with the latest research and tracing national and regional social policy groups.

Dictionaries and encyclopedias

Mizrahi, T. and Davis, L. E. (2008) *Encyclopedia of Social Work*, 20th edn, **Oxford University Press**

Prestigious four-volume set published in association with the National Association of Social Workers (USA). Over 400 articles covering all aspects of social work. Each entry has a bibliography to guide further reading.

Pierson, J. and Thomas, M. (2010) *Dictionary of Social Work: the definitive A to Z of social work and social care*, **Open University**

Designed for students. Contains over 1500 concise definitions of terms and concepts relating to all aspects of social work and social care.

Journal article indexes

ASSIA: Applied Social Sciences Index and Abstracts on the Web (subscription required)
www.csa.com/factsheets/assia-set-c.php

Indexes over 500 titles covering health and social science information, with a focus on applied information for the professional.

Social Care Online
www.scie-socialcareonline.org.uk

Maintained by the Social Care Institute for Excellence (SCIE). Provides free access to a searchable database of references to journal articles, government reports and grey literature covering all aspects of social welfare, social work and social care. Main emphasis on the UK, although other English-language areas of the world are also well covered. Links are provided to full text where available.

Social Policy and Practice (subscription required)
www.ovid.com/site/catalog/DataBase/1859.jsp

Brings together materials indexed by several leading databases: *Child Data* from the National Children's Bureau; *Planex* from IDOX; *Acompline* from the Greater London Authority; *Social Care Online* from the Social Care Institute for Excellence; *AgeInfo* from the Centre for Policy on Ageing. These provide thousands of references to journal articles, books and reports covering all aspects of social welfare and social services. There is a strong emphasis on research relating to Britain and Europe with an evidence-based focus.

Social Policy Digest
journals.cambridge.org/spd/action/home

Produced by the Social Policy Association as a companion to its scholarly journals the *Journal of Social Policy* and *Social Policy and Society*. A valuable resource for students and researchers which provides brief news and research summaries covering all areas of social policy. Access to some full-text journal articles requires a subscription. Archives of summaries available from 2002 onwards.

Social Services Abstracts (subscription required)
www.csa.com/factsheets/ssa-set-c.php

Indexes over 1300 serials and includes abstracts of journal articles Topics covered include social work, human services, social welfare, social policy and community development. Coverage is from 1979 onwards.

Social Work Abstracts (subscription required)
www.ovid.com/site/catalog/DataBase/150.jsp

Produced by the National Association of Social Workers (USA). Leading index to articles and reports covering social work. Coverage from 1977 onwards.

Internet gateways and portals

E-Library for Global Welfare
www.globalwelfarelibrary.org

Site created by academic staff from the Open University, University of Sheffield, University of Bath and STAKES Finland. Provides free access to an excellent searchable catalogue of links to key resources covering all aspects of comparative social policy.

Information for Practice

ifp.es.its.nyu.edu

Site edited by Dr Gary Holden, New York University Silver School of Social Work, which aims to keep social service professionals up to date with news and research. Includes some tables of contents from key journal titles, books reviews, news (mainly from the USA) and conference listings.

Learning Exchange

lx.iriss.org.uk

Digital library developed by IRISS (the Institute for Research and Innovation in Social Services, Scotland) which aims to provide free access to evidence-based teaching and learning resources covering all aspects of social services. Access case studies, news and reports. There is some emphasis on Scottish materials; however, coverage of other areas of the UK is also good.

Social welfare of children

Key libraries

National Children's Bureau

resources.ncb.org.uk/resources

Specialist multi-disciplinary library covering all aspects of children's services (with a major focus on the UK). Use the website to access the catalogue and consult some news and research guides. Some research and parliamentary current awareness digests are offered for subscribers only.

NSPCC Information Service

www.nspcc.org.uk/inform/research/information_service/
safeguarding_information_service_wda47732.html

The UK's leading specialist library for child protection and welfare literature. Open to the public for reference. Use the website to search the catalogue and consult reading lists.

Journal article indexes

Child Data (subscription required)

www.childdata.org.uk

Maintained by the National Children's Bureau. Indexes the complete holdings of the library plus journal articles, reports and press coverage of children's issues from 1996 onwards.

OntheWeb

www.nfer.ac.uk/what-we-offer/information/ontheweb

Monthly current awareness newsletter produced by the National Foundation for Educational Research. While its main focus is on education, it also covers schooling and the care of children generally. Current and past issues can be viewed via the website.

Online libraries and portals

Centre for Excellence and Outcomes in Children and Young People's Services

www.c4eo.org.uk

UK organization. The website aims to gather together in one place an evidence base of what works in providing care and services for children. Key topics include childhood poverty, safeguarding vulnerable children, schooling, disability and childhood, and family services. Access research news, full-text reports, case studies of good practice and statistical data.

Child Welfare Information Gateway

www.childwelfare.gov

Maintained by leading US government departments. Provides free access to information and US government resources relating to children. Key areas are child abuse and neglect, foster care and adoption.

Children's House

www.child-abuse.com/childhouse

Collaboration between a number of leading child welfare organizations including Child Abuse Prevention Network, Children's Rights Centre, Childwatch International, UNESCO and WHO. Maintains a detailed directory of links to key websites.

NSPCC Inform

www.nspcc.org.uk/Inform/informhub_wda49931.html

Specialist website designed for childcare professionals and researchers. Consult examples of the latest research reports and sign up to get regular news updates of developments covering all aspects of child welfare. Main focus is on the UK.

Research in Practice

www.rip.org.uk

Site produced in collaboration between the University of Sheffield and the Association of Directors of Children's Services. Aims to support evidence-informed practice with children and families. Provides free access to news stories, case studies and a database of research reviews.

Statistical data

Use these in conjunction with the sources suggested in the main **Statistical Data** section.

Child Trends

www.childtrends.org

Non-profit organization which specializes in providing research relating to all aspects of children's lives in the USA. Its website has an excellent data section with graphs covering all stages of the child's life and topic areas such as health and safety and economic and social well-being.

Department of Education

www.education.gov.uk/

Responsible for education and children's services. Access key government reports and statistics.

OECD

www.oecd.org/els/social/family/database

Produces statistics on social expenditure from OECD nations. Coverage includes benefits and public expenditure. Some materials are offered to subscribers only. Site also has an excellent collection of links to other data suppliers.

Poverty Site

www.poverty.org.uk

Site maintained by Guy Palmer using major statistical resources. Aims to track UK levels of poverty and social exclusion in income, work, health and education. Offers free access to over 100 statistical indicators.

United Nations Children's Fund (UNICEF)

www.unicef.org/statistics

Key UN agency focusing on children worldwide. Publishes an annual report called *The State of the World's Children*. Each issue has themed articles and a range of economic and social indicators relating to the health and welfare of children in specific nations. These can be accessed via its specialist website **ChildInfo, www.childinfo.org,** which also contains other free reports and country profiles.

Social welfare of older persons

Key libraries

Centre for Policy on Ageing

www.cpa.org.uk/information/information_services.html

Independent UK-based research organization. Its reference library has a specialist collection of books, journals and grey literature. Search the catalogue for references and consult some of its reading lists on key topics. The website also maintains the **National Database of Ageing Research,** **www.cpa.org.uk/research/ndar_about.html,** which focuses on current and on-going projects from academic departments, research units and government bodies covering all aspects of old age and related social policy. Main emphasis is on the UK.

GeroLit

vzlbs2.gbv.de:8080/DB=41

Online catalogue of the Deutsches Zentrum für Altersfragen/DZA (German Centre of Gerontology Library). Useful for tracing references to key publications from European nations. Key topics include work and retirement, economy of old age, health and social care, family and social relations of older persons.

Journal article indexes

AgeInfo

www.cpa.org.uk/ageinfo

Cross-disciplinary database containing references to journal articles and books which is produced by the library of the Centre for Policy on Ageing. Also offers detailed information on several thousand organizations which specialize in the field of ageing and an international calendar of forthcoming events.

Ageline (subscription required)

www.ebscohost.com/public/ageline

Leading journal index database originally produced by the American Association of Retired Persons (AARP). Coverage from 1978 onwards. Encompasses all aspects of the health, welfare and social policy of persons aged 50 plus.

Statistical data

Specialist services include:

World Health Organization
www.who.int/ageing/en
Consult reports and the latest data.

Internet gateways and portals

AgeSource/AgeStats Worldwide
www.aarpinternational.org/database/database_list.htm
Maintained by AARP (American Association of Retired Persons). Provides free access to a directory of links to hundreds of quality websites relating to all aspects of ageing from over 25 nations worldwide. AgeStats offers links to sources of statistical data. These focus on comparisons of economic and social conditions in many different regions of the world.

Worldwide Resources in Ageing
www.cpa.org.uk/ageinfo/worldres.html
Free directory of links to key organizations worldwide. Coverage is stronger in terms of the UK and Europe.

SOCIOLOGY

Typical questions

- Where can I get a list of recent articles by Anthony Giddens?
- I need a brief summary of symbolic interactionism.

Points to consider

- Increasing numbers of classic (out of copyright) Sociology texts can now be found online. However, students need to check the details of the edition and/or translation carefully before use.
- Many sociologists need to conduct social surveys, so the section on **Social Research Methods** may also be relevant.

Where to look

Key organizations

Use these to find examples of specialist research groups, key journals and lists of conferences.

American Sociological Association

> **www.asanet.org**
>
> National association for sociologists. Website has sections on research news and resources for lecturers.

British Sociological Association

> **www.britsoc.co.uk**
>
> Professional association for the UK. Large section for students with guidance on where and what to study.

European Sociological Association (ESA)

> **www.europeansociology.org**
>
> Supports teaching and research in Europe. Get lists and news about specialist research networks in Europe, plus lists of national sociological associations.

Higher Education Academy

> **www.heacademy.ac.uk**
>
> Specialist support for UK lecturers. Subject coverage includes Sociology. Access advice, training and free resources, including the **Companion for Undergraduate Dissertations: Sociology, Anthropology, Politics, Social Policy, Social Work and Criminology, www.socscidiss.bham.ac.uk,** a survival guide which contains useful tips on literature searching skills and preparing a dissertation at undergraduate level.

International Sociological Association
www.isa-sociology.org
International organization founded in 1949 which has special consultative status with the United Nations. Supports international conferences and specialist research networks. Also publishes key journals such as the *International Sociology Review of Books*, which highlights significant new publications. Website has news, conference calendars.

Libraries and archives

British Library
www.bl.uk/reshelp/findhelpsubject/socsci/sociol/sociologypage.html
Holds an extensive collection of books and journals covering all aspects of Sociology. Also available are many social surveys.

LSE Library
www2.lse.ac.uk/library/home.aspx
Established in 1896, the working library of the London School of Economics and Political Science. Use the library catalogue to locate relevant books and journals. The LSE Archives also holds papers from the **British Sociological Association, www2.lse.ac.uk/library/archive/ holdings/social_policy.aspx**.

Dictionaries and encyclopedias

Blackwell Encyclopedia of Sociology Online (subscription required)
www.sociologyencyclopedia.com
More than 1700 entries written by experts in the field. Covers theories, concepts and key individuals. Includes a timeline of Sociology. Updated regularly to cover new developments.

Turner, B., Abercrombie, N. and Hill, S. (2006) *The Penguin Dictionary of Sociology*, **6th edn, Penguin**
Useful for introducing students to key concepts, theories and persons, covering all aspects of Sociology.

Journal article indexes

International Bibliography of the Social Sciences (IBSS) (subscription required)
www.proquest.co.uk/en-UK/catalogs/databases/detail/ibss-set-c.shtml
Interdisciplinary database; one of the main areas covered is Sociology. Materials from 1952 onwards.

Sociological Abstracts (subscription required)
www.csa.com/factsheets/socioabs-set-c.php
Long established resource, indexing over 1800 journal titles, plus book chapters and conference papers. Covers all fields of Sociology from 1951 onwards.

Internet gateways and portals

Use these to locate examples of high-quality Sociology websites.

SocioLog
www.sociolog.com
Maintained by academic Julian Dierkes. A well regarded directory of links to themes in Sociology, professional associations, Sociology departments and much more.

Sociology Central
www.sociology.org.uk
Resource guide maintained by Chris Livesey. Although mainly aimed at providing resources for A-level Sociology teachers, it offers a wealth of information on different aspects of Sociology that would appeal to a wider audience. There are introductory guides, course notes and handouts on topics such as social class, deviance, divorce, many of which can be downloaded free of charge.

SocioSite
www.sociosite.net
Comprehensive directory of Sociology websites maintained by the faculty of Social Sciences at the University of Amsterdam. The subject areas section provides references to key websites for specialist sub-fields of Sociology. The sociologists section has links to online works and personal websites of famous writers. Many of these contain full-text articles and books.

SPEECHES

Typical questions
- Where can I get the text of Martin Luther King's 'I have a dream' speech?
- Last week the Prime Minister made a speech to the European Parliament. Can I get it online?

Points to consider
- The internet has revolutionized access to speeches. It is increasingly possible to access transcripts and audio files online. However, in order to search successfully try to find out as much information as possible about the speech, its date and possible location.
- Many governments provide free access to recent and historic speeches by prime ministers and presidents. Transcripts of speeches made in parliament can be found in parliamentary proceedings. Colleges and universities often create podcasts and/or webcasts of speeches by famous visitors, and some famous politicians and personalities provide free access to materials via their personal websites. National libraries may also hold sound archives of some key speeches. Some important speeches are also indexed in the resources listed in the **Quotations** section.
- Remember to check whether a speech is abridged or transcribed in full and its copyright status before using!

Where to look
MacArthur, B. (ed.) (1996) *Penguin Book of Historic Speeches*, **Penguin**
Over 100 summaries of famous examples from Plato to Mandela.

MacArthur, B. (ed.) (1998) *Penguin Book of Twentieth-Century Speeches*, **2nd edn, Penguin**
Good overview of key speeches ranging from Churchill to Hitler. Mainly European and North American speakers. Book gives summaries, not full transcripts.

Digital libraries
American Rhetoric.com
> **www.americanrhetoric.com/speechbank.htm**
> Useful online speech bank site maintained by Dr Michael E. Eidenmuller. Indexes over 5000 items, including speeches by politicians, show business stars and famous Americans. Most include transcripts and audio files.

British Library Sound Archive

www.bl.uk/reshelp/bldept/soundarch

National collection includes an oral history section containing historic speeches and addresses by British politicians from the late 19th century onwards. The website has a searchable catalogue plus access to a selection of online historic recordings, **sounds.bl.uk**. Some materials can be downloaded free of charge.

Library of Congress

www.loc.gov/rr/record/matrices.html

Recorded sound collection contains some 2.5 million audio recordings, including of many famous Americans. The **National Jukebox**, **www.loc.gov/jukebox**, provides free access to historic recordings. These include some presidential speeches (mainly early 20th century).

Presidential Speech Archive

millercenter.org/scripps/archive/speeches

Maintained by the Scripps Library, Miller Center of Public Affairs, University of Virginia. Offers free access to transcripts and, for more recent examples, audio and video files of important speeches from 1789 to the present day. They include inaugural addresses, State of the Union speeches and farewell addresses.

Vincent Voice Library

vvl.lib.msu.edu

Specialist archive of Michigan State University. Holds over 40,000 hours of spoken-word recordings, dating back to 1888. Includes speeches by many US presidents. Website offers free access to some sound clips.

SPORTS STUDIES

Typical questions

- I need to find articles on women's participation in sport in the 20th century.
- Where can I locate information on footballers' transfer fees?

Points to consider

- Studies of sport are becoming increasingly popular in higher/further education. Courses can cover Social Studies (see **Sociology**); Physiotherapy (see **Medicine and Nursing**) and the Economics of Sport (see **Economics**).
- There are many internet resources available. In particular, sporting events, such as the Olympic Games, often have their own dedicated websites which offer the most up-to-date information. However, beware! Many sites are created by fans, who may have little academic background. Always check the origin and currency of the information provided. This section focuses on scholarly resources.

Where to look

Key organizations

Academic and scholarly

Use these to locate references to academic research, conferences and publications.

British Philosophy of Sport Association
www.philosophyofsport.org.uk
Concerned with the nature, ethics and value of sport.

Higher Education Academy
www.heacademy.ac.uk
Seeks to support UK lecturers. Subject coverage includes sport. Website provides free access to case studies of good practice for lecturers plus full-text articles from the *Journal of Hospitality, Leisure, Sport and Tourism Education (JoHLSTE)*. The latter regularly publishes research articles and reviews of educational resources.

Leisure Association
www.leisure-studies-association.info
Scholarly society covering all areas of sport, leisure and tourism. Website has tables of contents and abstracts of all its scholarly publications.

International

International Association for the Philosophy of Sport (IAPS)
iaps.net
Aims to promote scholarship internationally. Get references to conferences and research projects on sports philosophy and ethics worldwide.

International Council of Sport Science and Physical Education (ICSSPE)
www.icsspe.org
Strong emphasis on applying academic sports science research to the practical field of physical education. Website contains surveys of physical education in schools, plus free access to other articles from issues of its bulletin.

International Society for the History of Physical Education and Sport (ISHPES)
ishpes.org
Key starting-point for sports historians. Trace references to publications and events.

International Society of Sport Psychology (ISSP)
www.issponline.org
Focuses on the study of the psychological aspects of physical activity, sport and exercise.

International Sociology of Sport Association
www.issa.otago.ac.nz
Umbrella organization for scholars and organizations worldwide. Useful for tracing specialist research about social aspects of sport.

Professional and sporting bodies

Use these to locate careers information, codes of ethics and sporting rules and standards. Most should also have details of recent, forthcoming and historic sporting events.

UK

Association for Physical Education (afPE)
www.afpe.org.uk
Subject association for UK physical education and sports teachers. Use the website to get information on sport in schools.

British Association of Sport and Exercise Sciences (BASES)
www.bases.org.uk

Professional association covering sports psychology, physiology and coaching.

British Olympic Committee
www.olympics.org.uk

Prepares British athletes for summer and winter games. Website has lists of current Olympic sports, news about forthcoming games and profiles of elite athletes. Some historical information on past games. Note that there is a separate **Paralympics Association**, with details of paralympic games and athletes, **www.paralympics.org.uk**.

Institute of Sport and Recreation Management
www.isrm.co.uk

Professional body for those involved in managing and developing sport and recreation services in the UK. Topics covered include swimming pool and leisure facility management.

UK Sport
www.uksport.gov.uk

Established in 1997. Body responsible for investing public funds in sport. Its website is a comprehensive guide to UK sports governance, funding and events. Look at a library of recent photos and videos from sporting events, profiles of key athletes, and its comprehensive directory of links to national and international governing bodies for specific sports, **www.uksport.gov.uk/ links**. Note that this organization is broader in scope than the British Olympic Committee, as not all sports are included in the Olympic Games!

International

Association of Recognised IOC International Sports Federations (ARISF)
www.arisf.org

Covers sports recognized by the International Olympic Committee. Get news from their international governing bodies.

International Association of Athletics Federations
www.iaaf.org

Website has good online news and video content covering sporting events and world records. Also has sections on anti-drug, anti-doping measures.

International Olympic Committee
www.olympic.org

Official site of the Olympic Games. In addition to current news stories, search a list of past medalists, look at profiles of famous athletes and get links and information on over 200 national Olympic committees worldwide.

SportAccord
www.sportaccord.com

Formerly General Association of International Sports Federations (GAISF). Umbrella organization for all (Olympic and non-Olympic) international sports federations. Get information on national and international bodies governing specific sports.

Government bodies

Remember that government departmental structures often change. When seeking information on historical bodies, refer to the **Government Publications** section.

Department for Culture, Media and Sport
www.culture.gov.uk/sport

Body currently responsible for UK policy. Use the website to trace information on legislation, funding and regulation. Also includes coverage of UK bids to host major sporting events. Remember to explore the links on the site to associated organizations. These often give more details on how money is invested in specific sports. For example, **Sport England**, **www.sportengland.org**, promotes sports in England. Its website has details of grants, community projects and a research section with academic studies on sports participation and the economic impact of sport.

European Commission
ec.europa.eu/sport/index_en.htm

Find details of new policy and reports on sport from the EU. It also includes some coverage of individual European nations.

House of Commons Culture, Media and Sport Committee
www.parliament.uk/business/committees/committees-archive/
culture-media-and-sport

Monitors the policy, administration and expenditure of the Department for Culture, Media and Sport. Read minutes and reports which discuss and analyse policy and performance.

Libraries and archives

British Library
www.bl.uk/reshelp/findhelpsubject/socsci/sport/sport.html

Collections cover all aspects of sports science and theory, including government documents, journals, trade publications and technical reports.

Website provides guides to current and historical holdings, including special collections covering the history of football and cricket.

University of Central Lancashire Library
www.uclan.ac.uk/students/library/outdoor_studies_guide.php
Holds the Sport England National Collection, comprising over 8000 books and reports covering Sports Science, Sports Management and training in specific sports. The website also has a guide to key resources for researching sports studies.

Dictionaries

Malcolm, D. (2008) *The SAGE Dictionary of Sports Studies*, **Sage Publications**
Designed to help students to understand concepts relating to the history, politics, economics and theory of sport. Each entry has a definition and list of key readings.

Tomlinson, A. (2010) *A Dictionary of Sports Studies*, **Oxford University Press**
Over 1000 entries covering the social, political and economic concepts of sport. Also has some biographies of famous sports persons and sporting organizations. Appendices include lists of medal winners at Olympic Games.

Journal article indexes

Leisure Tourism (subscription required)
www.cabi.org/leisuretourism
Wide coverage of tourism and all aspects of leisure, including Sport. Sports coverage encompasses the use of drugs in sport, sports psychology, education and employment and the impact of major sporting events on the regions. Materials from 1973 onwards.

SPORTDiscus (subscription required)
www.ebscohost.com/academic/sportdiscus-with-full-text
Comprehensive index covering Sports and Sports Medicine from 1985 onwards. Includes references to journal articles, reports, book chapters.

Statistical data

Most of the international federations and sporting bodies listed in the key organizations sub-section offer some statistics. Government department websites may contain financial allocation figures. Additionally, the following sites may be of value.

Statistics in Sport

www.amstat.org/sections/SIS

Special-interest section of the American Statistical Association. Website provides some links to sources. Also highlights key journals covering academic studies of sports statistics.

UK National Statistics

www.statistics.gov.uk/hub/people-places/people/culture-and-sport/index.html

Provides information on recent social surveys relating to leisure, culture and sport. Get statistics on participation from approximately 2000 onwards.

Internet gateways and portals

Restrictions of space mean that this section cannot provide lists of good reference sources for individual sports. Use these resources to trace more detailed recommendations!

Scholarly Sports Sites

www.starkcenter.org/research/web/sportswebsites

Comprehensive site maintained by H. J. Lutcher Stark Center for Physical Culture and Sports. Extensive sub-sections covering sports organizations, sub-fields, journals and more.

SocioSite

www.sociosite.net/topics/leisure.php

Based at the faculty of Social Sciences at the University of Amsterdam. It covers Sociology in the broadest sense; its leisure and sports section has links to major organizations, journals and websites.

STANDARDS

Typical questions

- What is kitemark certification?
- How can I get hold of BS EN ISO/IEC 7810:1996?
- I need a list of standards relating to the food industry.

Points to consider

- A standard is a published specification that establishes a common language and contains a technical specification or other precise criteria to enable consistency and reliability. Standards are applied to many products, materials and services.
- Standards are prepared through discussions in European (CEN) and international (ISO) committees. In the UK they are made available as British Standards and the published documents are prefixed with the letters BS.
- ES means the standard is a European Standard and is used throughout Europe. ISO means the standard is an International Standard and may be used throughout the world.

Where to look

American National Standards Institute (ANSI)

www.ansi.org

Oversees the creation and use of standards in the USA. Its website has information about and a catalogue of standards. Full access for subscribers only.

British Standards Institution (BSI)

www.bsigroup.com

UK standards and quality services organization. Website has a searchable catalogue of standards where you can browse standards by industry sector. Online access to full text is for subscribers only.

BSI Education website

www.bsieducation.org/Education/about/default.shtml

Really useful educational website created by the British Standards Institution. Find out what a British Standard is and how to locate them. Sections for school children contain classroom activities. The higher education section highlights useful standards for specific courses and offers tips on research. A resources section has a useful list of UK libraries where full standards can be found.

International Organization for Standardization (ISO)
www.iso.org/iso/home.html
Network of the national standards institutes of over 150 nations. Its website offers a catalogue, plus detailed information on the nature and development process of standards. It also includes a useful directory of national organizations.

STATISTICAL DATA

Typical questions

- I need some data on unemployment in Germany.
- Where can I get UK GDP figures?

Points to consider

- The trend for free data to be made available on the internet seems to be increasing students' usage. However, they should be reminded to evaluate carefully the date, sources and methodology of compilation. Nor should they forget that many libraries have older printed materials and/or subscription services which are more extensive!
- This section provides support in tracing general sources. Many of the subject sections also have statistical data sub-sections.

Where to look

Open data

Many governments worldwide are releasing statistical data onto the internet. Increasingly this is done through specialist open data websites which aggregate data from many departments. However, check dates and extent of coverage because not all may be included.

National governments

Data.Gov
> **www.data.gov**
> United States government.

Data.Gov.UK
> **data.gov.uk**
> UK government. Many new, interesting and topical datasets are also discussed on the **Guardian datablog, www.guardian.co.uk/news/datablog**.

Note that many countries which do not have a central data store post statistics online on departmental websites. A good starting-point is to trace the central statistical office. The **World Bank** has a directory, **go.worldbank.org/AT0N3TZW40**. Data.gov has an index of other key examples, **www.data.gov/opendatasites**, as does the **Open Government Data** website **opengovernmentdata.org**, a project of the Open Knowledge Foundation, which is seeking greater access to government information.

International organizations

The following are key examples.

Eurostat (European Union)
 epp.eurostat.ec.europa.eu

OECD
 stats.oecd.org/Index.aspx

United Nations
 data.un.org

World Bank
 data.worldbank.org

Data archives

Specialist organizations for curating large-scale digital qualitative and quantitative datasets. Many nations have national centres where extensive data (including items not available on the internet) can be downloaded. This often requires registration, so check locally about access agreements.

UK

EDINA
 edina.ac.uk
 Academic data archive based at the University of Edinburgh. Renowned for GIS and mapping data, although other social science areas are also covered.

UK Data Archive
 www.data-archive.ac.uk
 Holds the largest collection of social sciences and humanities data in the UK. Core services include:

- **Economic and Social Data Service (ESDS) www.esds.ac.uk**. Key starting-point for tracing economic and social qualitative and quantitative data series. There are separate sections for UK government and international data (including IMF, Eurostat and OECD). There is also the specialist Qualidata (qualitative data) unit. Search the catalogue or browse by theme. Registered users (including many UK institutions) can perform online data analysis. There are user support sections for teachers with advice and sample exercises for using data in teaching and learning.

- **History Data Service hds.essex.ac.uk**. Search the online catalogue and user guides. Key resources include historical population and census reports.

International

Council of European Social Science Data Archives (CESSDA)
www.cessda.org
Network of data archives in Europe. Cross-search a growing number of their catalogues online and get information and news about holdings.

Inter-University Consortium for Political and Social Research (ICPSR)
www.icpsr.umich.edu/icpsrweb/ICPSR
International network. It hosts thousands of social science data sets. These include North American and international coverage. Key areas are ageing, education, health, criminal justice and population. Online catalogues and tutorials available.

International Household Survey Network Catalog
www.ihsn.org
Maintained by the World Bank Data group. Enables users to quickly identify surveys undertaken in a specific nation by national or international agencies. They include census and population surveys, household and economic surveys. Typical entries give dates, sampling methods and links to websites where information on access can be obtained. The site also has an extensive question bank, plus tools and guidelines on microdata collection and questionnaire design and analysis. Entries for some countries date from the 1950s onwards.

Support services

Designed to support specialist data librarians. Good for locating specialist training, discussion of new open data sites and technical issues relating to data curation.

DISC-UK (Data Information Specialists Committee – United Kingdom)
www.disc-uk.org

International Association for Social Science Information Services & Technology (IASSIST)
www.iassistdata.org
International membership organization.

STUDENT UNIONS

Typical questions

- Where can I get a list of student unions in Europe?
- I want to find out about national campaigns regarding student funding.

Points to consider

- Student unions can help with questions regarding finance and grants, accommodation, tax issues and study skills. Their websites also offer comments on national issues regarding education policy and funding.
- All universities will have their own local student unions. These should be the first point of contact for specialist advice. The resources listed here offer supplementary guidance. There are more specific sections for **Disabled** and **International Students**. Other starting-points are the scholarly associations listed in the subject sections.

Where to look

European Students' Union

www.esu-online.org

Umbrella association of over 40 unions from European nations. Use the website to find information on student concerns and contact national European bodies.

International Union of Students

www.stud.uni-hannover.de/gruppen/ius

Worldwide association of national unions. Website has contact details of members plus information on world student congresses.

National Union of Students (NUS)

www.nus.org.uk

National voice for the UK. Has a directory of local student unions, campaign news and discounts for students.

United States Student Association

www.usstudents.org

THESES AND DISSERTATIONS

Typical questions

- Where can I get a list of recent theses on management theory?
- I want to look at a copy of this thesis. How can I get it?
- Are there any websites where I can download examples of PhD theses?

Points to consider

- Masters dissertations are not usually held in academic libraries. They may be available in the relevant academic department of the university, either in print or on the website.
- Increasing numbers of countries are now digitizing PhD theses and placing them on open access online. Examples of these are included below. However, many websites are not yet comprehensive. Check which universities and dates are covered.
- Individual universities may also have examples of PhD theses from their alumni. Again, check years of coverage.
- The sources below are recommended. Another good source of advice is your local interlibrary loans/interlending department.

Where to look

UK

EthOS

> **ethos.bl.uk**
>
> Working to build a centralized store of digitized theses from UK higher education institutions. Users can register free of charge and download increasing numbers of full-text PhD dissertations covering all subject areas. Abstracts are available for other items which can then be digitized on demand. This is a fee-based service and users should refer to their local interlibrary loans department for advice before use. Note that at the present time the site does not maintain a comprehensive historical listing of all UK PhDs. Also, some universities are not participating in the project. Further details on coverage are given on the website. Students requiring a comprehensive literature search should refer to *Index to Theses*.

Index to Theses (subscription required)

> **www.theses.com**
>
> Catalogue of all theses accepted for higher degrees by higher education institutions in Great Britain and Ireland from 1715 onwards. Includes

abstracts and links to items available in full text on *EthOS* and a number of UK university websites.

International

Australasian Digital Theses

adt.caul.edu.au

Free access to thousands of titles from Australian and New Zealand universities. Mainly 1990s onwards. Covers all subject areas.

DART-Europe E-theses Portal (DEEP)

www.dart-europe.eu

This service (which is currently under development) allows you to search for the full texts of research theses from a growing number of European countries. Note that it does not include all European universities.

Database of African Theses and Dissertations (DATAD OnLine)

www.aau.org/data

Project of the Association of African Universities which aims to increase the visibility of African research. Searchable catalogue of abstracts of masters and doctoral theses from a number of African colleges. Check website for list of participating universities.

Networked Digital Library of Theses and Dissertations

www.ndltd.org

Excellent starting-point for tracing the existence of online theses. Maintains a searchable catalogue of e-theses and a directory of links to key websites.

Proquest Dissertations and Theses (subscription required)

www.proquest.co.uk

Access the full text of thousands of doctoral theses submitted from 1997 onwards. Coverage mainly from North American institutions. Earlier titles (from 1861 onwards) and some Masters theses have abstracts. The site provides free access to some full-text titles at **pqdtopen.proquest.com**.

Theses Canada Portal

www.collectionscanada.ca/thesescanada/index-e.html

Free access to a database of the full-text of thousands of Canadian theses and dissertations. Bibliographic records for older items submitted since the 1960s.

THINK-TANKS/POLICY INSTITUTES

Typical questions
- Where can I get a list of social policy think-tanks?
- Who funds the Pensions Policy Institute?

Points to consider
- It can be quite difficult to define what constitutes a think-tank or policy institute. Very generally, the terms encompass organizations that conduct research and engage in advocacy in policy areas such as social welfare, economics and technology. Sources of funding can range from government, political party and business backing to charitable status. Therefore it is a good idea to check the status of the organization before relying on its results.
- Students/academic staff are often interested in the research outputs of think-tanks because these frequently include cutting-edge project reports and pamphlets. Increasingly, materials are published on websites rather than being purchased in paper by libraries. Therefore internet searches for the organizations are advised.
- This section offers a starting-point to tracing major think-tanks. Many of the internet gateways in the subject sections of the book also offer links to key policy websites.

Where to look

FPRI Security and International Affairs Think Tank Directory
  thinktanks.fpri.org
  Maintained by the Foreign Policy Research Institute (USA). Lists over 1000 influential international relations and foreign policy think-tanks and research centres worldwide. Offers contact names and web addresses.

Global Go-To Think Tanks report
  www.gotothinktank.com/thinktank
  Annual report on the leading public policy research organizations in the world edited by the University of Pennsylvania International Relations Think Tanks and Civil Society Program. The report gives statistics on the total number of think-tanks, new launches, and lists what it regards as the top think-tanks by world region and research area. The methodology for nominations and rankings is explained on the website. Individual entries offer contact details and summarize activities and funding.

NIRA's World Directory of Think Tanks
www.nira.or.jp/past/ice/index.html
Maintained by the National Institute for Research Advancement (NIRA), Japan. Provides a description of activities, sources of funding and area of interest for hundreds of organizations worldwide. Indexed by name and country.

TOURISM AND HOSPITALITY

Typical questions

- Where can I find up-to-date statistics on the number of tourists visiting the UK?
- I need to find materials relating to sustainable tourism.

Points to consider

- Many websites provide commercial services relating to tourism. This section offers starting-points in researching academic sources.
- Students studying these subject areas often wish to enter the tourist industry; they may therefore find the resources listed in the **Business Studies** section of this book useful.
- Others may be focusing on the impact of tourism upon the environment (covered in **Environment**) and sustainable development (covered in **Development Studies**).

Where to look

Key organizations

Academic associations

Association for Tourism and Leisure Education (ATLAS)
  www.atlas-euro.org
  Transnational organization which seeks to promote the academic study of tourism and leisure. Website provides information on conferences, research projects and publications.

Higher Education Academy
  www.heacademy.ac.uk
  UK organization which supports teaching. Subject coverage includes hospitality, leisure and tourism. Website includes case studies of good practice, plus lists of conferences and training events.

Leisure Studies Association
  www.leisure-studies-association.info
  Founded in 1975. Seeks to promote the teaching and research of all aspects of leisure (including sport, holidays and tourism). Website has news about recent and forthcoming events and publications.

International organizations

United Nations Environment Programme (UNEP) Tourism Programme
www.unep.fr/scp/tourism

Covers ecotourism and sustainable tourism. Website includes news, full-text publications, guidelines and reports.

World Tourism Organization (UNWTO)
unwto.org

Specialized agency of the United Nations, and the leading international organization in the field of tourism. Website has codes of practice, reports and some access to statistical data. Includes coverage of tourism and development, tourism and the economy and sustainable tourism.

Trade organizations

Use these to locate careers information, plus news about market trends and projections.

UK

Association of British Travel Agents (ABTA)
www.abta.co.uk

Website includes a searchable directory of tour operators who are members.

Association of Independent Tour Operators (AITO)
www.aito.co.uk

Association of small to medium-sized independent tour operating companies in the UK which specialize in particular areas or types of holiday.

British Hospitality Association
www.bha.org.uk

Represents hotels, restaurants and food service providers. Website includes some free access to headline statistics and reports on the impact of the trade on the British economy.

Federation of Tour Operators (FTO)
www.fto.co.uk

Point of contact for the UK government on all UK out-bound tour operation-related issues. Co-ordinates member activity in the key areas of crisis handling, health and safety, sustainable tourism, operational issues and establishing best-practice standards. News and publications on these subject areas can be found on the website.

People1st

www.people1st.co.uk

Sector skills council for the hospitality industry. In addition to careers advice, website also provides some free access to industry reports and statistics.

Tourism Society

www.tourismsociety.org

Professional body for people who work in the tourist industry. Website has extensive careers advice and jobs listings.

International

Association of National Tourist Offices and Representatives

www.tourist-offices.org.uk

Lobbying organization for the world's tourist offices. Its website is a good starting-point for tracing the contact details of national tourist boards worldwide. These are useful sources of information on national tourist statistics and market trends.

European Travel Commission

www.etc-corporate.org

Membership forum for national tourism organizations based in Europe. Website offers news and some market intelligence statistics about trends in European tourism.

World Travel and Tourism Council (WTTC)

www.wttc.org

International forum for business leaders in the industry. Supports research into the economic impact of tourism on national and world economies. Website has a large resource centre where full-text reports and economic datasets can be downloaded.

Libraries

British Library Business and IP Centre

www.bl.uk/bipc/aboutus/index.html

Open to the public. Offers specialist support in business research, including access to trade publications and online databases covering the tourist industry. Website contains a guide to researching the industry.

British Library of Development Studies

blds.ids.ac.uk/guides/tourism.html

Europe's largest specialist research collection on development studies. Holdings include coverage of tourism policy and tourism and development.

Dictionaries and encyclopedias

Collins, V. R. (2008) *Tourism Society's Dictionary for the Tourism Industry,* **CABI Publishing**

Intended for those working in the industry. Offers a handy guide to everyday terms used within the tourism, travel, leisure and airline sectors.

Jafari, J. (ed.) (2003) *Encyclopedia of Tourism,* **Routledge**

Over 1000 detailed entries. Topics covered include: key organizations, institutions and journals in the field, trends in the tourist trade and country-specific profiles.

Journal article indexes

Hospitality and Tourism Complete (subscription required)
www.ebscohost.com/academic/hospitality-tourism-complete

Covers all areas of scholarly research and industry news. Includes full-text e-journals. Coverage from 1960s onwards.

Leisure Tourism Database (subscription required)
www.cabi.org/leisuretourism

Indexes articles, book chapters and industry news relating to all aspects of leisure, tourism and hospitality. Includes extensive coverage of tourism and development. Materials from 1973 onwards.

News services

Travel Trade Gazette
www.ttglive.com

Leading UK trade journal. Website has news from the industry and job listings.

Travel Weekly
www.travelweekly.co.uk

Weekly newspaper for the UK travel industry, containing industry news and job advertisements for travel professionals. There are online supplements on destinations and types of holiday.

Statistical data

Explore the websites of these organizations to access recent datasets. Note that not all may be free.

Euromonitor (subscription required)
www.euromonitor.com/Travel_And_Tourism

Leading source of market analysis and data. Includes country and industry resources.

Office for National Statistics (ONS)

www.statistics.gov.uk/cci/nscl.asp?id=8131

Official statistics from the British government covering tourism and the tourist industry. Covers domestic and overseas tourism, visitor expenditure in the UK and employment in the tourist industry. A key publication is *Travel Trends*, which reports annually on trends in overseas travel and tourism from the *International Passenger Survey (IPS)*. It covers visits to the UK by overseas travellers and visits overseas made by UK residents.

VisitBritain

www.visitbritain.org

Works in association with the government and industry to market British tourism. In addition to general news, the website has a statistics section with data on UK tourism trends. This includes market data and projections, and demographic information about visitors.

World Economic Forum

www.weforum.org/s?s=tourism

Publishes a *Travel and Tourism Competitiveness Report*, which compares the relative competitiveness of national tourist industries.

World Tourism Organization (UNWTO)

unwto.org

Publishes extensive statistics. Some data offered free of charge on the website. Key publications include *The Yearbook of Tourism Statistics* and *Budgets of National Tourism Organisations*.

TRADE UNIONS

Typical questions

- Where can I get statistics on trends in union membership?
- How can I trace the archives of a union that no longer exists?

Points to consider

- Trade unions can be rich sources of information on industrial relations, labour and employment policy. Their websites can offer information on legislation, pension entitlements and workers' rights. They frequently publish comment on government policy which can offer a different perspective to that offered by academic journals or the government departments themselves!
- When searching for trade unions, try national and international federations as a key starting-point, because most have directories. However, bear in mind that not all unions may be affiliated.
- It can be difficult to trace historic name changes of trade unions. Good starting-points are the national federations, which may maintain their own listings.
- Finally, when looking for literature on unions remember to search for alterative spellings (such as 'labour' or 'labor') and synonyms (e.g. trade unions or labor unions, strikes or industrial action).

Where to look

UK

Current

Trade Union Congress Library collections
　　www.londonmet.ac.uk/services/sas/library-services/tuc
　　Based at London Metropolitan University. Major research library for the study of contemporary and historic unions. Search its online library catalogue and research guides. Holdings strongest in terms of British and Commonwealth unions.

Trades Union Congress (TUC)
　　www.tuc.org.uk
　　National body representing over 50 of Britain's major unions. Its website has information on campaigns and policy. It also includes sections for workers (on their pension and employment rights) and a current union directory by name of organization and sector. Note that this does not include all British unions, only those affiliated to the TUC. A full register

can be found at the **Certification Office** website, **www.certoffice.org**. Has lists of registered unions with their annual returns. Data available from approximately 2003 onwards. Includes mainly current unions.

Historical

Marsh, A. and Smethurst, J. (1980 –) *Historical Directory of Trade Unions,* **Ashgate**

Major multi-volume set. Entries are arranged by subject area. Each one traces the history of the union, its founding dates, amalgamations, and gives guidance on sources for its archives and minute books.

Union Makes Us Strong: TUC History Online

www.unionhistory.info

Award-winning site created by the TUC. Provides free access to a timeline of union history, documents relating to the General Strike of 1926, the full text of all Congress reports from 1868 to 1968 and the full text of the classic *The Ragged Trousered Philanthropists* by Robert Tressell. Links are provided to other historical sources.

International

European Industrial Relations Observatory (EIRO)

www.eurofound.europa.eu/eiro/index.htm

European Union (EU) body providing news and analysis of European industrial relations. Website includes information on major unions in EU nations and statistics on membership.

European Trade Union Federation

www.etuc.org

Represents trade unions in European nations. Website contains information on recent activity, concerns and worker's rights in Europe. It also covers European Works Councils. The website has a directory of links to member organizations.

Global Union Research Network (GURN)

www.gurn.info/en

Supports international research into trade unions. Website has news and a database of research publications. A good place for finding out about the latest academic research.

International Labour Organisation (ILO)

www.ilo.org

United Nations agency responsible for labour standards. Its website has useful policy reports and news on industrial relations and workers' rights. It includes free access to a number of databases, **www.ilo.org/global/ statistics-and-databases/lang--en/index.htm**. These include:

- *NATLEX*. A database of national labour, social security and related human rights legislation
- *Labordoc*. The ILO Library's database. Contains references to books and articles covering all aspects of work
- *LaborStat*. The ILO's labour statistics database. Topics covered include national and international data on disputes, strikes and lock-outs.

International Trade Union Confederation (ITUC)
www.ituc-csi.org
International organization founded in 2006 from the International Confederation of Free Trade Unions (ICFTU) and the World Confederation of Labour. Get international news and listings of members.

World Federation of Trade Unions
www.wftucentral.org
International federation of trade unions. Website provides details of events, policy and membership.

TREATIES

Typical questions

- I need a list of bilateral trade treaties between the USA and Asia.
- Is this treaty still in force?

Points to consider

- There are many different types of treaties. Research can involve complex legal queries. If a local law specialist is not available, good starting-points are the research guides listed below.
- Searches are more likely to be effective if the user is specific about the type of treaty they need. Basic questions to ask include: is the treaty bilateral or multilateral? Is it related to a specific international organization or national government? Is it historic or recent?
- Good starting-points include the websites of national governments and international organizations. Most will list and/or provide the full text of treaties to which they are a signatory. However, be careful to check when the website was last updated!
- Note that there are often long delays between the registration/ratification dates of a treaty and its entry into force.

Where to look

Research guides

ASIL Guide to Electronic Resources for International Law: Treaties
www.asil.org/treaty1.cfm
Compiled by the American Society for International Law. Excellent annotated guide which highlights key resources for US and international treaties. Links are provided to websites where available.

Columbia University Law Library Research guides
library.law.columbia.edu/guides/Guide_to_Treaty_Research
Good starting-point for novices. Highlights key resources, including printed volumes, commercial databases and websites. Has sections for USA, UK, international and bilateral treaties. Website has a separate detailed guide for historical treaty research, **library.law.columbia.edu/guides/Historical_Treaties**.

National

These are examples of national government websites. To trace those of other countries, search for the foreign ministry. The UK Foreign and Commonwealth Office website also has links to many foreign offices worldwide.

Treaties in Force
www.state.gov/s/l/treaty/tif/index.htm
Prepared annually by the US Department of State. Covers multilateral and bilateral treaties to which the USA is a signatory.

UK Treaties Online
www.fco.gov.uk/en/publications-and-documents/treaties/
uk-treaties-online
The Foreign and Commonwealth Office (FCO) maintains a full-text database of all treaties since 1896.

International

Avalon Project
avalon.law.yale.edu
Provides free access to documents in law, history and diplomacy. Includes the full text of some USA and non-USA historical treaties from earliest times.

Council of Europe Treaty Office
conventions.coe.int
Access the text of all Council of Europe treaties, their explanatory reports, the status of signatures and ratifications since 2005.

European Union, Treaties Office
ec.europa.eu/world/agreements/default.home.do
Contains all bilateral and multilateral treaties concluded by the European Union (EU) and its predecessors. Does not include the EU founding treaties or treaties between individual member nations. Founding and accession treaties of the EU can be found on the **Eur-Lex** website, **eur-lex. europa.eu/en/treaties/index.htm**.

Flare Index to Treaties
ials.sas.ac.uk/library/flag/introtreaties.htm
Maintained by the Institute of Advanced Legal Studies. A searchable database of basic information on over 1500 of the most significant multilateral treaties from 1856 onwards. Entries include details of where the treaty was published and a link to an online version (where available).

International Legal Materials (subscription required)
www.asil.org/ilm.cfm

Bimonthly journal published by the American Society of International Law. Each issue contains the full texts of important agreements. These regularly include treaties.

Multilaterals Project
fletcher.tufts.edu/multilaterals
Project of Fletcher School, Tufts University. Provides free access to several hundred full-text treaties covering a number of subject areas, including the environment, human rights and trade.

United Nations Treaty Collections
treaties.un.org
Key website; it includes:

- *Status of Multilateral Treaties Deposited with the Secretary-General*. Covers over 500 treaties deposited with the UN Secretary-General. Useful for tracing information on whether treaties have been signed or ratified.
- *United Nations Treaty Series*. Contains the text of all treaties registered and filed with the UN since 1946.
- *League of Nations Treaty Series*. The full text of historic treaties 1920–44.
- *Treaty Reference*. Definitions of key terms.

Historical treaties

Consolidated Treaty Series, edited and annotated by Clive Parry, Oceana
Over 200 printed volumes published 1969–81. Contains the full text of bilateral and multilateral treaties from 1648 to 1949 (when the UN series began). All texts are in their original languages, later modifications are shown. Indexes are by party and region.

Index to Multilateral Treaties: a chronological list of multi-party international agreements from the sixteenth century through 1963 (1965)
Harvard Law School Library
Key starting-place for tracing historic treaties. Contains a chronological list of 3859 multilateral treaties and other agreements from 1596 to 1963. Provides information on where the full text of the treaty can be found within a range of primary sources. Includes subject and regional indexes.

UNITED NATIONS

Typical questions

- Where can I get a list of all the UN Secretaries-General?
- I want to consult recent UN Security Council resolutions relating to Libya.

Points to consider

- Increasing amounts of UN information are now available on the internet. This includes reports, statistics and legislation. These can be of particular value when studying developing nations that may not have reliable websites of their own. They are also invaluable in providing updates on conflict zones and humanitarian crises.
- However, a common problem is the large number of UN organizations and the complexity of their websites. One of the best overall guides is the Dag Hammarskjöld Library website. This, and other recommended resources, are described below.

Where to look

United Nations website

www.un.org
Official website. Key features include:

- **Charter of the UN, www.un.org/en/documents/charter/index.shtml**.
- **United Nations Cyberschool Bus, cyberschoolbus.un.org**. Educational site designed for schools. Includes easy-to-understand introductions to the work of the UN, plus links to news and key websites.
- **UNData, data.un.org**. Open access to major statistical indicators from UN bodies. Search by country or subject area.
- **Documents, documents.un.org**. Official Document System (ODS), provides free access to resolutions of the General Assembly, Security Council and Economic and Social Council from 1946 onwards. Other documents generally date from at least 1993 onwards.
- **UN Press Releases, www.un.org/News**. Includes multimedia broadcasts.
- **RefWorld, www.unhcr.org/cgi-bin/texis/vtx/refworld/rwmain**. UN system containing reports on the status of refugees worldwide.
- **UN Treaty Collection, treaties.un.org**. Provides access to the United Nations and League of Nations treaty series from 1926 onwards, information on the status of major multilateral treaties deposited with the UN and monthly updates on treaties and international agreements.

- **United Nations Yearbook Collection, unyearbook.un.org**. Detailed annual summaries of UN activity, including details of all resolutions. Cross-search the historical collection from 1946.

Scholarly organizations

Academic Council on the United Nations System (ACUNS)
www.acuns.org
International association of scholars and research institutions worldwide.

United Nations Association (UK)
www.una.org.uk
Aims to raise awareness and debate about the role of the UN. Website includes guides to UN resources for the public and researchers. Also offers access to its briefings. Topics covered include UN reform.

World Federation of United Nations Associations
www.wfuna.org
Global network. Find out about events and trace the websites of national organizations.

Libraries

Dag Hammarskjöld Library,
www.un.org/depts/dhl
New York-based library of the UN. Its website offers free access to many valuable research resources. These include:

- **UN Documentation: research guide,**
  www.un.org/depts/dhl/resguide/index.html.
- **UNBISNET, unbisnet.un.org**. Library catalogue of the Dag Hammarskjöld Library and the Library of the UN Office at Geneva. Useful for tracing references to UN documents, commercial publications and publications about the UN (most published since 1979). The service also has an index to UN voting records from 1946 onwards and an index to speeches (with links to the full text where available) for the General Assembly, the Security Council and the Economic and Social Council from 1983 onwards.
- **UN-I-QUE, lib-unique.un.org/lib/unique.nsf**. Useful tool for locating the document numbers of UN materials.
- **UN Pulse, unhq-appspub-01.un.org/lib/dhlrefweblog.nsf**. Current awareness blog linking to the latest UN publications.

UN Depository Libraries
www.un.org/depts/dhl/deplib/index.html
Over 400 libraries in 140 countries worldwide receive copies of UN documents as part of a deposit agreement. Find their details using this directory. In the UK major collections are available at the **British Library**, **www.bl.uk** and the **LSE Library, www2.lse.ac.uk/library/home.aspx.**

VOLUNTEERING

Typical questions
- Do volunteers working abroad have to pay tax?
- Can you give me a list of environmental groups that accept volunteers?

Points to consider
- Students may wish to volunteer for a variety of reasons. Those requiring unpaid work experience in specific industries should be directed to the appropriate professional organizations because these often maintain their own directories.
- Don't forget that most universities have careers services and/or volunteering units which maintain lists of local opportunities. The **Charities** section also has key contact addresses.

Where to look

UK

Voluntary Agencies Directory, NCVO
Published annually by the National Council for Voluntary Organisations. Gives facts, figures and contact addresses for over 2000 top UK charities and voluntary organizations.

Volunteering England
www.volunteering.org.uk
Charity committed to promoting volunteering. Website includes useful advice for potential volunteers.

International

International Association for Volunteer Effort (IAVE)
www.iave.org
Global network of volunteers, volunteer organizations with members in over 70 countries. Website includes links to national volunteering centres worldwide.

Pybus, V. (2007) *The International Directory of Voluntary Work*, **Vacation Work Publications**
Details over 700 organizations worldwide. Includes short- and long-term postings.

WOMEN'S STUDIES

Typical questions

- Where can I get up-to-date statistics on women's political representation in India?
- I need a definition of second-wave feminism.
- How can I find journal articles on the 'glass-ceiling'?

Points to consider

- Women's studies is an inter-disciplinary subject area. It can encompass feminist theory as well as economics, politics, history and a range of other subjects from a female perspective. Many of the professional organizations listed in the subject sections have special-interest groups relating to research or lobbying for women.

Where to look

Key organizations

UK

Fawcett Society
 www.fawcettsociety.org.uk
 Leading campaigner for gender equality. Website provides free access to many of its research papers as well as campaign materials. Topics covered include women and politics, the gender pay gap and gender and the criminal justice system.

Feminist and Women's Studies Association (UK and Ireland)
 fwsa.org.uk
 Scholarly society. Website has a blog with news, conference and events listings.

Home Office
 www.homeoffice.gov.uk/equalities
 UK government body leading on gender equality policy. Website has the text of relevant legislation, research papers and links to related government bodies such as the Equality and Human Rights Commission (EHRC).

International

National Council for Research on Women
 www.ncrw.org
 Network of over 120 research and public policy institutes focusing on

women's lives. Many are US based. Website offers free access to some of their publications.

National Women's Studies Association (USA)
www.nwsa.org
Get news and conference listings.

UNwomen
www.unwomen.org
Created in 2010. Co-ordinates UN activity towards gender equality. Website has news, events, links to reports and statistics.

Libraries and archives

The Women's Library
www.londonmet.ac.uk/thewomenslibrary
Reference library based at London Metropolitan University. Collections cover women's political, social and economic history. Holdings strongest in terms of the UK and the Commonwealth. Catalogue available online.

Locate other UK libraries with historic women's collections using the **Genesis** website, **www.genesis.ac.uk**.

Office of the University of Wisconsin System Women's Studies Librarian
womenst.library.wisc.edu
Although intended for local students, this has many excellent services. These include:

- *Women's Audiovisuals in English (WAVE)*. A database that lists documentary, experimental and feature film productions by and about women.
- *Feminist Periodicals – a current listing of contents*. Annotated listings of tables of contents from major journals.
- Also available are gender topic research guides, bibliographies of readings.

Locate other libraries using:

Mapping the World of Women's Information Services
www.aletta.nu/aletta/eng/collections/informatiecentra
An online directory of information on women's libraries and information centres in over 100 nations hosted by the International Information Centre and Archives for the Women's Movement (IIAV).

Dictionaries and encyclopedias

Davis, K., Evans, M. and Lorber, J. (eds) (2006) *Handbook of Gender and Women's Studies*, **Sage**
Volume of 26 scholarly essays on the current state of women's studies.

Heywood, L. (2005) *The Women's Movement Today: an encyclopedia of third-wave feminism*, **ABC-CLIO**
Two-volume set containing over 200 articles introducing key concepts, figures and theories. Volume 1 contains 77 primary resource documents critical to understanding the movement.

Journal article indexes

Because of the interdisciplinary nature of the subject, students are advised to combine these with resources listed in the general **Journal Article Indexes** section.

LGBT Life (subscription required)
www.ebscohost.com/academic/lgbt-life-with-full-text
Indexes more than 100 historically important journal and newspaper titles for the study of gay, lesbian, bi-sexual and transgender history, economics, politics and culture. Can be purchased in a full-text version.

Women in Politics Database
www.ipu.org/bdf-e/bdfsearch.asp
Maintained by the Inter-Parliamentary Union (IPU). Provides free references to articles about women, politics and political representation worldwide.

Women's Studies International (subscription required)
www.ebscohost.com/academic/womens-studies-international
Combines a number of leading databases: *Women Studies Abstracts*, *Women's Studies Bibliography Database*, *Women's Studies Database*, *Women Studies Librarian*. Coverage from 1972 onwards. All subject areas covered.

Statistical data

National

Office of National Statistics (UK)
www.statistics.gov.uk/default.asp
Provides free access to many economic, social and political indicators that compare the position of men and women.

Women in America: Indicators of Social and Economic Well-Being
www.whitehouse.gov/administration/eop/cwg/data-on-women
Aims to draw together statistics from federal agencies. First published 2011.

International

FAO Gender and Land Rights Database
www.fao.org/gender/landrights
Free access to recent statistics, reports and legislation on women's access to land worldwide.

GenderStats
go.worldbank.org/T1WTTF4II0
World Bank website which provides free access to gender-related statistics from the Bank and other international agencies. Includes country and regional files. Most information from 2000 onwards.

OECD Gender, Institutions and Development Database
www.oecd.org/dev/gender/gid
Covers 60 indicators on gender discrimination in over 100 nations.

United Nations Statistics and Indicators on Women and Men
unstats.un.org/unsd/demographic/products/indwm
Get the latest data on six areas: population, families, health, politics, education, work. It is also possible to download the regular World's Women reports from the website.

Digital libraries and internet gateways

Many full-text writings can increasingly be found online. The **E-books**, **History** and **Literature** sections also list valuable resources.

Defining Gender, 1450–1910 (subscription required)
www.ampltd.co.uk/online/Defining-Gender/index.aspx
Over 120,000 pages of original documents and prints taken from the holdings of the Bodleian Library and the British Library. Themes include domesticity, the body, conduct, education and leisure.

Gerritsen Collection – Women's History Online (subscription required)
gerritsen.chadwyck.com/home.do
More than 4700 publications from continental Europe, the USA, the UK, Canada and New Zealand, dating from 1543 to 1945.

UK Web Archive: Women's Issues
www.webarchive.org.uk/ukwa/collection/98537/page/1
Archived snapshots of key women's studies websites, many dating from 2006 onwards. Includes organizations, pressure groups, think-tanks and e-zines. It is possible to search and retrieve full-text documents from the websites.

WSS Links
libr.org/wss/wsslinks/general.htm
Maintained by the Women's Studies section of the Association of College and Research Libraries/American Library Association. Directory of annotated links to key websites. Many US based.

WORKING PAPERS

Typical questions
- I need an IMF working paper.
- I want to find recent research on product placement.

Points to consider
- Working papers, pre-prints and technical reports are often useful sources of cutting-edge research. In some subject areas, such as Economics, they are a well established means of publishing the latest research before it appears in mainstream journals.
- However, older print titles may be difficult to trace because many libraries do not include them in their catalogues. Remember to check by both individual title and series name.
- More recent items can often be found on the internet. Listed below are some good starting-points. These are general sources; subject-specific services are listed in the relevant sections. They should be used to supplement references found in literature searches of **Journal Article Indexes.**

Where to look

OpenDOAR

www.opendoar.org

Cross-search the open access repositories of thousands of universities worldwide. Many of these contain full-text working papers, alongside references to other journal articles, theses and reports. Full text is often available where copyright allows. Particularly useful for tracing references to research from developing nations. However, remember to allow time to evaluate the results. Some may be draft versions of papers or may have incomplete references.

SSRN Working Papers (subscription required)

www.ssrn.com

Enormous online library hosted by the Social Science Research Network. Comprised of subject-specific networks which include: Health, Legal Scholarship, Accounting, Philosophy. The database may be searched free of charge. Full-text access usually requires a subscription.

WRITING AND STYLE GUIDES

Typical questions

- Can you recommend a book on writing skills?
- Should I use a colon or semi-colon in this sentence?

Points to consider

- A style guide is a set of standards to ensure uniformity in the writing and publication of documents. It can cover grammar, punctuation and referencing.
- Some universities have accepted styles. Students should check their course regulations for advice.
- Students who ask about style guides often require advice on **Citing and Referencing**. They can be referred to the sources listed in that section.
- Lecturers preparing materials for journal or book publication should first be advised to check the publisher's/journal's website to see if there is any advice for authors on preferred style.

Where to look

Burchfield, R. W. (1996) *Fowler's Modern English Usage*, **3rd edn, Oxford University Press**
In-depth coverage of British and American English, covering syntax, grammar, style and usage. Many newspapers also produce style guides for journalists. A key example is:

The Economist Style Guide (2010) **Economist Books, 10th edn**
A shortened version is online at **www.economist.com/research/styleguide**.

Times style and usage guide
www.timesonline.co.uk/tol/tools_and_services/specials/style_guide
Offers a quick guide for checking contentious points of grammar.

Student writing guides

Many general essay-writing handbooks cover style and presentation.

Companion for undergraduate dissertations: sociology, anthropology, politics, social policy, social work and criminology
www.socscidiss.bham.ac.uk
Free access to a survival guide published by the Higher Education Academy's Centre for Sociology, Anthropology and Politics, the Centre for

Social Work and Policy and Sheffield Hallam University. Provides useful tips on literature-searching skills and preparing a dissertation at undergraduate level.

Royal Literary Fund writing resources
www.rlf.org.uk/fellowshipscheme/writing/index.cfm
Includes sections on essay writing for undergraduates, and on preparing dissertations for graduates. In addition to literature-searching skills they also cover drafting, editing and the style of writing. There is also coverage of English as a second language.

Index

Know It All, Find It Fast

An A–Z source guide for the enquiry desk
3rd edition
Bob Duckett, Peter Walker and Christinea Donnelly

Know It All, Find It Fast remains a book to be kept to hand, not on the reference shelf...The word 'essential' is often over-used by reviewers, but it covers this book, just as it is essential that the compilers continue to keep it up to date with regular new editions.
REFERENCE REVIEWS

... there is much to treasure in this new edition of KIAFIF and it is an essential source for anyone dealing with enquiries. Buy it if you have not already done so.
REFER

This book should still be kept at hand by everyone providing an enquiry service.
UPDATE

This award-winning sourcebook is an essential guide to where to look to find the answers quickly. It is designed as a first point of reference for LIS practitioners, to be depended upon if they are unfamiliar with the subject of an enquiry – or wish to find out more. It is arranged in an easily searchable, fully cross-referenced A-Z list of around 150 of the subject areas most frequently handled at enquiry desks.

Each subject entry lists the most important information sources and where to locate them, including printed and electronic sources, relevant websites and useful contacts for referral purposes. The authors use their extensive experience in reference work to offer useful tips, warn of potential pitfalls, and spotlight typical queries and how to tackle them. This new edition has been brought right up-to-date with all sources checked for currency and many new ones added, especially subscription websites. The searchability is enhanced by a comprehensive index to make those essential sources even easier to find – saving you valuable minutes!

2008; 496pp; paperback; 978-1-85604-652-7; £44.95
Order online at: www.facetpublishing.co.uk